MACHINE
SCHEDULING PROBLEMS

Classification, complexity and computations

A. H. G. RINNOOY KAN

MARTINUS NIJHOFF / THE HAGUE / 1976

ISBN-13: 978-90-247-1848-1   e-ISBN-13: 978-1-4613-4383-7
DOI: 10.1007/978-1-4613-4383-7

To the memory of my mother

Preface

This book is the result of a doctoral dissertation written under the supervision of professor dr. G. de Leve of the University of Amsterdam. I am very grateful to him for suggesting the subject and for his guidance and support during the preparation. Professor dr. ir. J. S. Folkers has carefully read various drafts of the manuscript; I would like to thank him for his many helpful comments and suggestions. I have also greatly benefited from the advice of Gene Lawler, who spent the summer of 1975 in Amsterdam at the invitation of the Stichting Mathematisch Centrum.

A quick glance at the bibliography already indicates how much I owe to the extensive cooperation with Jan Karel Lenstra. Many of the results in this book are the outcome of our joint research. I am similarly grateful to Ben Lageweg, who actively participated in many projects and who was in charge of all computational experiments.

The Graduate School of Management in Delft provided a stimulating professional environment. In particular I want to acknowledge the inspiring advice of David Brée and the useful contributions by Erik de Leede, Hans Geilenkirchen, Jaap Galjaard and Jan Knipscheer.

I would like to thank Peter Brucker, Robbert Peters, K. Boskma, Michael Florian and Graham McMahon for their valuable written reactions. I am also grateful to Hendrik Lenstra II and Peter van Emde Boas for various illuminating conversations and to Bernard Dorhout for his kind cooperation.

As to the technical realisation of this book, I owe many thanks to Elly van Buuren who impeccably typed several drafts, and to Messrs. J. K. van der Sluys and P. J. van der Horst of Stenfert Kroese for their generous assistance.

The gratitude that I feel toward my parents and other family requires no further comment. My wife Happy suffered bravely through many months of neglect and provided badly needed moral support on many occasions.

Alexander Rinnooy Kan

Contents

1. INTRODUCTION 1

2. PROBLEM FORMULATION 5
   2.1. Notations and representations 5
   2.2. Restrictive assumptions 10
   2.3. Optimality criteria 16
      2.3.1. Regular measures 16
         2.3.1.1. Criteria based on completion times 18
         2.3.1.2. Criteria based on due dates 18
         2.3.1.3. Criteria based on inventory cost and utilization 19
      2.3.2. Relations between criteria 20
      2.3.3. Analysis of scheduling costs 24
   2.4. Classification of problems 28

3. METHODS OF SOLUTION 30
   3.1. Complete enumeration 31
   3.2. Combinatorial analysis 34
   3.3. Mixed integer and non-linear programming 36
      3.3.1. [Bowman 1959] 36
      3.3.2. [Pritsker et al. 1969] 37
      3.3.3. [Wagner 1959] 37
      3.3.4. [Manne 1960] 38
      3.3.5. [Nepomiastchy 1973] 39
   3.4. Branch-and-bound 39
   3.5. Dynamic programming 43
      3.5.1. [Held and Karp 1962; Lawler 1964] 44
      3.5.2. [Lawler and Moore 1969] 44
   3.6. Complexity theory 45
   3.7. Heuristic methods 50
      3.7.1. Priority rules 51
      3.7.2. Bayesian analysis 52

4. ONE-MACHINE PROBLEMS 56
  4.1. $n|1||c_{max}$ problems 57
    4.1.1. The $n|1||C_{max}$ problem. 57
    4.1.2. The $n|1||L_{max}$ problem. 57
    4.1.3. The general $n|1||c_{max}$ problem 58
  4.2. $n|1|\Gamma|c_{max}$ problems. 59
    4.2.1. The $n|1|r_i \geqq 0|c_{max}$ problem 59
      4.2.1.1. Lower bound by job splitting 62
      4.2.1.2. The algorithm of McMahon and Florian . . . 62
      4.2.1.3. Precedence constraints 64
    4.2.2. The $n|1|seq\,dep|c_{max}$ problem 66
    4.2.3. The $n|1|prec|c_{max}$ problem 66
  4.3. $n|1||\sum c_i$ problems 67
    4.3.1. The $n|1||\sum w_i C_i$ problem. 67
    4.3.2. The $n|1||\sum w_i T_i$ problem. 68
    4.3.3. The general $n|1||\sum c_i$ problem 71
      4.3.3.1. Elimination criteria 71
      4.3.3.2. A branch-and-bound algorithm 76
  4.4. $n|1|\Gamma|\sum c_i$ problems. 79
    4.4.1. The $n|1|r_i \geqq 0|\sum c_i$ problem 79
    4.4.2. The $n|1|seq\,dep|\sum c_i$ problem 84
    4.4.3. The $n|1|prec|\sum c_i$ problem 87

5. TWO-MACHINE AND THREE-MACHINE PROBLEMS. 89
  5.1. The $n|2|\gamma, \Gamma|c_{max}$ and $n|3|\gamma, \Gamma|c_{max}$ problem. 89
  5.2. The $n|2|F|\sum c_i$ problem 100
  5.3. The $n|2|P|C_{max}$ problem with time lags 105

6. GENERAL FLOW-SHOP AND JOB-SHOP PROBLEMS 106
  6.1. The $n|m|P|\delta$ problem 106
    6.1.1. Elimination criteria for the $n|m|P|C_{max}$ problem . . . 107
    6.1.2. Lower bounds for the $n|m|P|c_{max}$ problem 109
  6.2. The $n|m|F|\delta$ problem 115
  6.3. The $n|m|G|\delta$ problem 115
    6.3.1. Lower bounds 116
    6.3.2. Branching rules 119
      6.3.2.1. The procedure 'actsched' 120
      6.3.2.2. Branching on disjunctive arcs 120
  6.4. The $n|m|\gamma, no\,wait|\delta$ problem. 125

7. CONCLUDING REMARKS 131
   7.1. Complexity of scheduling problems 131
   7.2. Practical scheduling problems 135
   7.3. Conclusions 139

LIST OF NOTATIONS 143

Appendix 1. The $n|1|r_i \geqq 0|L_{\max}$ problem 146
Appendix 2. The $n|1||\sum c_i$ problem 150
Appendix 3. The $n|m|P|C_{\max}$ problem 156
Appendix 4. The $n|m|G|C_{\max}$ problem 163

REFERENCES 167

AUTHOR INDEX 176

SUBJECT INDEX 179

1

Introduction

The problems that form the object of this study can be summarized as follows.

Suppose that we have to perform a number of *jobs*, each of which consists of a given sequence of *operations*, by using a number of *machines*. To *perform* a job, each of its operations must be processed in the order given by the sequence. The *processing* of an operation requires the use of a particular machine for a given duration, the *processing time* of the operation. Each machine can process only one operation at a time. Given a *cost function* by which the cost of each possible solution can be measured, we want to find a processing order on each machine such that the corresponding cost is minimized.

Such problems occur under widely varying circumstances. The terminology used above already suggests that the problem arose originally in an industrial production context. However, various other interpretations are possible: jobs and machines can stand for patients and hospital equipment, classes and teachers, ships and dockyards, dinners and cooks, programmes and computers, or cities and (travelling) salesmen. Each of these situations fits into the framework sketched above and thus falls within the scope of machine scheduling theory and algorithms. The class of models suggested by the above formulation obviously requires elaboration. It will be necessary to explore in detail under what conditions an actual problem situation can be satisfactorily represented by one of these models. Also, the overall cost function referred to above will have to be specified in such a way that the result is not only computationally tractable, but also reflects actual cost factors. The first purpose of this study is to investigate the above aspects in order to arrive at a satisfactory **classification** of machine scheduling problems.

This investigation is carried out at length in chapter 2. First, some fundamental concepts, notations and representations are introduced. Among the latter is the problem representation known as the disjunctive graph model, allowing a simple and attractive characterization of feasible solutions to scheduling problems. For the time being, a distinction will be made here between sequences and schedules. A feasible *sequence* simply corresponds to an ordering of the operations on each machine that allows the sequence of operations corresponding to each job to be processed in the proper order. Corresponding to each feasible sequence there is an infinity of feasible *schedules* obtained by further specifying the exact starting time and finishing time of each operation. In particular a schedule determines for each job a completion time at which its last operation is finished.

Two other important concepts also emerge in the context of the feasibility question: it turns out to be useful to distinguish between *flow-shop* problems and *job-shop* problems. In the former case each job passes the machines in the same order, whereas in the latter case the machine order may vary per job.

Chapter 2 continues with an extensive discussion of various assumptions implicitly underlying the problem formulation. Particularly vital among these is the restriction to deterministic problems, in which stochastic aspects are ignored, and the restriction to machines of capacity equal to one. Generally, it will be examined to what degree these and other assumptions are crucial with respect to the applicability of scheduling theory. Quite often, complicating circumstances can be readily incorporated in the model; the resulting special cases are discussed separately in later chapters.

A further restriction on the applicability of scheduling theory arises out of the choice of specific cost functions as optimality criteria. Here a restriction will be made to so-called regular measures, criteria whose value with respect to a given schedule is completely determined by the job completion times. It may seem a serious restriction to let the quality of a schedule be determined solely by the job completion times. However, further investigations reveal that the class of regular measures is rich enough to accommodate a large variety of criteria. Six regular measures turn out to represent through equivalence relations all criteria encountered in the literature. Furthermore, together with two general measures they can be used to approximate a general cost function for scheduling problems, arrived at through economic analysis.

The study of representations, assumptions, and criteria finally leads to a detailed problem classification that determines to a large extent the structure of the later chapters. Not only is this classification validated by previous scheduling research, but also by results concerning the computational complexity of scheduling problems, that will be discussed shortly.

The exposition continues in chapter 3 with a general discussion of solution methods available to solve the class of problems outlined in chapter 2. Essentially, each scheduling problem is an optimization problem defined on the finite set of so-called active schedules. The cardinality of this set is usually so large that complete enumeration of all elements is not feasible within a reasonable time. More subtle solution methods are required, taking into account the specific structure of scheduling problems. These solution methods are of varying quality. On one hand, combinatorial analysis may lead to very efficient algorithms that produce an optimal schedule in a predictable number of steps, with this number increasing at most polynomially with the size of the problem. On the other hand, it often seems necessary to resort to far less predictable enumerative methods such as branch-and-bound. Inevitably, the question arises whether the **complexity** of a problem is such that the latter step is unavoidable.

A partial answer to this question can be obtained by applying some recent results from the area of computational complexity. There turns out to exist a class of difficult combinatorial problems with the property that an efficient algorithm for any of these problems would provide a similarly efficient algorithm for all the others as well. No such efficient algorithm has been found so far, and given the fact that many notorious problems such as the 0–1 programming problem, the knapsack problem and the travelling salesman problem are in this class, the existence of such an algorithm is highly unlikely. Thus, if a particular scheduling problem can be shown to belong to this class as well, the use of an enumerative method for its solution is justified reasonably well; no substantially better method is likely to exist. Along these lines, a great deal of attention will be paid to questions of problem complexity in chapters 3 to 6 in order to draw the borderline between 'easy' and 'hard' problems as accurately as possible.

Chapters 4, 5 and 6 are organized along the lines of the classification obtained in chapter 2. With respect to each type of problem, these chapters contain complexity results and methods for actual **computations**. From the complexity results it appears that efficient algorithms exist only for a very limited class of problems. Hence, many of the described algorithms are of an enumerative nature. One-machine algorithms can be found in chapter 4, two- and three-machine algorithms in chapter 5, and general flow-shop and job-shop algorithms in chapter 6. Some results given in these chapters are not new, but have been included to obtain a reasonably complete survey; occasionally, new and shorter proofs are provided.

This study should be of interest not only to researchers, but also to practitioners involved in actual scheduling problems. Although the growth of scheduling literature has been spectacular since Johnson's pioneering work in 1954, relatively few applications of scheduling theory have been reported so far. The discussion of assumptions and criteria in chapter 2 should facilitate the recognition of scheduling problems that fit in the framework used in this study. Of course, in most practical situations a scheduling problem can be considered to be satisfactorily solved if a good, not necessarily optimal solution has been found. The complexity results confirm that the search for an optimal schedule would often be too time-consuming in any case. However, even in the construction of heuristic solution methods a study of optimizing methods may contribute valuable insights and lead to better heuristics than the very general ones discussed in chapter 3. In chapter 7, following a summary of the complexity results, some limited experience with an actual scheduling problem is described, where knowledge of optimizing algorithms clearly influenced the design of a satisfactory heuristic. The general approach sketched and illustrated in this last chapter merits further experimentation in varying scheduling situations.

A final note on some prerequisites. Familiarity will be assumed with some basic results from linear programming theory and basic notions from graph theory. By convention undirected graphs will be defined by nodes and edges, and directed graphs by vertices and arcs. Important notations can be found in the index following chapter 7.

2

Problem formulation

As announced in chapter 1, this chapter deals with various aspects of problem formulation. In section 2.1 we discuss problem representations, including the important disjunctive graph model, and introduce notations to designate several concepts involving jobs, machines and operations. Whatever the interpretation of such concepts may be, several conditions have to be fulfilled before scheduling theory and algorithms can be applied; such restrictive assumptions are examined in section 2.2. The choice of optimality criteria will be discussed in section 2.3. Finally, in section 2.4 we combine previous notations to arrive at a classification of scheduling problems that determines to a large extent the structure of later chapters.

2.1. NOTATIONS AND REPRESENTATIONS

We introduce a number of basic definitions and relations leading to a mathematical model that will serve as a framework throughout the following chapters.

Let $\mathcal{O}$ be the set of *operations* (also called *tasks*). $\mathcal{O}$ can be partitioned into disjoint subsets in two ways:

$$(2\text{-}1) \quad \mathcal{O} = J_1 \cup \ldots \cup J_n$$

and

$$(2\text{-}2) \quad \mathcal{O} = M_1 \cup \ldots \cup M_m.$$

Subset J_i ($i = 1, \ldots, n$) contains the operations defining a *job* (also called *(commodity, production lot* or *job lot)*. Within our model, subset M_k $(k = 1, \ldots, m)$ defines a *machine* (also called *facility, production center, work station* or *(process) stage*), on which these operations are to be *processed*. Let $\mathcal{J}$ denote the set of jobs $\{J_1, \ldots, J_n\}$ and $\mathcal{M}$ the set of machines

$\{M_1, \ldots, M_m\}$, and let $\iota: \mathcal{O} \to \{1, \ldots, n\}$ and $\mu: \mathcal{O} \to \{1, \ldots, m\}$ be the functions induced by (2-1) and (2-2).

We assume the *processing order* per job to be known: each J_i is linearly ordered by an ordering relation $\prec$ and we can index the operations O_r in J_i $(i = 1, \ldots, n)$ accordingly:

$$O_{N_{i-1}+1} \prec O_{N_{i-1}+2} \prec \ldots \prec O_{N_i},$$

where $N_i \overset{\triangle}{=} \sum_{j=1}^{i} |n_j|$, $n_j \overset{\triangle}{=} |J_j|$, $(i, j = 1, \ldots, n)$.* If $O_r, O_s \in J_i$ and $r < s$, we say that O_r *precedes* O_s and write $O_r \lll O_s$; if $s = r + 1$, O_r *directly precedes* O_s.

The *processing time* p_r of operation O_r is also assumed to be given for each $O_r \in \mathcal{O}$. We assume p_r to be an integer number.

If $|J_i \cap M_k| = 1$, the unique operation of J_i on M_k will sometimes be denoted by O_{ik}. Occasionally this notation will be used to indicate the k-th operation of J_i $(k = 1, \ldots, n_i)$. In both cases, its processing time will be denoted by p_{ik}.

There are several ways to represent relevant problem data. For instance, if $|J_i \cap M_k| = 1$, we can introduce an $n \times m$ matrix $\mathcal{P} = [p_{ik}]$ containing the processing times of $O_{ik} \in J_i \cap M_k$ and an $n \times m$ matrix $\mathcal{S} = [v_i(k)]$ indicating the machine order of the operations of J_i by means of the permutation v_i of $\{1, \ldots, m\}$ with

$$O_{iv_i(1)} \prec O_{iv_i(2)} \prec \ldots \prec O_{iv_i(m)}.$$

A more useful representation is provided by the concept of a *disjunctive graph* $\mathcal{G} = (\mathcal{V}, \mathcal{C}, \mathcal{D})$ [Roy and Sussmann 1964], where

– $\mathcal{V} \subset \mathbb{N} \cup \{*\}$ is the set of *vertices* representing the operations, including dummy operations indicating start and finish; vertex r corresponds to O_r, the starting operation corresponds to vertex 0 and the finishing operation to vertex $*$.
  We define $A_0 \overset{\triangle}{=} \{r | r = N_i + 1, \ i = 0, \ldots, n-1\}$ and $B_* \overset{\triangle}{=} \{r | r = N_i, \ i = 1, \ldots, n\}$ to be the sets of first and last vertices (operations) respectively.
– $\mathcal{C} \subset \mathcal{V} \times \mathcal{V}$ is the set of *conjunctive arcs*, whose directions represent the given processing orders per job; $(r, s) \in \mathcal{C}$ *iff* (if and only if)
  (i) $r = 0$ and $s \in A_0$, or
  (ii) $O_r \prec O_s \ (s = r + 1)$, or
  (iii) $r \in B_*$ and $s = *$.

---

* $\overset{\triangle}{=}$: is by definition equal to.

– $\mathscr{D} \subset \mathscr{V} \times \mathscr{V}$ is the set of *disjunctive arcs* representing the machines; $(r, s) \in \mathscr{D}$ iff $\mu(O_r) = \mu(O_s)$.

We attach weight p_r to each vertex r, taking p_0 and p_* to be 0.*

Example. Consider the 3-job, 2-machine example with

$$\mathscr{S} = \begin{bmatrix} 1 & 2 \\ 2 & 1 \\ 1 & 2 \end{bmatrix}$$

and

$$\mathscr{P} = \begin{bmatrix} 2 & 3 \\ 1 & 4 \\ 6 & 5 \end{bmatrix}$$

The disjunctive graph is drawn in figure 2.1.

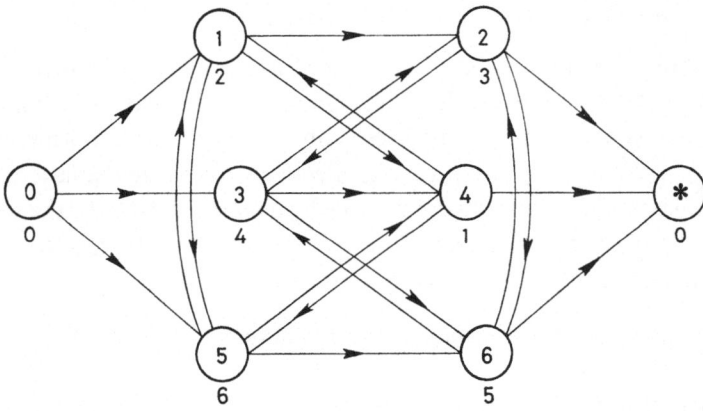

Figure 2.1.

We define the *inverse* disjunctive graph $\mathscr{G}^\dagger = (\mathscr{V}^\dagger, \mathscr{C}^\dagger, \mathscr{D}^\dagger)$ with respect to $\mathscr{G} = (\mathscr{V}, \mathscr{C}, \mathscr{D})$ by

– $\mathscr{V}^\dagger \triangleq \mathscr{V}$;
– $(r, s) \in \mathscr{C}^\dagger$ iff
  (i) $r = 0$ and $(N_n - s + 1, *) \in \mathscr{C}$, or
  (ii) $(N_n - s + 1, N_n - r + 1) \in \mathscr{C}$, or
  (iii) $(0, N_n - r + 1) \in \mathscr{C}$ and $s = *$;

---

* For yet another representation by means of Gantt charts, we refer to section 3.1.

$-\ (r, s) \in \mathscr{D}^\dagger$ iff $(N_n - r + 1, N_n - s + 1) \in \mathscr{D}$;

$-\ p_r^\dagger \triangleq p_{N_n - r + 1}.$

Informally, $\mathscr{G}^\dagger$ is obtained by reversing all conjunctive arcs. Given a problem, defined by $\mathscr{G}$, we can now construct an *inverse problem* defined by $\mathscr{G}^\dagger$. For some optimality criteria, these two problems are strongly related. We shall use this construction in chapters 4 and 5.

The disjunctive graph representation leads to a number of useful insights, including the following simple characterization of feasible sequences. A pair of disjunctive arcs $((r, s), (s, r))$ is called *settled* if one of the two arcs (say, (r, s)) has been added to an (initially empty) set $D \subset \mathscr{D}$ of *chosen* arcs and the other one (s, r) has been added to a set $D' \subset \mathscr{D}$ of *rejected* arcs; by doing so, we assign precedence to O_r over O_s on $M_{\mu(O_r)} = M_{\mu(O_s)}$. If all pairs in $\mathscr{D} \times \mathscr{D}$ have been settled (*i.e.*, $D \cup D' = \mathscr{D}$), a processing order has been defined for each pair of operations in each M_k ($k = 1, \ldots, m$). In order that these define a feasible sequence, we clearly require *transitivity on each machine*:

$-$ if $(r, s) \in D$ and $(s, t) \in D$, then $(r, t) \in D$.

If the above condition is fulfilled, we need not yet have obtained a feasible sequence: the processing order on each machine also has to be compatible with the given processing order per job (cf. figure 2.3). Within the disjunctive graph representation we can effectively formalize the latter requirement and combine it with the former one by defining $\mathscr{G}(D)$ to be the weighted directed graph with vertex set $\mathscr{V}$ and arc set $\mathscr{C} \cup D$ and weight p_r on vertex r; then evidently

$-$ D defines a *feasible sequence* iff $\mathscr{G}(D)$ contains no (directed) cycle.

Example. If in the previous example $D = \{(1, 4), (4, 5), (5, 1), (2, 6), (3, 6), (2, 3)\}$, there is a cycle on M_1 (figure 2.2). If $D = \{(4, 1), (5, 4), (5, 1), (2, 3), (2, 6), (3, 6)\}$, there is a cycle $(1, 2, 3, 4, 1)$ between M_1 and M_2 (figure 2.3). If $D = \{(1, 4), (4, 5), (1, 5), (3, 2), (3, 6), (2, 6)\}$, D defines a feasible sequence with processing order $(1, 4, 5)$ on M_1 and $(3, 2, 6)$ on M_2 (figure 2.4).

The disjunctive graph representation also suggests a further classification according to the type of machine order per job.

If $|J_i \cap M_k| = 1$ for all (i, k) and the v_i are identical for $i = 1, \ldots, n$, the problem is called a *flow-shop* problem. The symbol F will be used to indicate these problems. The following theorem now applies.

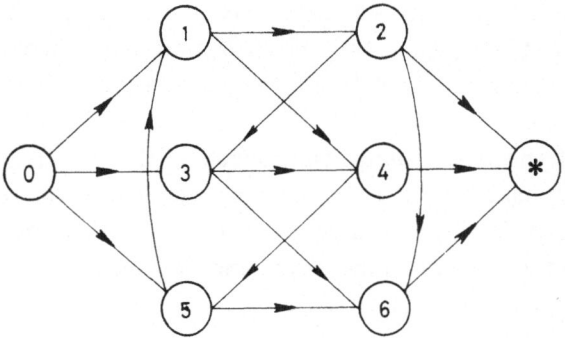

Figure 2.2.

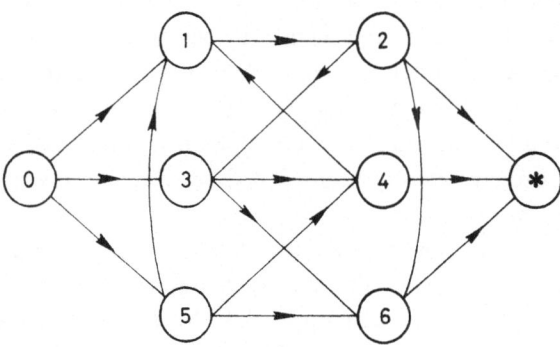

Figure 2.3.

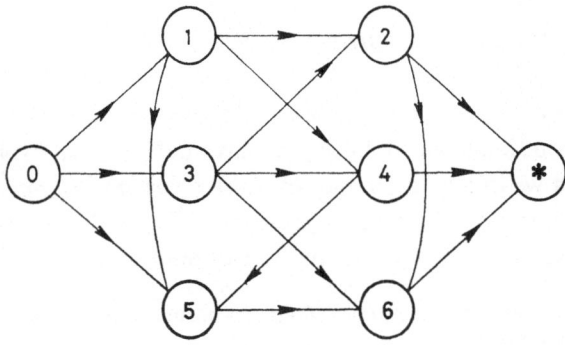

Figure 2.4.

THEOREM 2.1. If $M_1, \ldots, M_m$ can be numbered in such a way that $O_r \prec O_{r+1}$ implies that $\mu(O_r) < \mu(O_{r+1})$, then, given D, transitivity on each machine is a sufficient requirement for $\mathscr{G}(D)$ not to contain a cycle.

PROOF. The transitivity requirement excludes cycles on one machine. Any cycle between machines must contain a conjunctive arc $(r, r+1)$ with $\mu(O_r) < \mu(O_{r+1})$. If s is a third vertex in the cycle, then on one hand we have $\mu(O_{r+1}) \leqq \mu(O_s)$ and on the other hand we have $\mu(O_s) \leqq \mu(O_r)$, contradicting that $\mu(O_r) < \mu(O_{r+1})$.   (Q.E.D.)

Flow-shop problems have a number of other useful properties as well, some of which tend to simplify the search for the optimal schedule. More specifically, it turns out that in certain circumstances an optimal flow-shop schedule exists whereby the processing order is identical on all machines (cf. theorems 5.1 and 5.2). Such a schedule is completely specified by one permutation of $\{1, \ldots, n\}$ and hence is called a *permutation schedule*. Although often an optimal flow-shop schedule will feature non-identical processing orders on some machines (see sections 5.1 and 6.2 for examples), it is sometimes advantageous from a computational point of view to search only for the optimal permutation schedule. Such a restriction will be designated by the symbol P.*

The symbol G will be used to indicate the *general job-shop* problem where the processing order may be different for each job.

It seems useful to stress the importance of a good problem representation such as the disjunctive graph. This model will lead to an additional number of simplified proofs and definitions and has been especially crucial in the development of general job-shop algorithms to be described in chapter 6.

2.2. RESTRICTIVE ASSUMPTIONS

For application of scheduling theory to be possible it is usually necessary that certain conditions are fulfilled that have not yet been explicitly stated. In this section we discuss a number of those *restrictive assumptions*, formulated again in terms of jobs and machines. We shall find that they are sometimes essential, but that usually we can refer to later sections or other

---

* In section 5.4 the restriction to permutation schedules will be made within a general job-shop (notation: G, P).
Everywhere else, the symbol P implicitly indicates a flow-shop situation.

Table 2.1.

(J1)	$\mathcal{J}$ is known and fixed.	(M1)	$\mathcal{M}$ is known and fixed.
(J2)	All jobs are available at the same instant and independent.	(M2)	All machines are available at the same instant and independent.
(J3)	All jobs remain available during an unlimited period.	(M3)	All machines remain available during an unlimited period.
(J4)	Each job can be in each one of three states: waiting for the next machine, being operated by a machine or having passed its last machine.	(M4)	Each machine can be in each one of three states: waiting for the next job, operating on a job or having finished its last job.
(J5)	All jobs are equally important.	(M5)	All machines are equally important.
(J6)	Each job is processed by all the machines assigned to it.	(M6)	Each machine processes all the jobs assigned to it.
(J7)	Each job is processed by one machine at a time.	(M7)	Each machine processes one job at a time.

(JM1)	All processing times are fixed and sequence-independent.
(JM2)	Each operation once started must be completed without interruption.

(JM3)	The processing order per job is known and fixed.	(JM4)	The processing order per machine is unknown and has to be fixed.

literature for a discussion of what can be done if an assumption is not met.

We note in passing that application of the results from succeeding chapters is further restricted by our choice of optimality criteria (section 2.3). In section 2.3.3 we examine how serious this additional restriction is.

Table 2.1 summarizes a number of restrictive assumptions. We shall take a closer look at some of them below. Whenever appropriate, we shall introduce notation to indicate that some condition does *not* hold.

Assumptions (J1) and (M1) are truly crucial; they distinguish the *static/ deterministic* problem from the *dynamic/stochastic* one. We refer to [Conway *et al.* 1967, chapters 7–10] for an introduction to the theory developed for the stochastic problem, where concepts such as *queue* and *waiting line* are fundamental.

On the other hand, assumption (J2) is an example of a far less stringent condition on the applicability of scheduling theory. We shall study later on two situations in which this assumption does not hold (sections 4.2.1, 4.2.3, 4.4.1, 4.4.3, 5.1).

In the first one jobs J_i become available at non-equal integer *ready times* or *release dates* r_i ($i = 1, \ldots, n$). We use the notation $r_i \geqq 0$ to indicate these problems; they will be discussed in sections 4.2.1 and 4.4.1. If at most one r_i can be strictly positive (say for $i = n$), this will be indicated by $r_n \geqq 0$. Everywhere else we shall assume that $r_1 = \ldots = r_n = r^*$, and without loss of generality that $r^* = 0$.

The second situation in which non-simultaneous availability and mutual dependency of jobs arises, occurs when *precedence constraints* exist between jobs, where precedence of J_i over J_j (notation: $J_i \prec J_j$) implies that the processing of J_j cannot start before the completion of J_i. These constraints can be conveniently represented by means of a directed acyclic *precedence graph* $H = (V, A)$ with vertex set $V = \{1, \ldots, n\}$ and arc set $A = \{(i,j) | J_i \prec J_j\}$. Since obviously $(i, j) \in A$, $(j, k) \in A$ implies $(i, k) \in A$, a more efficient representation is obtainable through construction of the *transitive kernel* $H' = (V, A')$ of H, defined to be the minimal subgraph of H such that addition of (i, k) whenever $(i, j_1), (j_1, j_2), \ldots, (j_{r-1}, j_r), (j_r, k)$ are in A' yields H. With respect to the general problem, these precedence constraints can be incorporated in the disjunctive graph representation in a straight-forward manner. In special situations it is sometimes convenient (notably in section 4.4.3) to distinguish between the case that H' is a *branching*, i.e. a set of directed trees with either indegree or outdegree at most equal to 1, and the case in which H' can be any acyclic directed graph. An example of the first mentioned case is provided by H and H' as drawn in figures 2.5

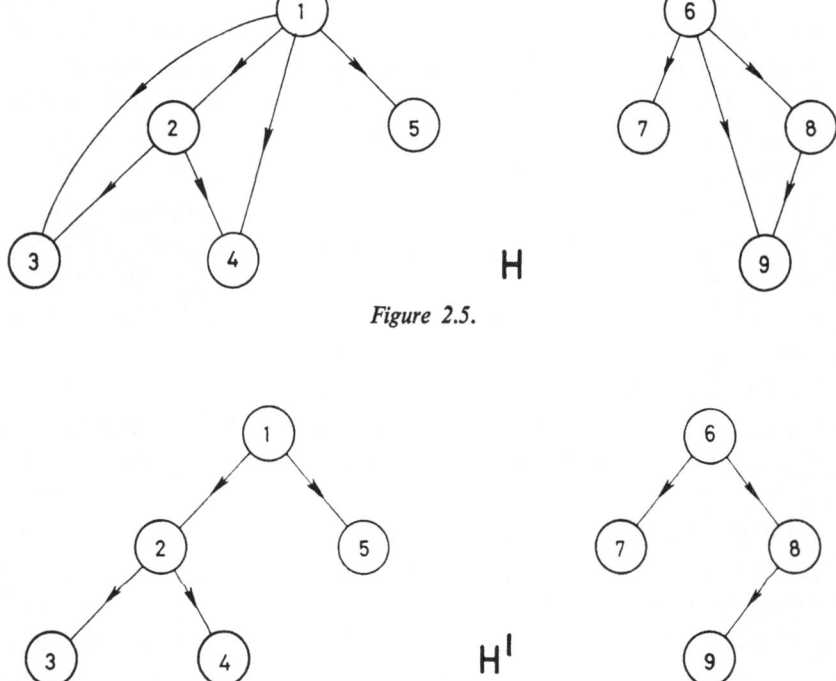

Figure 2.5.

Figure 2.6.

and 2.6. We will indicate this type of problem by means of the notation *tree*, whereas *prec* will denote the general problem.

Although we shall sometimes ignore the presence of delivery dates on which a job should be finished, in many cases assumption (J3) is evidently unrealistic and *due dates* d_i $(i = 1, ..., n)$ will have to be incorporated in our model. Several optimality criteria are formulated explicitly in terms of the d_i (section 2.3.1.2); it is not necessary to define additional notation to indicate their presence.

Assumptions (M2) and (M3) also may be unrealistic: under certain interpretations of the concept of machine, it seems highly unlikely that all or some machines would never be temporarily unavailable due to break-downs, labour shortage or irregular pauses. Relatively little research has been conducted along these lines; we refer to [Sahney 1972] for a simple model involving a limited supply of labour.

With respect to (J4), a number of situations exist in which *intermediate storage* facilities for jobs in process are limited or non-existent. The former situation arises in a computer system where buffer space is limited and costly; the latter situation is met for instance in steel or aluminium rolling where the high temperature of the metal has to be maintained throughout the production process. In either situation, assumption (J4) is not met. We shall be especially interested in the situation in which no waiting time is allowed between machines once a job has started. These problems are discussed in section 6.4 and will be indicated by *no wait*.

The similar restriction (M4) on the possible states of a machine is almost never dropped. Note that (M4) implies that no alternative employment is provided for the machines until the last job has been finished. We may, of course, indicate by our choice of optimality criterion that idle time on some or all machines should occur as rarely as possible. In that case we may also wish to indicate the relative importance of a machine by an appropriate numerical *weight* v_k attached to M_k. This violation of assumption (M5) will be clear from the context and requires no further notation, just as it will be immediately clear from our choice of optimality criterion if assumption (J5) is dropped by attaching *weight* w_i to J_i.

Assumptions (J6) and (M6) again stress the deterministic character of the scheduling problems that will be discussed. If we drop either of them and assume that jobs may be rejected or left unfinished under certain circumstances, the problem changes drastically. Thus, (J6) and (M6) will never be dropped. On the contrary, assumptions (J7) and (M7) exclude certain problems that can sometimes be handled quite easily by extension of available techniques. For instance, *assembly-type* production can be represented

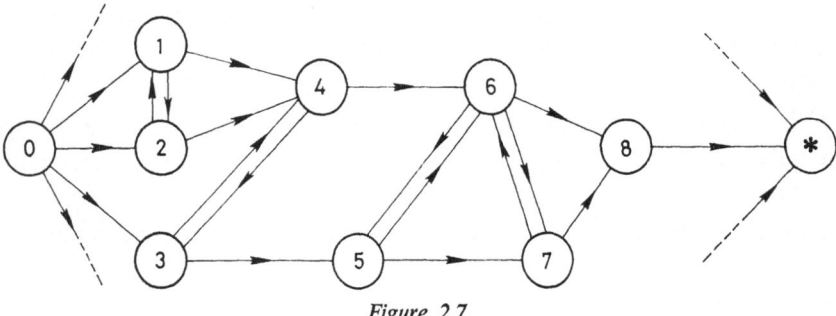

Figure 2.7.

in the disjunctive graph model by replacing a chain of operations representing a job by a directed tree with outdegree at most one. Standard job-shop algorithms can be applied to this model without any complication (figure 2.7).

Another relaxation of (J7) will be studied in section 5.3, where we shall allow a job to start on its second machine before being completely finished on the first one.

An important relaxation of (M7) occurs when we allow a machine M_k to process γ_k jobs at a time with $\gamma_k > 1$, *i.e.* when we increase the *capacity* of M_k from 1 to γ_k. Equivalently, we may assume that γ_k identical machines of type M_k are available. Natural further relaxations then lead to the class of interesting and well-researched problems of *resource constrained project scheduling*. Here, each operation may require more than one machine at a time; the number γ_k of each type of machine that is available may even vary over time. More generally still, the fixed precedence constraints between the operations may be of any type: $\mathscr{G}(\emptyset)$ is then an arbitrary acyclic directed graph. The resulting problem is generally a very difficult one (see [Lenstra *et al.* 1975]). The concept of the disjunctive graph has to be adjusted [Balas 1970a; Gorenstein 1972; MacMahon 1971] and only for problems of small size the optimal schedule can be found within reasonable time (see, for instance, [Davis and Heidorn 1971; Fisher 1973; Fisher 1973a; Lofts 1974; Mason and Moodie 1971; Moodie and Mandeville 1965]. Use of heuristic methods (e.g., [Wiest 1967]) is unavoidable for larger problems. We refer to three surveys [Davis 1966; Davis 1973; Bennington and McGinnis 1973] for further references to the general problem. Special attention has been paid to the case in which each job consists of one operation, to be performed on any of *m identical* or *parallel* machines. In this situation various types of problems can indeed be solved efficiently [Bruno *et al.* 1974; Coffman and Graham 1972; Elmaghraby and Park 1974; Fujii *et al.* 1969; Horn 1974; Hsu 1966; Hu 1961; Root 1965; Rothkopf 1966]. The general problem is also very complicated (see [Lenstra *et al.* 1975; Bruno *et al.* 1974; Ullman 1972]) and again heuristics are often unavoidable (e.g., [Baker and Merten 1973]). Some of these latter methods have been analyzed thoroughly with respect to their worst case behaviour in [Coffman 1975; Garey and Graham 1975; Graham 1969; Graham 1972; Liu 1972]; see also [Eastman *et al.* 1964]. We refer to [Coffman and Denning 1972] and [Liu 1971] for further details, especially with regard to the applicability of this model in the context of computer operating systems.

Finally, in a number of places we will make the more drastic and usually simplifying assumption that one or more M_k are *non-bottleneck machines* that can process all jobs simultaneously (*i.e.*, $\gamma_k \geqq n$). The notation M_k *non-bott* will refer to this violation of (M7).

Turning to assumptions (JM1) and (JM2) that concern the interaction of jobs and machines, we mention first that in sections 4.2.2 and 4.4.2 we shall examine the consequences of *sequence dependent change-over times* between jobs and *job dependent set-up times* on a machine (notation: *seq dep*) in the context of one-machine scheduling. Dropping (JM2) by allowing *job splitting* or *preemption* may actually simplify a problem and will sometimes play a role in developing a solution method. Thus the relaxed problem, indicated by *job spl*, will be studied separately on several occasions.

The final two assumptions (JM3) and (JM4) are again very crucial ones characterizing the type of problem that we shall be interested in.

The above discussion should make it possible to determine the applicability of theory and algorithms presented in the rest of this work. Table 2.2 summarizes the assumptions that we shall drop occasionally and the notation we shall use to indicate this. We now complete our description of the model by discussing in the next section several available optimality criteria and the relations between them.

Table 2.2.

$r_i \geqq 0$	Non-equal release dates.
$r_n \geqq 0$	At most one release date $r_n \geqq 0$.
prec	Arbitrary precedence relations in $\mathscr{J}$.
tree	Transitive kernel of precedence graph is a branching.
no wait	No waiting time between machines once a job has started.
M_k *non-bott*	M_k can process up to n jobs simultaneously.
sep dep	Sequence dependent change-over times and job dependent set-up times.
job spl	Job splitting (preemption) allowed.
—	Due dates d_i.
—	Weights v_k and w_i.

2.3. OPTIMALITY CRITERIA

The objective in any scheduling environment will generally be to minimize the costs that are imputable to the scheduling decision. Hence we have to define cost functions in terms of our model that correspond to various real world conditions. In section 2.3.1 we survey optimality criteria that have been used in previous research and examine a few natural extensions. Relations between those criteria are discussed in section 2.3.2. To facilitate the choice of an appropriate criterion, we briefly analyze scheduling costs from an economic point of view in section 2.3.3.*

2.3.1. Regular measures

A schedule is determined by *starting times* S_r for operation O_r $(O_r \in \mathcal{O})$; if $O_r \in J_i \cap B_*$, $S_r + p_r$ is equal to the *completion time* C_i of J_i.

In seeking to express the costs associated with a particular schedule, we shall restrict ourselves to *regular measures, i.e.* real functions $f(C_1, \dots, C_n)$ such that $f(C_1, \dots, C_n)$ is non-decreasing in every variable:

$$f(C_1, \dots, C_n) < f(C'_1, \dots, C'_n)$$

implies that

$$C_i < C'_i$$

for at least one i. The latter condition seems reasonable enough; it may, however, be questioned if the quality of a schedule should not be judged by more than just the completion times C_i, but actually the class of regular measures turns out to be sufficiently rich to accommodate a large variety of criteria.

Restriction to regular measures has the additional advantage that it allows us to skip our distinction between sequences and schedules. Of course, every schedule uniquely determines a sequence; conversely, given a (feasible) sequence determined by $D \subset \mathcal{D}$, we can calculate S_r for operation O_r by finding its earliest possible starting time in the acyclic graph $\mathcal{G}(D)$ through

---

* In a few studies, more than one criterion has been discussed in the sense that an optimal schedule according to some criterion was sought among those that are optimal with respect to another one [Smith 1956; Heck and Roberts 1972; Emmons 1973; Bratley *et al.* 1971]. See [Lenstra *et al.* 1975] for some results on the complexity of these problems. No particular applications of the theory of *multiple objective programming* [Roy 1971] to scheduling problems have been reported; solution by complete enumeration is presented in [Ashour 1972].

the familiar recursive equations:

$$(2\text{-}3) \quad \begin{cases} S_0 = 0 \\ S_r = \max_{(q,r) \in \mathscr{C} \cup D} \{S_q + p_q\}. \end{cases}$$

The starting times S_r define a schedule with the property that the starting time of no operation can be decreased without altering the processing order on some machine. These schedules are called *semi-active*. It follows from the above discussion that the class $\mathscr{F}$ of all semi-active schedules, being in one-one correspondence with feasible sequences, has finite cardinality of at most $(n!)^m$.

THEOREM 2.2. $\mathscr{F}$ contains at least one optimal schedule with respect to any regular measure.

PROOF. Suppose that we have an optimal schedule not in $\mathscr{F}$. If it is possible to decrease some starting time while maintaining feasibility and the same processing order on each machine, this will not increase $S_r + p_r$ for any r, in particular not for $O_r \in J_i \cap B_*$ with $C_i = S_r + p_r$. Accordingly no C_i will increase, and hence the value of $f(C_1, \ldots, C_n)$ will not increase either. As soon as it is no longer possible to decrease any S_r, we have a semi-active schedule, the cost of which cannot exceed the cost of the original schedule.

(Q.E.D.)

Actually, we shall restrict our choice of criteria somewhat further by assuming the existence of *cost functions* $c_i(t)$ $(i = 1, \ldots, n)$ that are non-decreasing in the time variable t. There are then two types of criteria: either we shall seek to *minimize the maximum cost*

$$(2\text{-}4) \quad c_{\max} = \max_i \{c_i(C_i)\}$$

or *minimize the total cost*

$$(2\text{-}5) \quad \sum c_i = \sum_{i=1}^{n} c_i(C_i).$$

In some situations algorithms can be developed that are suitable for any non-decreasing $c_i(t)$ (e.g., see sections 4.1.3 and 4.3.3). However, it is often advantageous from a computational point of view to use (possibly piecewise) linear cost functions. The most common ones among those will be mentioned in sections 2.3.1.1 and 2.3.1.2.

2.3.1.1. Criteria based on completion times

In the simple case that $c_i(t) = t$, (2-4) corresponds to the *maximum completion time*

(2-6) $C_{max} \overset{\triangle}{=} \max\limits_{1,\dots,n} \{C_i\}.$

C_{max} represents the time interval needed to finish all jobs; it is also called the *schedule time*, *total production time* or *make-span*.

   In this case (2-5) corresponds to the *sum of completion times*

(2-7) $\sum C_i \overset{\triangle}{=} \sum\limits_{i=1}^{n} C_i.$

Dropping assumption (J6), we obtain a more sophisticated criterion by assuming costs per time unit w_i for each job J_i $(i = 1, \dots, n)$. In that case $c_i(t) = w_i t$ and (2-5) becomes the *weighted sum of completion times*

(2-8) $\sum w_i C_i \overset{\triangle}{=} \sum\limits_{i=1}^{n} w_i C_i.$

If $w_i = 1/n$ $(i = 1, \dots, n)$, (2-8) becomes the *average completion time*

(2-9) $\bar{C} \overset{\triangle}{=} \dfrac{1}{n} \sum\limits_{i=1}^{n} C_i.$

Clearly, (2-7) and (2-9) are equivalent from an optimizing point of view. All such relations are collected in section 2.3.2.

   If not all r_i are equal to 0 (*i.e.*, if assumption (J2) is dropped), we can distinguish between C_i and the *flow time* $F_i \overset{\triangle}{=} C_i - r_i$. Analogously to (2-7)–(2-9), we may then choose to minimize the *sum of flow times* $\sum F_i$, the *weighted sum of flow times* $\sum w_i F_i$ and the *average flow time* $\bar{F}$.*

   Finally we may define the *waiting time* W_i by $W_i \overset{\triangle}{=} C_i - (r_i + \sum\limits_{O_r \in J_i} p_r).$

Putting $c_i(t) = t - (r_i + \sum\limits_{O_r \in J_i} p_r)$, we obtain criteria corresponding to the *sum of waiting times* $\sum W_i$, the *weighted sum of waiting times* $\sum w_i W_i$ and the *average waiting time* $\bar{W}$.*

2.3.1.2. Criteria based on due dates

As pointed out in section 2.2, it is sometimes convenient to assume that due dates d_i $(i = 1, \dots, n)$ have been set for each job. Taking $c_i(t) = t - d_i$, we define the *lateness* L_i by $L_i \overset{\triangle}{=} C_i - d_i$ and arrive at criteria corresponding

---

   * F_{max} and W_{max} will not be considered; no non-trivial results on these criteria have been obtained.

to the minimization of the *maximum lateness* L_{max}, the *sum of latenesses* or *total lateness* $\sum L_i$, the *weighted sum of latenesses* $\sum w_i L_i$ and the *average lateness* $\bar{L}$.

Clearly $L_i < 0$ if $C_i < d_i$. Hence, using these criteria implies that we assume negative costs to be incurred if we finish the job before the due date. Sometimes, it may be more realistic to assume that costs are only incurred if a due date is not met. Representing this situation by $c_i(t) = \max(0, t - d_i)$, we define the *tardiness* T_i by $T_i \triangleq \max(0, L_i)$ and we may then seek the minimization of the *maximum tardiness* T_{max}, the *sum of tardinesses* or *total tardiness* $\sum T_i$, the *weighted sum of tardinesses* $\sum w_i T_i$ or *the average tardiness* $\bar{T}$.

2.3.1.3. Criteria based on inventory cost and utilization

We have already mentioned that criteria given by (2-4) or (2-5) may be criticized on the grounds that the costs should be related to the production process as a whole and not just to its outcome as reflected by the C_i. In this section we shall introduce a number of possible alternative criteria that seem more suitable in this respect. Some of them will turn out to be closely related to the criteria introduced in sections 2.3.1.1 and 2.3.1.2 (see section 2.3.2), justifying our restriction to criteria of that type.

Suppose we have a schedule leading to starting time S_r for operation O_r. Then *the number of jobs being processed at time t* is defined by

$$N_p(t) \triangleq |\mathscr{J}_p(t)|$$

with $\mathscr{J}_p(t) \triangleq \{J_i | \exists O_r \in J_i : S_r \leqq t \leqq S_r + p_r\}$. Similarly the *number of jobs waiting at time t* is defined by

$$N_w(t) \triangleq |\mathscr{J}_w(t)|$$

with $\mathscr{J}_w(t) \triangleq \{J_i | \exists O_r, O_{r+1} \in J_i : S_r + p_r < t < S_{r+1}\}$, the *number of jobs finished at time t* by

$$N_f(t) \triangleq |\mathscr{J}_f(t)|$$

with $\mathscr{J}_f(t) = \{J_i | C_i < t\}$, and the *amount of work in progress at time t* by

$$A_p(t) \triangleq \sum_{S_r \leqq t \leqq S_r + p_r} p_r$$

Letting $\bar{f}$ denote the average value of a function $f(t)$ over the interval $[0, C_{max}]$, we can seek to find schedules that minimize $\bar{N}_w$ or $\bar{N}_p + \bar{N}_w$ (roughly reflecting in-process inventory costs), minimize $\bar{N}_f$ (reflecting inventory costs of finished goods) or maximize $\bar{N}_p$ or $\bar{A}_p$ (reflecting the need for efficient use of the available machines).

The importance of efficient utilization of machines can also be expressed by the following three criteria. Defining *idle time* I_k on M_k by

$$I_k \triangleq C_{max} - \sum_{O_r \in M_k} p_r,$$

we can seek to minimize the *total idle time* $\sum I_k \triangleq \sum_{k=1}^{m} I_k$ or the *weighted sum of idle times* $\sum v_k I_k \triangleq \sum_{k=1}^{m} v_k I_k$. Finally, we can be interested in the minimization of the *mean utilization* given by

$$\bar{U} \triangleq \frac{\sum_{i=1}^{n} \sum_{O_r \in J_i} p_r}{m.C_{max}}.$$

As indicated already, there exist several relations between the criteria introduced so far, which makes them effectively equivalent. The next section is devoted to a discussion of these aspects.

2.3.2. Relations between criteria

In this section we examine the relations between the 26 criteria introduced in section 2.3.1. More specifically, we shall be interested to know which criteria happen to be *equivalent* in the sense that a schedule that is optimal with respect to one of them is also optimal with respect to the other(s). Knowledge of these equivalence relations reduces the number of separate problems that we have to deal with in chapters 4, 5 and 6. As usual all conditions from section 2.2 are assumed to hold here, except possibly (J3), (J5) and (M5) that are dropped whenever due dates d_i, weights w_i for J_i and weights v_k for M_k appear in the criterion, and (J2) that may be assumed dropped whenever a flow time criterion is used, since $r_i = 0$ implies $F_i = C_i$.

THEOREM 2.3. The following criteria are equivalent:

  (i) C_{max}
  (ii) $\bar{N}_p$
  (iii) $\bar{A}_p$
  (iv) $\sum I_k$
  (v) $\sum v_k I_k$
  (vi) $\bar{U}$

PROOF. (i) and (ii): from the definition, we deduce

$$\overline{N}_p = \frac{\sum\limits_{i=1}^{n} \sum\limits_{O_r \in J_i} p_r}{C_{\max}} \; ;$$

hence maximizing $\overline{N}_p$ is equivalent to minimizing $C_{\max}$.
(i) and (iii): from the definition, we deduce

$$\overline{A}_p = \frac{\sum\limits_{i=1}^{n} \sum\limits_{O_r \in J_i} p_r^2}{C_{\max}} .$$

(i), (iv) and (v): we have

$$\sum I_k = m C_{\max} - \sum_{k=1}^{m} \sum_{O_r \in M_k} p_r$$

and

$$\sum v_k I_k = (\sum_{k=1}^{m} v_k) C_{\max} - \sum_{k=1}^{m} v_k \sum_{O_r \in M_k} p_r.$$

(i) and (vi): immediate from the definition of $\overline{U}$.   (Q.E.D.)

Remark. Note from (2-3) that $C_{\max}$ is equal to the length of a maximum weight path in $\mathscr{G}(D)$ (also called longest or 'critical' path). From the definition in section 2.1, this must also be the length of a critical path in the inverse disjunctive graph $\mathscr{G}^\dagger$. In fact, if $D \subset \mathscr{D}$ defines an optimal schedule with respect to $\mathscr{G}$, then $D^\dagger \stackrel{\triangle}{=} \{(r, s)|(N_n - s + 1, N_n - r + 1) \in D\} \subset \mathscr{D}^\dagger$ defines an optimal schedule with respect to $\mathscr{G}^\dagger$.

THEOREM 2.4. The following criteria are equivalent:

(i) $\sum C_i$
(ii) $\sum F_i$
(iii) $\sum W_i$
(iv) $\sum L_i$
(v) $\overline{C}$
(vi) $\overline{F}$
(vii) $\overline{W}$
(viii) $\overline{L}$

PROOF. (i), (ii), (iii) and (iv): we have

$$\sum_{i=1}^{n} C_i$$

$$= \sum_{i=1}^{n} F_i + \sum_{i=1}^{n} r_i$$

$$= \sum_{i=1}^{n} W_i + \sum_{i=1}^{n} r_i + \sum_{i=1}^{n} \sum_{O_r \in J_i} p_i$$

$$= \sum_{i=1}^{n} L_i + \sum_{i=1}^{n} d_i.$$

(i) and (v), (ii) and (vi), (iii) and (vii), (iv) and (viii): trivially by definition.

(Q.E.D.)

Remark. By a similar proof $\bar{T}$ and $\sum T_i$ are equivalent criteria.

THEOREM 2.5. The following criteria are equivalent:

(i) $\sum w_i C_i$
(ii) $\sum w_i F_i$
(iii) $\sum w_i W_i$
(iv) $\sum w_i L_i$

PROOF. Similar to the first half of the proof of theorem 2.4.   (Q.E.D.)

THEOREM 2.6. A schedule optimal with respect to L_{max} is also optimal with respect to T_{max}.

PROOF. Given two schedules with latenesses L_i and L_i' and tardinesses T_i and T_i' respectively, we have that $L_{max} = \max_{i}\{L_i\} \leq L_{max}' = \max_{i}\{L_i'\}$ implies that

$$T_{max} = \max_{i}\{\max(0, L_i)\}$$

$$= \max(0, L_{max})$$

$$\leq \max(0, L_{max}')$$

$$= T_{max}'.$$

Remark. Note that L_{max} and T_{max} are not equivalent: a schedule with $T_{max} = 0$ may be suboptimal with respect to L_{max}.

THEOREM 2.7. The following criteria are equivalent:

(i) $\bar{N}_p + \bar{N}_w$
(ii) $\bar{N}_f$
(iii) $\bar{C}/C_{max}$

PROOF. (i) and (ii): from their definitions, we have:

$$\bar{N}_p + \bar{N}_w + \bar{N}_f = n.$$

(i) and (iii): similarly, it can be deduced that

$$(2\text{-}10) \quad \bar{N}_p + \bar{N}_w = \frac{\sum\limits_{i=1}^{n} C_i}{C_{max}}$$

$$= \frac{\bar{C}}{C_{max}} n. \qquad\qquad (Q.E.D.)$$

Remark. Equation (2-10) can be interpreted as the static counterpart of the fundamental relation from dynamic theory: $\bar{N}_p + \bar{N}_w = \lambda\bar{C}$, where λ is the *mean rate of job arrival* [Conway *et al.* 1967].

THEOREM 2.8. The following criteria are equivalent:

(i) $\bar{N}_w$
(ii) $\bar{W}/C_{max}$

PROOF. $\bar{N}_w = \dfrac{n\bar{C}}{C_{max}} - \bar{N}_p$

$$= \frac{n\bar{C}}{C_{max}} - \frac{\sum\limits_{i=1}^{n} \sum\limits_{O_r \in J_i} p_r}{C_{max}}$$

$$= n\,\frac{\bar{W}}{C_{max}}. \qquad\qquad (Q.E.D.)$$

Remark. The criteria from theorems 2.7 and 2.8 are not regular measures, unless C_{max} is sequence independent as in one-machine scheduling (see theorem 4.2), in which case $\bar{N}_p + \bar{N}_w$, $\bar{N}_f$ and $\bar{N}_w$ are equivalent to $\bar{C}$.

We conclude from the above discussion that the following criteria serve to represent all specific regular measures introduced so far:

    (a) C_{max}
    (b) $\sum C_i$
    (c) $\sum w_i C_i$
    (d) L_{max}
    (e) $\sum T_i$
    (f) $\sum w_i T_i$.

We will encounter these criteria again in chapters 4, 5 and 6, together with the general criteria (2-4) and (2-5). First, however, we shall proceed in the next section to be discuss briefly the adequacy of these criteria from an economic point of view.

2.3.3. Analysis of scheduling costs

Within the simple model, defined in sections 2.1 and 2.2, we shall now examine the actual cost related to a scheduling decision and compare the resulting expression to the six criteria (a)–(f) in section 2.3.2 (see also [Gupta 1971; Bornstein 1973]). The main purpose of this section is to justify our choice of these criteria on grounds other than tradition or computational convenience. By the very nature of this objective, the analysis will remain general: any scheduling situation will exhibit its own characteristic features and will require an approach that explicitly takes these features into account.

Our discussion wil again be in terms of the industrial scheduling problem involving jobs and machines; generalisation to other scheduling situations is straightforward.

Since by (JM1) the processing times are fixed and sequence independent, operation (running) costs are sequence independent as well. Thus, we shall consider only the four following cost components:

    (i)   capital costs;
    (ii) inventory costs;
    (iii) machine idle costs;
    (iv) costs due to early or late delivery.

Throughout, we may of course neglect all sequence independent terms; the notation $A \simeq B$ will indicate that $A - B$ is sequence independent.

(i) With respect to *capital costs*, let us assume that the value of raw materials needed to process J_i is equal to f_i and that these materials have to be available at time 0. Let the k-th operation O_{ik} of J_i add g_{ik} to the value of J_i. If we denote the starting time of O_{ik} by S_{ik}, we incur opportunity costs between $S_{i,k-1} + p_{i,k-1}$ and $S_{ik} + p_{ik}$ that are equal to the product of $\rho(S_{ik} + p_{ik} - S_{i,k-1} - p_{i,k-1})$ and the value of J_i at time $S_{i,k-1} + p_{i,k-1}$, where ρ is the net return on investment per time unit. Furthermore, if the job is delivered at time $d_i > C_i$, we incur similar costs during the period $d_i - C_i$. Summing these costs for J_i, we obtain:

$$(2\text{-}11) \quad \sum_{k=1}^{n_i} ((f_i + \sum_{r=1}^{k-1} g_{ir}) \rho (S_{ik} + p_{ik} - S_{i,k-1} - p_{i,k-1})) +$$

$$+ \rho(f_i + \sum_{O_r \in J_i} g_r) \max(0, d_i - C_i)$$

where $S_{i0} = p_{i0} = 0^*$ and $g_{N_{i-1}+k} \stackrel{\triangle}{=} g_{ik}$.

Eliminating sequence independent terms, (2-11) becomes after rearrangement

$$(2\text{-}12) \quad \rho(f_i + \sum_{O_r \in J_i - B*} g_r) C_i - \rho \sum_{O_r \in J_i - B*} g_r S_r + \rho(f_i + \sum_{O_r \in J_i} g_r) \max(0, d_i - C_i).$$

(ii) As to *inventory costs*, let us assume that these costs are equal to e_i per time unit for J_i ($i = 1, \ldots, n$). Hence, we can express them by evaluating for each i

$$\sum_{k=1}^{n_i} (e_i(S_{ik} - S_{i,k-1} - p_{i,k-1})) + e_i \max(0, d_i - C_i)$$

$$= e_i C_i + e_i \max(0, d_i - C_i) - e_i \sum_{O_r \in J_i} p_r$$

$$(2\text{-}13) \quad \simeq e_i C_i + e_i \max(0, d_i - C_i).$$

(iii) *Machine idle costs* have been discussed previously in section 2.3.1.3. If we assume by (M4) that no other employment than $J_1, \ldots, J_n$ is available for the machines from time 0 until $C_{\max}$, idle time costs are equal to

$$\sum_{k=1}^{m} v_k(C_{\max} - \sum_{O_r \in M_k} p_r)$$

$$(2\text{-}14) \quad \simeq (\sum_{k=1}^{m} v_k) C_{\max}$$

where v_k represents the opportunity costs of one unit idle time on M_k.

---

* If we assume that raw materials are available at time S_{i1}, $-f_i \rho S_{i1}$ should be added to (2-11) and to (2-12).

(iv) If, finally, we assume costs equal to a_i $(a_i \geqq 0)$ for each time unit of late delivery (costs due to penalty clauses or loss of goodwill) and allow for negative costs $-b_i$ $(b_i \geqq 0)$ for each time unit of early delivery, the *costs due to early or late delivery of* J_i are given by*

$$a_i \max(0, C_i - d_i) - b_i \max(0, d_i - C_i) =$$

$$= -b_i(d_i - C_i) + (a_i - b_i) \max(0, C_i - d_i) =$$

$$= -b_i d_i + b_i C_i + (a_i - b_i) T_i$$

$$(2\text{-}15) \quad \simeq b_i C_i + (a_i - b_i) T_i.$$

Summing both (2-12) and (2-13) over all i and adding the resultants leads to the following expression for the first two cost components:

$$(2\text{-}16) \quad \sum_{i=1}^{n} \left(\rho \big(f_i + \sum_{O_r \in J_i - B*} g_r \big) + e_i \right) C_i - \rho \sum_{O_r \in \mathcal{O} - B*} g_r S_r$$

$$+ \sum_{i=1}^{n} \left(\rho \big(f_i + \sum_{O_r \in J_i} g_r \big) + e_i \right) \max(0, d_i - C_i).$$

We may rewrite (2-16) in terms of C_i and T_i, sum (2-15) over all i and add (2-14) to arrive at the following expression for total costs:

$$(2\text{-}17) \quad w C_{\max} + \sum_{i=1}^{n} w_i' C_i + \sum_{i=1}^{n} w_i'' T_i - \rho \sum_{O_r \in \mathcal{O}} g_r S_r$$

where

$$w \triangleq \sum_{k=1}^{m} v_k$$

$$w_i' \triangleq b_i$$

$$w_i'' \triangleq \rho \big(f_i + \sum_{O_r \in J_i} g_r \big) + e_i + a_i - b_i.$$

Criterion (2-17) is not a regular one, due to the term $-\rho \sum_{O_r \in \mathcal{O}} g_r S_r$. Combined with the term involving T_i, this cost component reflects the objective to finish the job as near to d_i as possible; it can be traced to the inclusion of the (weighted) *earliness* $E_i \triangleq \max(0, d_i - C_i)$ in (2-12) and (2-13). The latter non-regular measure has been studied relatively little (see [Lawler and Moore 1969] for an isolated result on minimizing $\sum w_i E_i$) and we shall not pursue this matter here.

---

* If costs associated with late delivery increase very fast in time, the $L_{\max}$ or general $c_{\max}$ criterion may become appropriate.

Now, if all g_r are roughly equal, the last term in (2-17) becomes proportional to $\sum_{O_r \in \mathcal{O}} S_r$; it may be possible to ignore this term entirely if the g_r are small. The remaining terms in (2-17) represent a regular measure that under various circumstances may indeed be approximated by one of the criteria (a), (b), (c), (e) or (f). If w is relatively large, the $C_{\max}$ criterion may be used; if $wC_{\max}$ may be ignored, a $\sum c_i$ criterion emerges, which specializes into the $\sum T_i$ or $\sum w_i T_i$ criterion if w_i'' is relatively large, and into the $\sum C_i$ or $\sum w_i C_i$ criterion if w_i'' is relatively small.

If all coefficients are of the same order of magnitude, the situation is more complicated and merits some additional remarks. The first three terms of (2-17) may be rewritten as

$$(2\text{-}18) \quad \max_{j \in \{1,\dots,n\}} \left\{ \sum_{i=1}^{n} ((w_i' + \delta_{ij}w)C_i + w_i''T_i) \right\}$$

where $\delta_{ij} = 1$ if $i = j$ and $\delta_{ij} = 0$ otherwise.

Let us define φ_{jh} to be the value of the j-th component of (2-18) with respect to the h-th schedule ($h = 1, \dots, |\mathcal{F}|$):

$$(2\text{-}19) \quad \varphi_{jh} \triangleq \sum_{i=1}^{n} ((w_i' + \delta_{ij}w)C_i + w_i''T_i)$$

Accordingly, by (2-18) we are interested in finding j_0 and h_0 such that

$$\varphi_{j_0 h_0} = \min_{h}(\max_{j}\{\varphi_{jh}\})$$

Note that (2-19) represents a $\sum c_i$ criterion that again may specialize into $\sum C_i$, $\sum w_i C_i$, $\sum T_i$ or $\sum w_i T_i$. Hence, it is of interest to know under which circumstances there is a schedule with index h_1, such that both

$$(2\text{-}20) \quad \max_{j}\{\varphi_{jh_1}\} = \min_{h}(\max_{j}\{\varphi_{jh}\})$$

and

$$(2\text{-}21) \quad \varphi_{j_1 h_1} = \min_{h}\{\varphi_{j_1 h}\}$$

for some j_1. In this case we may restrict our attention to the n schedules minimizing (2-19) for $j = 1, \dots, n$. These can be found by the algorithms to be presented in chapters 4, 5 and 6.

In general, h_1 satisfying both (2-20) and (2-21) need not exist, as demonstrated immediately by an inspection of the simple case in which $w_i' = w_i'' = 0$, $w = 1$.

Suppose, however, that for some h_1 with

(2-22) $\varphi_{j_1 h_1} = \min_{h} \{\varphi_{j_1 h}\}$

for some j_1, we also find that

(2-23) $\varphi_{j_1 h_1} = \max_{j} \{\varphi_{j h_1}\}$.

In this case the matrix $[\varphi_{jh}]$ has a *saddle point* and it is well known, e.g. from the theory of games, that (2-22) and (2-23) together imply that

$$\varphi_{j_1 h_1} = \min_{h}(\max_{j} \{\varphi_{jh}\}),$$

i.e. we may take $j_0 = j_1$, $h_0 = h_1$. Moreover, it follows also that

$$\varphi_{j_1 h_1} = \max_{j}(\min_{h} \{\varphi_{jh}\}),$$

hence the only schedule that could possibly satisfy (2-22) and (2-23) is the one that maximizes the value of the j-th optimal schedule over all j. If this schedule does not satisfy (2-23), it may nevertheless be a heuristically satisfying solution.

We conclude that the traditional choice of criteria (a)–(f) or the general $c_{\max}$ or $\sum c_i$ criteria can be reasonably justified on economic grounds. It remains quite possible that an actual scheduling situation requires a more complicated or even non-regular measure of performance, but the insights obtained in this section can be quite useful in practice. We refer to chapter 7 for a simple illustration of this point of view.

Having explored the basic properties of our model in sections 2.1, 2.2 and 2.3, we are now in a position to introduce the classification of machine scheduling problems that will be used throughout the rest of this work.

2.4. CLASSIFICATION OF PROBLEMS

We now extend the scheme in [Conway *et al.* 1967] to obtain the following classification of machine scheduling problems.

The classification has the following format:

$$\alpha|\beta|\gamma, \Gamma|\delta$$

where:

- α represents the number of jobs; we shall in fact assume α to be an integer variable n.*
- β represents the number of machines; we shall find that it pays to distinguish between the cases in which β is equal to 1, 2 or 3 and the general case in which β is an integer variable m.
- γ indicates the type of machine ordering per job and the possible restriction to permutation schedules ($\gamma \in \{F, P, G\}$).
- Γ is a (possibly empty) parameter set indicating dropped assumptions by means of the notation developed in section 2.2, and possible limitations on the range of p_r, n_i, d_i or w_i.
- δ indicates the optimality criterion in the notation of section 2.3.

Example. A $n|1|seq\ dep|C_{\max}$ problem is the problem to minimize the maximum completion time of n jobs to be processed on 1 machine, when there are job dependent set-up times and sequence dependent change-over times.

The above classification affords more than just a notational convenience. It is exhaustive with respect to the framework developed so far and yet it is not too detailed: a change in some parameter often leads to a substantially different problem that has been the subject of separate research. Moreover, the value of parameters α, β, γ, Γ and δ will turn out to determine to a large extent the complexity of a problem, in a sense yet to be defined in section 3.6. These aspects largely justify the problem oriented approach taken in chapters 4, 5 and 6, where different $\alpha|\beta|\gamma$, $\Gamma|\delta$ problems will be studied separately.

Having delimited the types of problems that we shall be interested in, we shall in the next chapter present a general survey of various methods that have been used to solve such problems, and discuss some of the properties of these methods.

---

* See [Hardgrave and Nemhauser 1963] for an efficient algorithm for the $2|m|G|C_{\max}$ problem.

3

Methods of solution

In this chapter we examine the better known methods that have been used to solve machine scheduling problems. They will be treated in more or less detail in inverse proportion to the degree to which they reappear in chapters 4, 5 and 6. The presentation in sections 3.1 to 3.5 and 3.7 thus varies between the description of a common framework and a definite review. Since the choice of an appropriate solution method depends to some extent on the complexity of the problem, we consider this latter aspect more formally in section 3.6.

We shall now discuss the sections in more detail.

The combinatorial nature of machine scheduling problems has been noted before; the finite cardinality of $\mathscr{F}$ has been mentioned in the context of theorem 2.2. Accordingly, an optimal schedule could be found in principle by *complete enumeration* of all elements of $\mathscr{F}$. Although it turns out in section 3.1 that the enumeration can be restricted to a subset of $\mathscr{F}$, the number of elements in this subset is still too large for this method to be suitable for any but the smallest problems.

Hence, the search for an optimal schedule has to be conducted in a more efficient manner by exploiting characteristic features of the problem under consideration. Methods of *combinatorial analysis* often turn out to be useful in this context. With respect to scheduling problems, they frequently involve a close examination of the effect of a minor change in a particular schedule (notably the interchange of two – possibly adjacent – jobs). Section 3.2 contains a very general result due to W. E. Smith indicating circumstances under which this type of analysis will lead to an optimal schedule straightaway. Even if this is not the case this 'local' approach serves to reduce the number of candidates for the optimum on many occasions.

The evident approach to scheduling problems through *mixed integer and non-linear programming* methods is reviewed in detail in section 3.3. Several formulations of a general $n|m|G|\delta$ scheduling problem as a 0–1 or non-linear model turn out to be possible. Although the formulations are elegant and flexible, the very generality of these models has a predictably negative influence on their computational efficiency and more specific methods are necessary.

Many algorithms developed with the latter purpose are of a more 'global' nature: by successively partitioning $\mathscr{F}$ into smaller and smaller subsets each schedule is either explicitly or implicitly considered. The latter situation occurs if an entire subset $F \subset \mathscr{F}$ can be removed from further consideration, because a schedule at least as good as the ones in F has been previously obtained or because such a schedule is known to exist among the remaining ones on combinatorial analytical grounds.

Methods of branch-and-bound fall within this description and are introduced in section 3.4; the related method of *dynamic programming* is briefly discussed in section 3.5.

The behaviour of especially branch-and-bound methods is unfortunately very unpredictable. In most, if not all cases, these methods do not lead to algorithms that are *good* or *efficient* in the by now conventional sense [Edmonds 1965] that the total number of steps is bounded by a polynomial function of some input parameter(s). Thus it seems reasonable to ask if the *complexity* of a problem is such that an enumerative approach like branch-and-bound is unavoidable. Recent results in the theory of computational complexity allow at least a partial answer to this question and will be discussed in section 3.6.

One of the consequences of these results is that efficient algorithms are highly unlikely to be found for many types of machine scheduling problems. *Heuristic methods* producing suboptimal solutions therefore are unavoidable in many practical situations. In actual practice it seems possible to exploit known optimal algorithms to produce a good heuristic approach; we refer to section 7.2 for a small example. Two widely tested very general heuristics are discussed in section 3.7: section 3.7.1 briefly summarizes the many experiments involving *priority rules* and section 3.7.2 introduces and extends the approach based on statistical properties of randomly generated schedules, combined with *Bayesian analysis*.

3.1. COMPLETE ENUMERATION

The cardinality of $\mathscr{F}$ for a $n|m|\gamma$, $\Gamma|\delta$ problem is bounded from above by $(n!)^m$; if $\gamma = P$, this number reduces to $n!$. Even for small values of n and m the cardinality becomes very large. If $n = m = 5$, $(n!)^m = 24,883,200,000$, which implies that a computer evaluating 100,000 schedules a second would still need almost three days to evaluate them all.

Clearly then, this form of complete enumeration is not suitable even for small problems. The question arises whether it is possible to identify a subset of $\mathscr{F}$ containing an optimal schedule with respect to any regular measure, so that it is unnecessary to enumerate all elements in $\mathscr{F}$.

Such a subset is the set of *active schedules, i.e.* those semi-active schedules in which it is not possible to decrease the starting time of any operation without increasing the starting time of at least one other one. The set $\mathscr{F}_0$ of all active schedules is a subset of $\mathscr{F}$ and must contain an optimal schedule with respect to every regular measure.

The $2|3|F|\delta$ semi-active schedule with $p_{21} = p_{12} = p_{23} < p_{11} = p_{22} = p_{13}$ illustrated by the *Gantt-chart* in figure 3.1 illustrates the concept. (In a Gantt-chart (see [Porter 1968]) operations are represented by closed intervals on time-axes that represent the machines, the length of the interval being proportional to the processing time.)

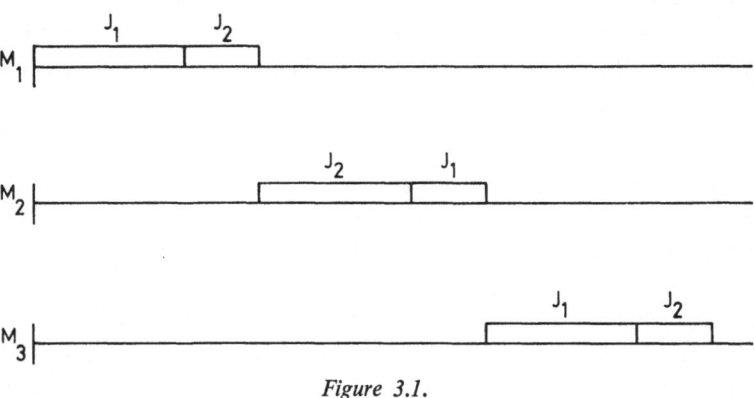

Figure 3.1.

S_{12} can be decreased by $p_{12} + p_{22}$ time-units, allowing a decrease of $p_{12} + p_{22}$ time-units in both C_1 and C_2. Clearly, the schedule in figure 3.1 is not an active one.

In theorem 3.1 we shall give a quasi-ALGOL procedure that generates each active schedule exactly once. We define the operation ':$\in$' in the statement '$s :\in S$' to mean that s becomes an arbitrary element selected from the set S.

THEOREM 3.1 (cf. [Giffler and Thompson 1960]). The following procedure generates each active schedule with respect to a disjunctive graph $\mathscr{G}$ exactly once.

procedure *actsched* $(\mathcal{G})$;
begin procedure *node* $(S, \{t(O_s)|O_s \in T\}, T)$;
    begin local Q, k;
        if $S = \emptyset$ **then**
        comment an active schedule has been generated
        else
        begin $k :\in \{l | \min \{t(O_s) + p_s | O_s \in S \cap M_l\}$
                $= \min \{t(O_s) + p_s | O_s \in S\}\}$;
             $Q := \{O_r | O_r \in S \cap M_k : t(O_r) < \min \{t(O_s) + p_s | O_s \in S\}\}$;
             while $Q \neq \emptyset$ **do**
             begin $O_r :\in Q$; $S_r := t(O_r)$;
                  $Q := Q - \{O_r\}$;
                  node (**if** $O_r \in B_*$ **then** $S - \{O_r\}$
                  else $(S - \{O_r\}) \cup \{O_{r+1}\}$,
                  $\{$**if** $O_s \in M_{\mu(O_r)} \cup J_{\iota(O_r)}$
                  then $\max(t(O_s), S_r + p_r)$
                  else $t(O_s)\}, T - \{O_r\})$
            end
        end
    end;
    node $(A_0, \{0\}, \emptyset)$;
end *actsched*;

PROOF. Whenever node $(S, \{t(O_s)|O_s \in T\}, T)$ is called, S contains all operations O_s such that all O_r with $O_r \ll O_s$ have been scheduled. Thus, we only have to prove that the restriction to $Q \subset S$ is the proper one, *i.e.* that:

    (i)   each schedule generated by actsched $(\mathcal{G})$ is active;
    (ii) a schedule that is not generated by actsched $(\mathcal{G})$ is not active;
    (iii) all schedules generated by actsched $(\mathcal{G})$ are different.

We prove (i) and (ii), (iii) being trivial.

(i) Suppose that in some schedule generated by actsched $(\mathcal{G})$ we try to decrease S_s for some O_s. If this is at all possible, it means that at some point we must have been able to choose O_s, but have chosen O_r instead. Hence, $S_r < t(O_s) + p_s$ and S_r would have to be increased.

(ii) Suppose that instead of $O_r \in M_k$ we choose $O_s \in M_l \cap (S - Q)$. If $O_{s+1} \in M_k$, it should not be scheduled immediately since $t(O_{s+1}) \geq$ $\geq t(O_s) + p_s \geq \min \{t(O_r) + p_r | O_r \in M_k \cap S\}$. Thus, if the resulting schedule is at all active (which need not be the case: possibly $O_{r+1} \in M_l$ and $t(O_{r+1}) + p_{r+1} \leqq t(O_s)$), it can be generated by actsched ($\mathscr{G}$).   (Q.E.D.)

The cardinality $|\mathscr{F}_0|$ of $\mathscr{F}_0$ is still too large for the set to be effectively enumerable, but the algorithm from theorem 3.1 reappears in an $n|m|G|C_{\max}$ algorithm to be described in section 6.3.

If in node $(S, \{t(O_s)|O_s \in T\}, T)$ we change the assignment of k and Q to

$$k :\in \{l|\min\{t(O_s)|O_s \in S \cap M_l\} = \min\{t(O_s)|O_s \in S\}\};$$

$$Q := \{O_r|O_r \in S \cap M_k : t(O_r) = \min\{t(O_s)|O_s \in S \cap M_k\}\};$$

the resulting schedule is called a *non-delay schedule*. An optimal schedule is not necessarily a non-delay one, as illustrated by the optimal $2|3|F|C_{\max}$ schedule with $p_{22} = p_{13} = 2p_{11} = 2p_{12}$ in figure 3.2.

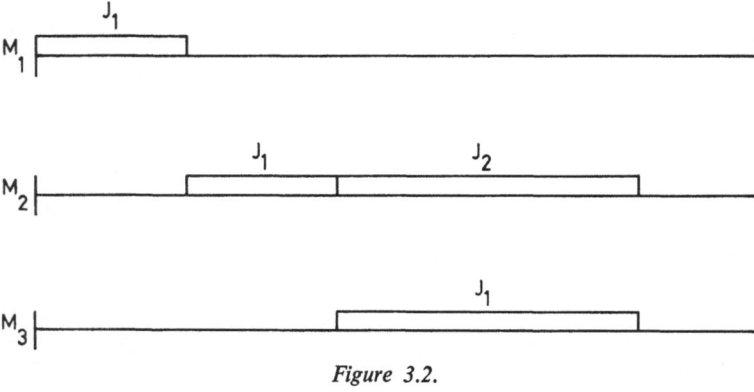

Figure 3.2.

It is none the less remarkable that random generation of a number of non-delay schedules seems to provide better schedules on the average than similar generation of active schedules, as reported in [Conway *et al.* 1967].

3.2. COMBINATORIAL ANALYSIS

The term combinatorial analysis here serves to indicate all analytical methods that are or might be used in designing algorithms for combinatorial problems. It has already been pointed out that in the context of scheduling problems these methods often involve close examination of the effect of some type of minor change in a particular schedule. If, as is the case with $n|m|P|\delta$ problems or $n|1||\delta$ problems, this schedule can be represented by a permutation $\pi: \{1, \ldots, n\} \to \{1, \ldots, n\}$, the type of change defines a *neighbourhood* *structure* of the set of all permutations (see [Reiter and Sherman 1965; Rau 1970; Nicholson 1971]). Thus, if we consider the effects of an interchange of two adjacent jobs, this defines the neighbourhood of π (represented as an ordered n-tuple $(\pi(1), \ldots, \pi(n))$)) to be the set containing all permutations $(\pi(1), \ldots, \pi(i-1), \pi(i+1), \pi(i), \pi(i+2), \ldots, \pi(n))$ for $i = = 1, \ldots, n-1$. Similarly, if we consider the interchange of two not necessarily adjacent jobs, the neighbourhood of $(\pi(1), \ldots, \pi(n))$ contains all permutations of the type $(\pi(1), \ldots, \pi(i-1), \pi(j), \pi(i+1), \ldots, \pi(j-1), \pi(i), \pi(j+1), \ldots, \pi(n))$ for $i = 1, \ldots, n-1, j = 1, \ldots, n, i < j$.

The analysis of neighbourhoods, especially the two types mentioned above, will often allow us to develop a partial ordering of the jobs that has to be respected by at least one optimal schedule. For certain types of problems, the analysis even leads to a total (linear) ordering of the jobs, in which case an efficient algorithm to solve the problem has been found. The following theorem indicates circumstances in which a *switching argument* indeed produces an optimum.

THEOREM 3.2 [Smith 1956]. If a function g exists such that

(3-1) $g(\pi(j+1), \pi(j)) \leqq g(\pi(j), \pi(j+1))$

implies that

$$\varphi(\pi(1), \ldots, \pi(j+1), \pi(j), \ldots, \pi(n)) \leqq$$

(3-2) $$\leqq \varphi(\pi(1), \ldots, \pi(j), \pi(j+1), \ldots, \pi(n))$$

where φ is the function to be minimized over all permutations, then a permutation π^* with

(3-3) $i < j$

implying that

(3-4) $g(\pi^*(i), \pi^*(j)) \leqq g(\pi^*(j), \pi^*(i))$

is optimal with respect to φ.

PROOF. Suppose π^* exists. Any $\pi \neq \pi^*$ must contain two adjacent elements $(\pi^*(j), \pi^*(i))$ with $i < j$. Interchanging them will produce a new permutation without increasing φ because of (3-3), (3-4), (3-1) and (3-2). Continuing in this way, π^* will be reached eventually.   (Q.E.D.)

Even if g exists, the ordering defined by (3-4) may not be transitive. However, when g is a function of only a single argument, this ordering is transitive, for in this case (3-1) becomes

$$g(\pi(j+1)) \leqq g(\pi(j))$$

and (3-4) becomes

$$g(\pi^*(i)) \leqq g(\pi^*(j)),$$

the transitivity now being obvious.

Some special functions φ for which g can be constructed are described in [Elmaghraby 1968] and [Rau 1970]; no non-trivial application of these results is known.

The techniques described in this section and theorem 3.2 in particular will be encountered frequently in chapters 4, 5 and 6.

3.3. MIXED INTEGER AND NON-LINEAR PROGRAMMING

A natural way to attack machine scheduling problems is to formulate them as mathematical programming models.

We shall present five different ways to do this in subsections 3.3.1 to 3.3.5 below; except for subsection 3.3.3, we are always referring to $n|m|G|\delta$ problems.

3.3.1. [Bowman 1959]

We introduce $|\mathcal{O}|.\tau$ $0-1$ variables X_{rt} where τ is some upper bound on $C_{\max}$; X_{rt} will be equal to 1 iff O_r is being processed at time t. This leads to the following constraints:

$$\sum_{t=1}^{\tau} X_{rt} = p_r \qquad\qquad (O_r \in \mathcal{O})$$

$$(3-5) \quad p_r(X_{rt} - X_{r,t+1}) + \sum_{u=t+2}^{\tau} X_{ru} \leqq p_r \qquad (O_r \in \mathcal{O}; t = 1, \ldots, \tau - 1)$$

$$\sum_{O_r \in M_k} X_{rt} \leqq 1 \qquad\qquad (k = 1, \ldots, m; t = 1, \ldots, \tau)$$

$$(3-6) \quad p_r X_{r+1,t} \leqq \sum_{u=1}^{t-1} X_{ru} \qquad (O_r \in \mathcal{O} - B_*; t = 1, \ldots, \tau)$$

Job splitting is prevented by (3-5); the processing order per job is enforced by (3-6). The objective function to be minimized if $\delta = C_{\max}$ is

$$(3\text{-}7) \quad \sum_{t=0}^{\tau-\tau_0} \sum_{O_r \in B_*} (n+1)^t X_{r,\tau_0+t}$$

where $\tau_0 \triangleq \max_i \{ \sum_{O_r \in J_i} p_r \}$.

The total number of constraints is $2|\mathcal{O}|.\tau + (m-n)\tau$.

In [Haehling Von Lanzenauer and Himes 1970] (3-5) and (3-6) are reformulated so as to make all coefficients equal to 0 or ± 1. The linear program that originates if all $0-1$ variables are treated as continuous ones in the closed interval $[0, 1]$ is claimed to have often a $0-1$ solution, but this cannot be guaranteed at all.

3.3.2. [Pritsker et al. 1969]

In a related approach, the model is reformulated in such a way that $X_{rt} = 1$ iff $S_r + p_r = t$. The constraints are the following.

$$\sum_{t=l_r}^{u_r} X_{rt} = 1 \qquad\qquad (O_r \in \mathcal{O})$$

with $l_r = \sum_{O_s \ll O_r} p_s$ and $u_r = \tau - \sum_{O_r \ll O_s} p_s$.

$$\sum_{t=l_r}^{u_r} t X_{rt} + p_{r+1} \leq \sum_{t=l_{r+1}}^{u_{r+1}} t X_{r+1,t} \qquad\qquad (O_r \in \mathcal{O} - B_*)$$

$$\sum_{O_r \in M_k} \sum_{u=t}^{t+p_r-1} X_{ru} \leq 1 \qquad\qquad (t = 1, \ldots, \tau - \min_{O_r \in M_k} \{p_r\};$$
$$k = 1, \ldots, m)$$

Again, (3-7) can be taken as the objective function. The number of constraints is at most equal to $2|\mathcal{O}| + m\tau - n$. This formulation is clearly more compact than the previous one, although the number of $0-1$ variables remains very large. We refer to [Redwine and Wismer 1974] for a successful application of this model.

3.3.3. [Wagner 1959]

This approach is only suitable for $n|m|P|\delta$ problems. We require n^2 $0-1$ variables X_{ij} where $X_{ij} = 1$ iff J_i is scheduled in the j-th position. Thus we have:

$$\sum_{i=1}^{n} X_{ij} = 1 \qquad\qquad\qquad (j = 1, \dots, n)$$

$$\sum_{j=1}^{n} X_{ij} = 1 \qquad\qquad\qquad (i = 1, \dots, n)$$

We introduce additional real variables Z_{jk} ($j = 1, \dots, n-1; k = 1, \dots, m$) to represent idle time on M_k between the j-th and $(j+1)$-th job and U_{jk} ($j = 1, \dots, n; k = 1, \dots, m-1$) to represent the waiting time for the j-th job between M_k and M_{k+1}:

$$Z_{jk} + \sum_{i=1}^{n} p_{ik} X_{i,j+1} + U_{j+1,k} =$$

$$= U_{jk} + \sum_{i=1}^{n} p_{i,k+1} X_{ij} + Z_{j,k+1} \qquad \begin{array}{l}(j = 1, \dots, n-1; \\ k = 1, \dots, m-1)\end{array}$$

where $Z_{j1} = 0$ for $j = 1, \dots, n-1$.

If $\delta = C_{\max}$, the objective function to be minimized is given by

$$\sum_{i=1}^{n} \sum_{j=1}^{m-1} p_{ij} X_{i1} + \sum_{i=1}^{n-1} Z_{im}$$

The number of constraints is $mn + n - m + 1$. Although the formulation seems quite attractive for this particular problem, computational experience as reported in [Muth and Thompson 1963] is not encouraging.

3.3.4. [Manne 1960]

Introducing real variables S_r to represent, as usual, the starting time of O_r, we have

(3-8) $S_{r+1} - S_r \geqq p_r$ \qquad\qquad\qquad ($O_r \in \mathcal{O} - B_*$)

We need $\frac{1}{2} \sum_{k=1}^{m} |M_k| \cdot (|M_k| - 1)$ $0 - 1$ variables Y_{rs} to represent machine interference, with $Y_{rs} = 1$ if O_r precedes O_s and $Y_{rs} = 0$ if O_s precedes O_r on their machine $M_{\mu(O_r)} = M_{\mu(O_s)}$:

(3-9) $\begin{cases} (c + p_s) Y_{rs} + (S_r - S_s) \geqq p_s & (O_r, O_s \in M_k; \\ (c + p_r)(1 - Y_{rs}) + (S_s - S_r) \geqq p_r & k = 1, \dots, m) \end{cases}$

where c is some large constant.

Constraints (3-9) insure that the *disjunctive constraint*

(3-10) $(S_r - S_s \geqq p_s) \vee (S_s - S_r \geqq p_r)$

is true for every pair (r, s) with $\mu(O_r) = \mu(O_s)$.

If we introduce an additional real variable S with

$$S \geqq S_r + p_r \qquad\qquad\qquad\qquad\qquad (O_r \in B_*)$$

minimizing $C_{\max}$ is simply equivalent to minimizing S.

The number of constraints with $0 - 1$ variables in $\sum\limits_{k=1}^{m} |M_k|(|M_k| - 1)$. This formulation is attractive, because it closely reflects the disjunctive graph structure. Computational experience with this model using general $0 - 1$ methods ([Balas 1967; Gupta 1971a; Raimond 1969]) has again not been particularly encouraging.

3.3.5. *[Nepomiastchy 1973]*

Using the real variables S_r introduced previously and again setting constraint (3-8), we replace the disjunctive constraint (3-10) by the following non-linear non-convex constraint

$$(S_r - S_s - p_s)(S_s - S_r - p_r) \leqq 0$$

We may again use the objective function S defined above. The resulting non-linear programming problem is solvable by penalty function methods leading to a local, possibly non-global optimum. Thus, this ingenious approach is essentially heuristic.

Notwithstanding the mathematical elegance of the five models presented above, it should be noted that no good general algorithm has been developed to solve $0 - 1$ or non-linear programming problems. Generally, it appears that these methods do not make sufficient use of the special structure of scheduling problems. Whenever we fail to find a good method for a particular scheduling problem (see section 3.6), we may just as well turn to more tailor-made forms of implicit enumeration to be discussed next.

3.4. BRANCH-AND-BOUND

Methods of *branch-and-bound* (*backtracking, branch-and-exclude,* etc.) are among the most widely used solution methods for combinatorial programming problems. They were developed and first used in the context of mixed integer programming [Land and Doig 1960] and the travelling salesman problem [Eastman 1959], but soon their wide applicability was perceived. The main reason for their present popularity seems to be the simplicity of the basic principles, combined with easy implementation (see [Lenstra and Rinnooy Kan 1975]) and often surprising computational efficiency. However, by their very nature the computational behaviour of these methods remains unpredictable.

Branch-and-bound methods find a solution $x^* \in X$ minimizing a function $c: X \to \mathbb{R}$, where $|X|$ is usually finite, by *implicit enumeration* of all $x \in X$ through examination of increasingly smaller subsets $Y \subset X$, until the latter either are singletons or definitely do not contain all x^*. The latter situation arises if we know that a solution superior to those in Y exists, either on combinatorial-analytical grounds or because we have explicitly obtained it previously.

The formal properties of branch-and-bound methods have been analyzed both for $|X|$ finite (*e.g.*, see [Agin 1966] or [Balas 1968]) and $|X|$ infinite [Mitten 1970; Rinnooy Kan 1974]. Such very general analyses do not seem to be required here. Since our description of the several branch-and-bound procedures to be encountered in chapters 4, 5 and 6 will be rather informal, we give in this section a general framework of a branch-and-bound algorithm and settle terminology.

Suppose then, that given a *set X of feasible solutions* and a *criterion function $c: X \to \mathbb{R}$*, we want to find an $x^* \in X$ such that $c(x^*) = \min_{x \in X} c(x)$. A branch-and-bound procedure to find such an *optimal solution* can be characterized as follows.

– Throughout the execution of the procedure, the *best solution x^* found so far* provides an *upper bound* $c(x^*)$ on the value of the optimal solution.
– A *branching rule* b associates to $Y \subset X$ a family $b(Y)$ of subsets such that
$$\bigcup_{Y' \in b(Y)} Y' = Y;$$
the subsets Y' are the *descendants* of the *parent* subset Y. This rule only has to be defined on a set $\mathscr{X}$ with $X \in \mathscr{X}$ and $b(Y) \subset \mathscr{X}$ for any $Y \in \mathscr{X}$.
– A *bounding rule* $lb: \mathscr{X} \to \mathbb{R}$ provides a *lower bound* $lb(Y) \leqq c(x)$ for all $x \in Y \in \mathscr{X}$. *Elimination* of Y occurs if $lb(Y) \geqq c(x^*)$.
– A *predicate* $\xi: \mathscr{X} \to \{true, false\}$ indicates if during the examination of Y (e.g. during the calculation of $lb(Y)$) a feasible solution $x(Y)$ is generated which has to be evaluated. *Improvement* of x^* occurs if $c(x^*) > c(x(Y))$.
– A *search strategy* chooses a subset from the collection of generated subsets which have so far neither been eliminated nor led to branching.

It turns out that, of the three search disciplines that have been used most frequently, two are suitable for *recursive implementation*. To illustrate this, we shall present three general procedures:

- 'bb jumptrack' implements a *frontier search* where a subset with minimal lower bound is selected for examination;
- 'bb backtrack1' implements a *depth-first search* where the descendants of a parent subset are examined in an arbitrary order; this type of tree search is known as *newest active node search*;
- 'bb backtrack2' implements a *depth-first search* where the descendants are chosen in order of non-decreasing lower bounds; this type is sometimes called *restricted flooding*.

During the tree search, parameters na and nb count the numbers of subsets that are eliminated and that lead to branching respectively. We define the operation ':$f\in$' in the statement 's :$f\in S$' to mean that $s := s^*$ with $f(s^*) = = \min_{s\in S} f(s)$; hence, ':$\in$' indicates an arbitrary choice, as in section 3.1.

procedure *bb jumptrack* $(X, c, x^*, b, lb, \xi, na, nb)$;
begin local $\mathscr{Y}, \mathscr{Y}', \mathscr{B} \subset \mathscr{X}, Y, Y' \in \mathscr{X}, LB: \mathscr{X} \to \mathbb{R}$;
    $na := nb := 0; \mathscr{Y} := \emptyset$;
    $LB(X) := lb(X)$; **if** $\xi(X)$ **then** $x^* :c\in \{x^*, x(X)\}$;
    if $LB(X) \geq c(x^*)$ **then** $na := 1$ **else** $\mathscr{Y} := \{X\}$;
    while $\mathscr{Y} \neq \emptyset$ **do**
    begin $Y : LB \in \mathscr{Y}$;
        $nb := nb + 1; \mathscr{B} := b(Y); \mathscr{Y} := (\mathscr{Y} - \{Y\}) \cup \mathscr{B}$;
        while $\mathscr{B} \neq \emptyset$ **do**
        begin $Y' :\in \mathscr{B}; \mathscr{B} := \mathscr{B} - \{Y'\}$;
            $LB(Y') := lb(Y')$; **if** $\xi(Y')$ **then** $x^* :c\in \{x^*, x(Y')\}$
        end;
        $\mathscr{Y}' := \{Y' | Y' \in \mathscr{Y}, LB(Y') \geq c(x^*)\}$;
        $na := na + |\mathscr{Y}'|; \mathscr{Y} := \mathscr{Y} - \mathscr{Y}'$
    end
end *bb jumptrack*;

procedure *bb backtrack1* $(X, c, x^*, b, lb, \xi, na, nb)$;
begin local $Y' \in \mathscr{X}$;
    procedure *node*(Y);
    begin local $\mathscr{B} \subset \mathscr{X}, LB \in \mathbb{R}$;
        $LB := lb(Y)$; **if** $\xi(Y)$ **then** $x^* :c\in \{x^*, x(Y)\}$;
        if $LB \geq c(x^*)$ **then** $na := na + 1$ **else**

$$\textbf{begin } nb := nb+1; \mathscr{B} := b(Y);$$
$$\textbf{while } \mathscr{B} \neq \emptyset \textbf{ do}$$
$$\textbf{begin } Y' :\in \mathscr{B}; \mathscr{B} := \mathscr{B} - \{Y'\};$$
$$\textbf{if } LB < c(x^*) \textbf{ then } node(Y')$$
$$\textbf{end}$$
$$\textbf{end}$$
$$\textbf{end};$$
$$na := nb := 0;$$
$$node(X)$$
$$\textbf{end } bb \ backtrack1;$$

$$\textbf{procedure } bb \ backtrack2 \ (X, c, x^*, b, lb, \xi, na, nb);$$
$$\textbf{begin local } \mathscr{B} \subset \mathscr{X}, Y' \in \mathscr{X}, LB: \mathscr{X} \to \mathbb{R};$$
$$\textbf{procedure } node(Y);$$
$$\textbf{begin local } \mathscr{Y} \subset \mathscr{X};$$
$$nb := nb+1; \mathscr{Y} := \mathscr{B} := b(Y);$$
$$\textbf{while } \mathscr{B} \neq \emptyset \textbf{ do}$$
$$\textbf{begin } Y' :\in \mathscr{B}; \mathscr{B} := \mathscr{B} - \{Y'\};$$
$$LB(Y') := lb(Y'); \textbf{if } \xi(Y') \textbf{ then } x^* :c \in \{x^*, x(Y')\}$$
$$\textbf{end};$$
$$\textbf{while } \mathscr{Y} \neq \emptyset \textbf{ do}$$
$$\textbf{begin } Y' : LB \in \mathscr{Y}; \mathscr{Y} := \mathscr{Y} - \{Y'\};$$
$$\textbf{if } LB(Y') \geqq c(x^*) \textbf{ then } na := na+1 \textbf{ else } node(Y')$$
$$\textbf{end}$$
$$\textbf{end};$$
$$na := nb := 0;$$
$$LB(X) := lb(X); \textbf{if } \xi(X) \textbf{ then } x^* :c \in \{x^*, x(X)\};$$
$$\textbf{if } LB(X) \geqq c(x^*) \textbf{ then } na := 1 \textbf{ else } node(X)$$
$$\textbf{end } bb \ backtrack2;$$

Actual branch-and-bound procedures may vary at minor points with the above descriptions. Notably, if the search discipline is newest active node, the heuristic ordering referred to above may be based on a first estimate $lb'(Y') \leqq lb(Y')$; $lb(Y')$ will only be calculated for subsets that are actually chosen. The essential difference between newest active node and the other disciplines remains that in the former approach lower bounds are not calculated before a choice has been made. Also, elimination of Y may be possible during the calculation of $lb(Y)$ or may be based on *elimination criteria* provided by dominance rules or feasibility considerations. Minor variations as described above do not influence the basic mechanisms of branch-and-bound.

Branch-and-bound search procedures can be conveniently represented by means of a *search tree* consisting in step 1 only of a single node representing X. In step 2, $|b(X)|$ nodes are created, each of them representing a particular $Y \in b(X)$. Edges are created between the node representing X and all the nodes representing some $Y \in b(X)$, etc. Nodes can be eliminated by means of lower bounds or elimination criteria.*

The unpredictability of branch-and-bound methods alluded to previously is clear from the above description. In most, if not all cases the number of possible nodes in the search tree will be superpolynomial or exponential in some problem parameters. There is no way of finding out in general how many of these nodes will not have to be examined because of sufficiently large lower bounds or elimination criteria. Hence the actual computational behaviour remains unpredictable and untractable: the algorithm is never good in the formal sense and large scale experiments are necessary to get an indication of its quality. This, in turn, raises the question of how to define and obtain 'fair' test data; any answer to such a question remains somewhat arbitrary and unsatisfactory. Altogether, branch-and-bound methods should certainly not be used before one feels reasonably sure (see section 3.6) that no substantially better approach can be found.

3.5. DYNAMIC PROGRAMMING

Methods of dynamic programming have been used to solve a number of (mainly) $n|m|P, \Gamma|\delta$ scheduling problems. Basically, these methods interpret scheduling and other combinatorial optimization problems as multistage decision problems. Bellman's principle of optimality is then invoked to draw up recursive equations that describe the optimal criterion function at step n in terms of previously obtained ones.

Thus, these methods lead to a search graph conceptually similar to the branch-and-bound tree. In many combinatorial applications a 'lower bound' is given by the costs incurred so far. Branches are pruned by means of this lower bound if they lead to subgraphs representing identical sets of alternatives.

---

* The search tree representation underlines that we are dealing with a fundamental type of search procedure that figures prominently in other branches of science as well. The resulting links between operations research and a discipline such as artificial intelligence seem little known and deserve further exploration.

We illustrate this approach by means of two typical examples that will be referred to later on.

3.5.1. [Held and Karp 1962; Lawler 1964]

In the $n|1||\sum c_i$ problem, denote by $c^*(S)$ the minimum costs incurred by scheduling $\{J_i | i \in S\}$ in the period from 0 to $\sum_{i \in S} p_{i1}$.
Then we have typically:

$$c^*(\emptyset) = 0$$

$$c^*(S) = \min_{i_0 \in S} \{c^*(S - \{i_0\}) + c_{i_0}(\sum_{i \in S} p_{i1})\}$$

The problem is solved by recursively calculating $c^*(\{1, \ldots, n\})$.

It is instructive to interpret these two equations in terms of the shortest path from vertex $v(\emptyset)$ to vertex $v(\{1, \ldots, n\})$ in a weighted directed search graph with 2^n vertices, with vertex $v(S)$ corresponding to subset $S \subset \{1, \ldots, n\}$. A directed arc from $v(S)$ to $v(T)$ exists whenever $T - \{i_0\} = S$, and has length $c_{i_0}(\sum_{i \in T} p_{i1})$. The recursive equation now simply states that the shortest path from $v(\emptyset)$ to $v(S)$ is a one step extension of the shortest path to one of the vertices directly preceding $v(S)$.

Better methods can be devised to solve the $n|1||\sum c_i$ problem (see section 4.3.3); the number of vertices in the search graph is large and $c^*(S)$ functions only as a weak lower bound on the costs of any complete schedule obtained from S. Comparing the structure of this graph to a branch-and-bound search tree described in section 4.3.3.2, we see that typically the dynamic programming approach leads to a smaller total number of possible vertices, but only at the expense of more complicated bookkeeping.

3.5.2. [Lawler and Moore 1969]

Consider an $n|1||\sum c_i$ problem with the special feature that the processing order of $J_1, \ldots, J_n$ is fixed, but that each job may be processed in two different ways.

The first one requires p_i' time-units, the second one p_i'' time-units; costs incurred if $C_i = t$ equal $c_i'(t)$ in the first case and $c_i''(t)$ in the second case.

Defining $c^*(j, t)$ to be the minimal total cost for the first j jobs under the constraint that these jobs are finished at time t at the latest, we have the knapsack-like equations:

$$c^*(0, t) = 0 \qquad\qquad (t \geqq 0)$$

$$c^*(j, t) = +\infty \qquad\qquad (t < 0)$$

$$c^*(j, t) = \min(c^*(j, t-1), c_j'(t) + c^*(j-1, t-p_j'),$$

$$c_j''(t) + c^*(j-1, t-p_j''))$$

The problem is then solved by calculating $c^*(n, \sum_{i=1}^{n} \max(p_i', p_i''))$.

The assumption of a fixed processing order seems to render this approach not suitable for our type of scheduling problem. However, it has been ingeniously adapted to solve the $n|1|d_i = d^*|\sum w_i T_i$ problem and a number of other scheduling problems. Some of these applications will be reported in due course.

The two examples above illustrate the elegance and simplicity of the dynamic programming equations. As mentioned, dynamic programming methods are not always computationally attractive; the size of the search graph is often superpolynomial and the pruning mechanism inherent in the equations may be rather weak.

3.6. COMPLEXITY THEORY

In view of the unpredictable behaviour of implicit enumeration methods as compared to the polynomial-boundedness of good algorithms, it seems natural to ask with respect to any particular problem if the use of the first mentioned type of method is really unavoidable. A partial answer to this question can be obtained through results from the theory of *computational complexity* concerning the relation between the classes $\mathscr{P}$ and $\mathscr{NP}$ of (*language recognition*) *problems* solvable on *deterministic* and *non-deterministic Turing machines* respectively, in a number of steps bounded by a polynomial in the size of the problem input.* However, in a combinatorial programming context we do not really require mathematically rigorous

---

* The influence of the particular encoding chosen forms a relatively neglected topic. Usually we shall assume a standard encoding in binary numbers; hence, if input consists of an integer A, the size of the inputstring is $\lceil^2\log A\rceil$. See, however, section 4.3.2 for a brief discussion of the effect of allowing *unary* encoding, in which the size of input A is proportional to A.

definitions of these concepts, and for our purpose we may in fact safely identify $\mathscr{P}$ with the class of problems for which a good (*i.e.* polynomial-bounded [Edmonds 1965]) algorithm can be found, and $\mathscr{NP}$ with the class of problems solvable by backtrack search in a search tree of polynomial-bounded depth. Clearly $\mathscr{P} \subset \mathscr{NP}$, and the question arises whether this inclusion is a proper one or if, on the contrary, $\mathscr{P} = \mathscr{NP}$.

Although this fundamental question must remain unanswered for the time being, there are results, to be discussed shortly, that render an affirmative answer to the $\mathscr{P} = \mathscr{NP}$ question highly unlikely; most bets (e.g., in [Knuth 1974]) have in fact been going in the other direction. To examine the consequences of an affirmative answer, let us define the following relation between problems P_1 and P_2: P_1 *is reducible to* P_2 ($P_1 \propto P_2$) if for any instance of P_1 an instance of P_2 can be constructed in a polynomial-bounded number of steps such that solving the instance of P_2 will solve the instance of P_1 as well. Thus, P_1 can informally be considered to be a special case of P_2. If $P_1 \propto P_2$ and $P_2 \propto P_1$, the two problems are called *equivalent*.

We have already encountered simple examples of these relations in previous sections: the $n|m|\gamma, \Gamma|T_{\max}$ problem is reducible to the $n|m|\gamma, \Gamma|L_{\max}$ problem by virtue of theorem 2.6 and $n|m|\gamma, \Gamma|\delta$ is equivalent to $n|m|\gamma, \Gamma|\delta'$ if δ and δ' are equivalent criteria (see theorems 2.3, 2.4, 2.5, 2.7). Note, however, that the $n|1||\sum c_i$ problem is not reducible to the shortest path problem, since the construction in section 3.5.1 is not polynomial-bounded, the number of vertices in the graph being equal to 2^n.

In 1971, S. A. Cook proved the remarkable result [Cook 1971] that all problems in $\mathscr{NP}$ are reducible to the so-called SATISFIABILITY problem, which consists of finding out if a given formula in Boolean variables can assume the value *true*. In Cook's paper, such a formula is explicitly constructed for any problem in $\mathscr{NP}$. It follows now that an affirmative answer to the $\mathscr{P} = \mathscr{NP}$ question is equivalent to the existence of a good algorithm for the SATISFIABILITY problem: if SATISFIABILITY $\in \mathscr{P}$, a good algorithm for any $P \in \mathscr{NP}$ could be found by first constructing the corresponding SATISFIABILITY problem and solving the latter problem. Both steps are polynomial-bounded and the resulting algorithm would obviously be good.

The same argument applies if we replace SATISFIABILITY by any problem P_1 in $\mathscr{NP}$ such that every $P_2 \in \mathscr{NP}$ is reducible to P_1. If we call such a problem P_1 *NP-complete* [Knuth 1974], then $\mathscr{P} = \mathscr{NP}$ *iff* a good algorithm exists for any NP-complete problem. A large number of such NP-complete problems have been identified by R. M. Karp in [Karp 1972]; the following theorem mentions a number of them. Since they are all notoriously difficult combinatorial problems, for which typically no good algorithm has been found so far, Karp's results afford strong circumstantial evidence that the equality of $\mathscr{P}$ and $\mathscr{NP}$ is highly unlikely.

THEOREM 3.3. The following problems are NP-complete.

(i) PARTITION

Given positive integers $a_1, \ldots, a_t$, does there exist a subset $S \subset T = \{1, \ldots, t\}$ such that $\sum\limits_{i \in S} a_i = \sum\limits_{i \notin S} a_i$?

(ii) KNAPSACK

Given positive integers $a_1, \ldots, a_t, b$, does there exist a subset $S \subset T = \{1, \ldots, t\}$ such that $\sum\limits_{i \in S} a_i = b$?

(iii) DIRECTED HAMILTONIAN CIRCUIT

Given a directed graph $G = (V, A)$, does G have a hamiltonian circuit (*i.e.*, a directed cycle passing through each vertex exactly once)?

(iv) DIRECTED HAMILTONIAN PATH

Given a directed graph $G' = (V', A')$, does G' have a hamiltonian path (*i.e.*, a directed path passing through each node exactly once)?

(v) TRAVELLING SALESMAN

Given a complete directed graph on n vertices with weight (length) c_{ij} attached to arc (i, j), what is the shortest hamiltonian circuit?

(vi) CLIQUE

Given an undirected graph $G = (N, E)$ and an integer k, does G contain a k-clique (*i.e.*, a complete subgraph on k nodes)?

PROOF. For proofs of (i), (ii), (iii) and (vi), we refer to [Karp 1972]. The problems under (iv) and (v) are both in $\mathscr{NP}$ and to prove NP-completeness it is sufficient to prove that an NP-complete problem such as DIRECTED HAMILTONIAN CIRCUIT is reducible to both of them.

(iv) DIRECTED HAMILTONIAN CIRCUIT $\propto$ DIRECTED HAMILTONIAN PATH:

Given $G = (V, A)$, choose $v_0 \in V$ and construct $G' = (V', A')$ with

$V' = V \cup \{v_0'\} \ (v_0' \notin V)$

$A' = \{(v, w) | (v, w) \in A, w \neq v_0\} \cup \{(v, v_0') | (v, v_0) \in A\}$

G has a hamiltonian circuit *iff* G' has a hamiltonian path.

(v)   DIRECTED HAMILTONIAN CIRCUIT $\propto$ TRAVELLING SALESMAN:

Given $G = (V, A)$, take $n = |V|$ and define

$$c_{ij} = \begin{cases} 0 & \text{if } (i, j) \in A \\ 1 & \text{if } (i, j) \notin A \end{cases}$$

G has a hamiltonian circuit *iff* there is a travelling salesman's route of length ≤ 0.   (Q.E.D.)

Note that in order to deal with the complexity of a minimization problem we transform it into the problem of finding a solution with value at most equal to some y. Many reductions in [Karp 1972] feature the same transformation that is required to make these problems compatible with problems requiring a yes/no answer.

The relevance of the concept of NP-completeness with respect to the opening question of this section is now clear: establishing NP-completeness for a machine scheduling problem renders the discovery of a good algorithm for the problem highly unlikely and thus serves as a formal justification to use branch-and-bound or similar methods of implicit enumeration. Embarrassing incidents such as the presentation in a standard text-book of a branch-and-bound approach to the undirected Chinese postman problem, for which a good algorithm had already been developed in [Edmonds 1965a], are then less likely to occur.

In a well-structured area such as machine scheduling, where a natural problem classification as developed in section 2.4 is available, it is particularly challenging to study the effect of various problem parameters on the complexity of the problem. More specifically, one would like to describe in terms of these parameters the borderline separating the 'easy' problems (in $\mathscr{P}$) from the 'hard' (NP-complete) ones. It has been noted in several problem areas that a minor change in some problem parameter (notably, for some as yet mystical reason, an increase from two to three) may transform an 'easy' problem into a 'hard' one. Similar results with respect to machine scheduling situations will be presented throughout chapters 4, 5 and 6. Gathering all these results in chapter 7, we shall find that a reasonable insight in the location of the above-mentioned borderline has been obtained, although some questions remain open.

Discussion of the complexity results will be facilitated by mentioning at this point a number of elementary results on reducibility among machine scheduling problems.

THEOREM 3.4.

(i)   If $n'|m'|\gamma', \Gamma'|\delta' \propto n|m|\gamma, \Gamma|\delta$ and $n|m|\gamma, \Gamma|\delta \in \mathscr{P}$, then $n'|m'|\gamma', \Gamma'|\delta' \in \mathscr{P}$.

(ii)   If $n'|m'|\gamma', \Gamma'|\delta' \propto n|m|\gamma, \Gamma|\delta$ and $n'|m'|\gamma', \Gamma'|\delta'$ is NP-complete, then $n|m|\gamma, \Gamma|\delta$ is NP-complete.

(iii) $n|m'|\gamma, \Gamma|\delta \propto n|m|\gamma, \Gamma|\delta$ if $m' \leqq m$ or if m' is constant and m is variable.

(iv) $n|m|F, \Gamma|\delta \propto n|m|G, \Gamma|\delta$

(v) $n|m|\gamma, \Gamma|\delta \propto n|m|\gamma, \Gamma \cup \Gamma'|\delta$ if $\Gamma' \subset \{r_i \geqq 0, r_n \geqq 0, prec, tree\}$

(vi) $n|m|\gamma, \Gamma \cup \Gamma'|\delta \propto n|m|\gamma, \Gamma|\delta$ if
$\Gamma' \subset \{n_i \leqq n^*, p_{ik} = 1, 0 \leqq p_{ik} \leqq p^*, w_i = 1\}$

(vii) $n|m|\gamma, \Gamma|C_{\max} \propto n|m|\gamma, \Gamma|L_{\max}$

(viii) $n|m|\gamma, \Gamma|T_{\max} \propto n|m|\gamma, \Gamma|L_{\max}$

(ix) $n|m|\gamma, \Gamma|\sum C_i \propto n|m|\gamma, \Gamma|\sum T_i$

(x) $n|m|\gamma, \Gamma|\sum w_i C_i \propto n|m|\gamma, \Gamma|\sum w_i T_i$

(xi) $n|m|\gamma, \Gamma|\sum C_i \propto n|m|\gamma, \Gamma|\sum w_i C_i$

(xii) $n|m|\gamma, \Gamma|\sum T_i \propto n|m|\gamma, \Gamma|\sum w_i T_i$

(xiii) $n|m|\gamma, \Gamma|\delta$ and $n|m|\gamma, \Gamma|\delta'$ are equivalent if δ and δ' are equivalent criteria.

(xiv) $n|1|r_n \geqq 0|\delta \propto n|2|F|\delta$

(xv) $n|2|r_n \geqq 0|\delta \propto n|3|F|\delta$

PROOF.

(i, ii)   By the definition of reducibility.

(iii, iv)   Trivial.

(v, vi, vii)   The problems on the left hand side are special cases of the problems on the right hand side.

(viii)   Theorem 2.6.

(ix, x, xi, xii) See (v, vi, vii) above.

(xiii)   By the definition of equivalence of criteria (section 2.3.2).

(xiv)   Given p_{i1} $(i = 1, \ldots, n)$, r_n, take
$$p'_{i1} = 0 \quad (i = 1, \ldots, n - 1)$$
$$p'_{n1} = r_n$$
$$p'_{i2} = p_{i1} \quad (i = 1, \ldots, n)$$

The $n|2|F|\delta$ problem defined by the p'_{i1} and p'_{i2} has a solution with value at most y *iff* the $n|1|r_n \geqq 0|\delta$ problem has a solution with value at most equal to y, as can be easily verified.

Note that the above construction involves processing times equal to 0, implying that the jobs in question visit the machine for an infinitesimally small period of time. In each case, however, where (xiv) will be used, it turns out to be possible by sufficiently inflating all problem data to make all of them strictly positive integers. Examples of such constructions can be found in theorem 5.12 (ii, iii).

(xv)   Similar to (xiv).   (Q.E.D.)

As announced, we shall frequently apply the concepts introduced in this section in chapters 4, 5 and 6. The NP-completeness of many scheduling problems as proved in these chapters again underlines the necessity of good suboptimal approaches. Two such approaches will be discussed in the next section.

3.7. HEURISTIC METHODS

Even if an actual scheduling problem can be fitted into the model developed in chapter 2, its complexity may be such that finding an optimal schedule would be too time consuming to be feasible. Under these circumstances *heuristic methods* that produce good, but possibly suboptimal schedules are of interest. A very general methodology to design heuristic methods that reflect the characteristic features of a particular problem situation, is discussed and illustrated in chapter 7. Basically, this approach involves the determination of *critical machines* in the production process that are important from a cost-minimizing point of view and whose functioning has a crucial influence on the production process as a whole. Often, insights derived from the study of optimal algorithms to be pursued in chapters 4, 5 and 6 can be used to develop good rules to schedule such critical machines; the resulting schedules are linked in a heuristic fashion to produce an overall schedule of reasonable quality.

In this section we propose to discuss briefly only two methods that have attracted attention because of their very general applicability (with the predictable negative effect on their general quality). Nevertheless, the *priority rules* to be mentioned in section 3.7.1 deserve attention if only for the enormous effort that has gone into experimenting with these rules on randomly generated problems. In section 3.7.2 we discuss and illustrate the possible application of *Bayesian analysis* to scheduling problems within the framework developed in [Raiffa and Schlaifer 1961].

3.7.1. Priority rules

A priority rule is a prescription determining which operation O_r should be chosen next from the set S of *scheduleable* operations appearing in the algorithm described in theorem 3.1.

Thus, instead of randomly selecting O_r from Q (i.e., using the RANDOM rule), we may grant highest priority to O_r such that

(i) $d_{\iota(O_r)}$ is minimal (all minima or maxima are to be taken over Q) (the earliest due date (EDD) rule);

(ii)   the *slacktime* $\sigma_r \triangleq d_{\iota(O_r)} - (p_r + \sum_{O_r \ll O_s} p_s)$ is minimal or maximal;

(iii) $\sigma_r/(|\bar{A}_r|+1)$ with $\bar{A}_r \triangleq \{O_s | O_r \ll O_s\}$ is minimal;

(iv) $t(O_r)$ is minimal (the first come, first served (FCFS) or first in, first out (FIFO) rule);

(v) $r_{\iota(O_r)}$ is minimal (if $r_i \geqq 0$ holds);

(vi) p_r is minimal (the shortest processing time (SPT) or shortest operation time (SOT) rule);

(vii)   the *workload* $\omega_r \triangleq p_r + \sum_{O_r \ll O_s} p_s$ is minimal (maximal);

(viii) $\sum_{O_s \in J_{\iota(O_r)}} p_s$ is minimal (maximal);

(ix) $|\bar{A}_r|$ is minimal (maximal);

(x) O_r has minimal set-up time (if *seq dep* holds).

Still other priority rules have been developed and can be found in [Gere 1966; Conway *et al.* 1967; Day and Hottenstein 1970]. The performance of most rules has been extensively investigated. Large scale experiments reported in [Conway *et al.* 1967] indicate that priority rules work best on non-delay schedules, that the SPT and RANDOM (!) rule are superior to most other rules on active schedules and that the 'maximal ω_r' rule performs quite well in general. No rule is obviously the best one, and this outcome is further confirmed in [Gere 1966]. Here it is reported that rules based on σ_r are slightly better than the SPT rule, which in turn outperforms the RANDOM and FIFO rule. However, when bolstered by some additional heuristics such as an 'alternative operation' rule where J_j is preferred to J_i if the choice of J_i threatens overdue delivery of J_j, and a 'look ahead' rule whereby J_i waits if an urgent job is on the way, all rules work about equally well. Finally, a mixture of the RANDOM rule and some priority rules reported in [Conway *et al.* 1967] involves the assignment to all operations in S of probabilities of choice that are to a certain degree influenced by the priority of the operations; surprisingly, some fixed degree of randomness consistently leads to schedules superior to those produced by either extreme method.

Having reported very briefly on some computational experiments, it seems to us that the relatively high quality of the RANDOM rule adequately illustrates the insufficiency of priority rules for complex scheduling problems. But then, all these rules are of a particularly simple type: decisions are taken in order of implementation (*dispatching procedures*) and are never revoked (*single pass procedures*). As yet, few *iterative heuristics* have been developed, but the few experiments conducted so far as reported in [Krone and Steiglitz 1974] certainly warrant a more thorough investigation of this possibility.* Generally speaking, most implicit enumeration methods can also be used to produce suboptimal solutions quickly: all lower bounds can be increased by a fixed constant or fixed percentage, or the procedure may simply stop when the first feasible solution has been found. Next to straight-forward simulation of human decision making (see [Dutton 1964]), these and other iterative heuristics seem to be much better equipped to deal with the complexity of many standard scheduling problems.

3.7.2. Bayesian analysis

A second heuristic approach to scheduling problems is based on the obser-vation [Ashour 1972; Heller 1960] that the number of distinct schedule times $C_{\max}$ is usually much smaller than the number of distinct semi-active schedules. Thus we can study the distribution of the random variable $\underline{C}_{\max}$ over the set $\mathscr{F}$ of all semi-active schedules. This distribution can be proved to be (asymptotically) normal [Heller 1959]; extensive numerical experi-ments [Heller 1960] have confirmed Heller's result.

Denoting the unknown parameters of this normal distribution by μ and σ, we can use methods of *Bayesian analysis* to generate random schedules until we have found a schedule, the schedule time of which is such that, roughly speaking, the probability of finding a smaller schedule time in the next experiment is not greater than some given α_0. Without entering into a general discussion on the relative merits of such an approach, we propose to indicate in more detail in this section how such an analysis could be carried out. Previous comparable approaches [Randolph *et al.* 1973; Cunningham and Turner 1973] have neglected to exploit the normal distribution of $\underline{C}_{\max}$. We shall make use of the notations and some general results in [Raiffa and Schlaifer 1961].

---

* From a theoretical point of view it would be very interesting to know more about the worst case behaviour of priority rules and other simple heuristics; the relation between worst case behaviour and problem size may well further characterize the complexity of a problem (see [Garey and Graham 1975; Gonzalez and Sahni 1975]).

Basically, we start by constructing a *prior distribution* on the parameters μ and $\underline{\sigma}$, reflecting our initial beliefs on their values. We then generate a random schedule, use its value to update parameters of the prior distribution to find the *posterior distribution* of $(\mu, \underline{\sigma})$ and calculate the probability p, given the posterior distribution, of finding a value $C_{\max}$ in the next experiment that is smaller than the currently best schedule time C^*. If $p \leq \alpha_0$, we stop; otherwise, the posterior distribution serves as a prior distribution to the next experiment, etc.

To construct a computationally tractable prior distribution, we note that the *likelihood* of outcomes $(x_1, \ldots, x_n)$ is given by

$$(3\text{-}11) \quad l(x_1, \ldots, x_n | \mu, \sigma) = \frac{1}{(\sqrt{2\pi}\,\sigma)^n} \, e^{-\sum_{i=1}^{n}(x_i - \mu)^2 / 2\sigma^2}.$$

Defining

$$m \triangleq \frac{1}{n} \sum_{i=1}^{n} x_i,$$

$$v \triangleq \frac{1}{n-1} \sum_{i=1}^{n} (x_i - m)^2,$$

(3-11) becomes

$$l(x_1, \ldots, x_n | \mu, \sigma) = \frac{1}{(\sqrt{2\pi}\,\sigma)^n} \, e^{-(n-1)v/2\sigma^2} \cdot e^{-n(m-\mu)^2/2\sigma^2},$$

so that (m, v, n) are *sufficient statistics* in the sense of [Raiffa and Schlaifer 1961]. Dropping constant factors, we write

$$(3\text{-}12) \quad l(x_1, \ldots, x_n | \mu, \sigma) \sim \frac{1}{\sigma^n} \, e^{-(n-1)v/2\sigma^2} \cdot e^{-n(m-\mu)^2/2\sigma^2}.$$

We select a prior distribution from the family of *natural conjugates* [Raiffa and Schlaifer 1961] of (3-12), *i.e.*

$$(3\text{-}13) \quad D(\mu, \sigma | m, v, n, v) \sim \frac{1}{\sigma} \, e^{-(\mu - m)^2 / 2(\sigma^2/n)} \cdot e^{-vv/2\sigma^2} \, \frac{1}{\sigma^{v+1}}.$$

If the prior distribution is given by (3-13), the posterior distribution after one experiment with value x is given by multiplying (3-13) and $l(x|\mu, \sigma)$; we then obtain $D(\mu, \sigma | m'', v'', n'', v'')$ with

$$(3\text{-}14) \quad m'' \triangleq \frac{n'm' + x}{n' + 1},$$

$$(3\text{-}15) \quad n'' \triangleq n' + 1,$$

(3-16) $v'' \triangleq \dfrac{v'v' + n'm'^2 + x^2 - n''m''^2}{v' + 1},$

(3-17) $v'' \triangleq v' + 1,$

so that the posterior distribution is of the same type as the prior distribution. Equations (3-14)–(3-17) describe the updating process referred to previously.

We may now calculate

$$p = \iiint_R l(x|\mu, \sigma)D(\mu, \sigma|m', v', n', v')dx\,d\mu\,d\sigma$$

with

$$R = \{(x, \mu, \sigma)| -\infty \leqq x \leqq C^*, -\infty < \mu < +\infty, 0 \leqq \sigma < \infty\}.$$

Putting $h = 1/\sigma^2$, we get

$$p \sim \iiint_R e^{-\frac{1}{2}h(x-\mu)^2} h^{\frac{1}{2}} e^{-\frac{1}{2}hn'(\mu-m')^2} h^{\frac{1}{2}} e^{-\frac{1}{2}v'v'h} h^{\frac{1}{2}v'-1}\,dx\,d\mu\,dh.$$

Since

$$(x-\mu)^2 + n'(\mu-m')^2 = n''(\mu-m'')^2 + n'''(x-m')^2$$

with

$$n''' \triangleq \dfrac{n'}{n'+1}$$

we have that

$$p \sim \iiint_R h^{\frac{1}{2}v'} e^{-\frac{1}{2}v'v'h - \frac{1}{2}h(n''(\mu-m'')^2 + n'''(x-m')^2)}\,dx\,d\mu\,dh$$

$$\sim \int_{-\infty}^{C^*} \int_0^{\infty} h^{\frac{1}{2}v'-\frac{1}{2}} e^{-\frac{1}{2}h(v'v'+n'''(x-m')^2)}\,dh\,dx$$

$$\sim \int_{-\infty}^{C^*} \left(v'v' + \dfrac{n'}{n'+1}(x-m')^2\right)^{-\frac{1}{2}(v'+1)}\,dx$$

$$\sim \int_{-\infty}^{C^{**}} (1 + z^2)^{-\frac{1}{2}(v'+1)}\,dz$$

with

$$C^{**} \triangleq \left(\dfrac{n'}{(n'+1)v'v'}\right)^{\frac{1}{2}} (C^* - m').$$

By putting $z = \text{tg } w$, we obtain

$$p = I\left(v', -\frac{\pi}{2}, \text{arctg } C^{**}\right)\Big/ I\left(v', -\frac{\pi}{2}, +\frac{\pi}{2}\right)$$

where

$$I(v', A, B) = \int_A^B \cos^{v'-1} w\, dw.$$

Thus, p can be evaluated using the familiar recursive expression

$$I(v', A, B) = \frac{1}{v'-1}\left(\sin B \cos^{v'-2} B - \sin A \cos^{v'-2} A\right) +$$

$$+ \frac{v'-2}{v'-1} I(v'-2, A, B).$$

If $p \leqq \alpha_0$, we stop; otherwise, we generate a new random schedule, update m', n', v and v', etc.

It remains to specify initial values m'_0, n'_0, v'_0 and v'_0. Traditionally, this is a relatively neglected aspect of the Bayesian approach. We refer to [De Leede and Rinnooy Kan 1975] for details on the choice of an initial prior distribution for this particular case. During some actual experiments on a $20|10|P|C_{\max}$ problem with data provided in [Heller 1960], convergence of the initial distribution to the final one turned out to be relatively independent of the particular prior distribution chosen. A near-optimal schedule was found in a few seconds CPU time after roughly 250 iterations in most cases.

None the less, it appears to us that the Bayesian approach through its dependency on asymptotic results for the distribution of $\underline{C}_{\max}$ is more of academic interest than of great practical use; it seems difficult to generalize this approach to less structured situations. Again, a (possibly iterative) approach along the lines briefly illustrated in chapter 7 seems a more fruitful way to attack actual scheduling problems.

4

One-machine problems

In sections 4.1 to 4.4 we examine the case that the number of machines m is equal to 1.

The structure of this chapter is summarized in tabel 4.1. Sections 4.1 and 4.2 deal with c_{max} criteria. In sections 4.1.1 and 4.1.2 we briefly deal with completion time and due date criteria; an efficient algorithm for a general non-decreasing cost function $c_i(t)$ is presented in section 4.1.3. In section 4.2 we consider $n|1|\Gamma|c_{max}$ problems in which some of the assumptions mentioned in section 2.2 are not met: we successively allow non-equal release dates (4.2.1), sequence dependent change-over times and job dependent set-up times (4.2.2) and precedence relations between jobs (4.2.3). Within each of these subsections, we consider the computational complexity of the problem and discuss available algorithms.

Sections 4.3 and 4.4 deal with $\sum c_i$ criteria in a similar way. Again we examine completion time and due date criteria in sections 4.3.1 and 4.3.2. The general $n|1||\sum c_i$ problem is NP-complete and will be discussed at length in section 4.3.3. In section 4.4, the same assumptions as in section 4.2 are successively dropped, and we examine the complexity and possible algorithms for the resulting special $\sum c_i$ problems.

We conclude this introductory section by giving a general result that will find application throughout chapter 4.

THEOREM 4.1. If all r_i are equal and $m = 1$, there exists an optimal schedule with respect to any regular measure without machine idle time and without job splitting.

PROOF. An active one-machine schedule will not exhibit idle time, and job splitting can never be advantageous.   (Q.E.D.)

We note finally that throughout this chapter we shall write p_i instead of p_{i1}.

Table 4.1.

		$c_{\max}$		Σc_i
completion time criteria		4.1.1		4.3.1
due date criteria	4.1	4.1.2	4.3	4.3.2
arbitrary non-decreasing $c_i(t)$		4.1.3		4.3.3
$r_i \geqq 0$		4.2.1		4.4.1
seq dep	4.2	4.2.2	4.4	4.4.2
prec		4.2.3		4.4.3

4.1. $n|1||c_{\max}$ PROBLEMS

4.1.1. The $n|1||C_{\max}$ problem

If $m = 1$, $C_{\max}$ is equal to $\sum\limits_{i=1}^{n} p_i$ and thus clearly a sequence independent constant. The following theorem is now a straightforward consequence of theorems 2.4, 2.7 and 2.8.

THEOREM 4.2. If $m = 1$, the following criteria are equivalent:

(i) $\bar{N}_p + \bar{N}_w$
(ii) $\bar{N}_f$
(iii) $\bar{N}_w$
(iv) $\sum C_i$.

PROOF. Trivial.   (Q.E.D.)

4.1.2. The $n|1||L_{\max}$ problem

THEOREM 4.3 [Jackson 1955]. The $n|1||L_{\max}$ problem is solved by the EDD rule, *i.e.* by ordering the jobs according to non-decreasing d_i.

PROOF. In order to prove that $g(i,j) = d_i$ satisfies the conditions of theorem 3.2, we consider the exchange of two adjacent jobs J_j and J_i with completion times C_j and $C_i = C_j + p_i$, and with $d_i < d_j$. For the resulting schedule with completion times C_i' and C_j', we have that

$$L_i' = C_i' - d_i \leqq C_i - d_i = L_i$$

$$L_j' = C_j' - d_j = C_i - d_j \leqq C_i - d_i = L_i,$$

so that

$$L_{max}' = \max\{L_h'\} \leqq L_{max}. \tag{Q.E.D.}$$

The above result is known as *Jackson's rule*.

Remark. The above procedure requires $O(n \log n)$ steps, necessary to order the d_i [Knuth 1973].

The effect of ordering the jobs according to non-decreasing $d_i - p_i$ (the *slack time rule*) can be analyzed in a similar way.

THEOREM 4.4 [Conway *et al.* 1967]. The minimum lateness $\min\{L_i\}$ and the minimum tardiness $\min\{T_i\}$ are maximized by ordering the jobs according to non-decreasing $d_i - p_i$.

PROOF. Again we consider the exchange of two adjacent jobs J_j and J_i with $d_i - p_i < d_j - p_j$:

$$L_j' = C_j' - d_j > C_j - d_j = L_j$$

$$L_i' = C_i' - d_i = C_i - p_j - d_i > C_i - p_i - d_j = L_j.$$

Hence,

$$\min_h \{L_h'\} \geqq \min_h \{L_h\}. \tag{Q.E.D.}$$

4.1.3. The general $n|1||c_{max}$ problem

THEOREM 4.5 [Lawler 1973]. The following procedure generates a permutation π^* such that $(J_{\pi^*(1)}, \ldots, J_{\pi^*(n)})$ is an optimal solution to the $n|1||c_{max}$ problem for arbitrary non-decreasing $c_i(t)$.

procedure *n1cmax* (p, π^*);
begin local S, k, i;
$\quad S := \{1, \ldots, n\}; k := n$;
$\quad$ **while** $S \neq \emptyset$ **do**
$\quad$ **begin** $i :\in \{j | j \in S, c_j(\sum_{g \in S} p_g) = \min_{h \in S}\{c_h(\sum_{g \in S} p_g)\}\}$;

$$\pi^*(k) := i;$$
$$k := k-1; \ S := S - \{i\}$$
end
end $n1cmax$;

PROOF. If J_f is chosen instead of J_i with $c_f(\sum\limits_{g \in S} p_g) > \min\limits_{h \in S} c_h(\sum\limits_{g \in S} p_g)$, then interchanging J_i with the jobs following it, up to and including J_f, will not increase $c_{\max}$, since $c_i(\sum\limits_{g \in S} p_g) < c_f(\sum\limits_{g \in S} p_g)$ and $c_f(\sum\limits_{\substack{g \in S \\ g \neq i}} p_g) \leqq c_f(\sum\limits_{g \in S} p_g)$.

(Q.E.D.)

Remark 1. Theorem 4.3 is easily seen to be a special case of theorem 4.5.

Remark 2. The procedure 'n1cmax' requires $O(n^2)$ steps.

4.2. $n|1|\Gamma|c_{\max}$ PROBLEMS

4.2.1. The $n|1|r_i \geqq 0|c_{\max}$ problem

THEOREM 4.6. The $n|1|r_i \geq 0|C_{\max}$ problem is solved by ordering the jobs according to increasing r_i.

PROOF. At no time can it be advantageous not to schedule one of the available jobs.   (Q.E.D.)

It is useful to view theorem 4.6 as the *inverse* version of Jackson's rule. The $n|1|r_i \geq 0|C_{\max}$ problem is equivalent to an $n|n+1|G|C_{\max}$ problem in which J_i is processed on M_i during r_i time units ($i = 1, \ldots, n$) before passing on to a last machine M_{n+1}, on which its processing time is p_i. Alternatively, $M_1, \ldots, M_n$ can be replaced by a single non-bottleneck machine. If we now take the inverse of this problem (cf. sections 2.1 and 2.3.2), we obtain an equivalent problem in which each job has a final operation of length r_i on a non-bottleneck machine. Instead of minimizing $C_{\max}$ on the non-bottleneck machine we can equivalently minimize $L_{\max}$ with respect to due dates $-r_i$ that are to be attained on the common first bottleneck machine. Application of Jackson's rule to this latter problem yields theorem 4.6.

Such an inversion oriented approach becomes particularly fruitful when we consider the $n|1|r_i \geqq 0|L_{\max}$ problem. A problem instance is defined by n triples (r_i, p_i, d_i) or, equivalently, by n triples (r_i, p_i, q_i) where the *tail* $q_i \overset{\triangle}{=} c - d_i$, $c \geqq \max\{d_i\}$. The r_i and the q_i can be interpreted as processing times on first and last non-bottleneck machines and the objective now is to minimize $L'_{max} \triangleq \max_i \{C_i + q_i\} = c + L_{max}$, where C_i is the completion time of J_i on the bottleneck machine.

Clearly, the optimal processing order with respect to this problem is the reverse of the optimal processing order with respect to the problem defined by (q_i, p_i, r_i).

Two special cases of this problem where either all r_i or all q_i are equal have been solved in theorems 4.3 and 4.6 above. A third special case in which $p_i = p^*$ for all i can be solved in $O(n \log n)$ steps if $p^* = 1$.

THEOREM 4.7 (cf. [Horn 1974]). The following procedure generates a permutation π^* such that $(J_{\pi^*(1)}, \ldots, J_{\pi^*(n)})$ is an optimal solution to the $n|1|r_i \geq 0, p_i = 1|L'_{max}$ problem.

procedure *n1ri0pi1lmax* (n, r, q, π^*);
begin local S, Q, t, k, i;
    $S := \{1, \ldots, n\}$; $t := 0$; $k := 1$;
    while $S \neq \emptyset$ **do**
    begin $t := \max(t, \min_{j \in S} \{r_j\})$;
        $Q := \{j | j \in S, r_j \leq t\}$;
        $i :\in \{j | j \in Q, q_j = \max_{g \in Q} \{q_g\}\}$;
        $\pi^*(k) := i$;
        $k := k+1$; $t := t+1$; $S := S - \{i\}$
    end
end *n1ri0pi1lmax*;

PROOF. No job can become available during the processing of another one. Thus, it can never be advantageous to postpone processing a job from $\{J_g | g \in Q\}$. Theorem 4.7 now follows from a switching argument as in theorems 4.3 and 4.4.   (Q.E.D.)

The algorithm described in theorem 4.7 does not generalize to the case that p^* does not divide all r_i: e.g., if $n = p^* = 2$, $r_1 = q_1 = 0$, $r_2 = 1$, $q_2 = 2$, postponing J_1 is clearly advantageous. The procedure 'n1ri0pi1lmax' will be used, though, in section 4.2.1.1 to solve the $n|1|r_i \geq 0, job spl|L_{max}$ problem by considering each job J_i as p_i jobs with release date r_i and due date d_i.

The following theorem indicates that a similarly efficient algorithm for the general $n|1|r_i \geq 0|L_{max}$ problem is unlikely to exist, even if only one release date can be not equal to 0.

THEOREM 4.8. The $n|1|r_n \geqq 0|L_{\max}$ problem is NP-complete.

PROOF. We prove NP-completeness by showing that the KNAPSACK problem (see theorem 3.3) is reducible to the $n|1|r_n \geqq 0|L_{\max}$ problem. Given integers $a_1, \ldots, a_t, b, A \triangleq \sum_{i=1}^{t} a_i$, we define a corresponding instance of the $n|1|r_n \geqq 0|L_{\max}$ problem by:

$$n = t + 1$$
$$r_i = 0, p_i = a_i, d_i = A + 1 \qquad\qquad (i = 1, \ldots, t)$$
$$r_n = b, p_n = 1, d_n = b + 1$$
$$y = 0.$$

If $\sum_{i \in S} a_i = b$ for some $S \subset T = \{1, \ldots, t\}$, i.e. if KNAPSACK has a solution, then a schedule with value $\leqq y$ is obtained by scheduling the jobs in the following order: $(\{J_i | i \in S\}, J_n, \{J_i | i \in T - S\})$ (see figure 4.1).

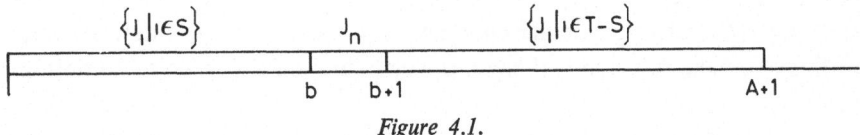

Figure 4.1.

Conversely, if KNAPSACK has no solution, then $\sum_{i \in S} a_i - b = c \neq 0$ for all $S \subset T$, and we have for a processing order $(\{J_i | i \in S\}, J_n, \{J_i | i \in T - S\})$ that

$$c > 0 \Rightarrow L_{\max} \geqq C_n - d_n$$
$$= (\sum_{i \in S} a_i + 1) - (b + 1) > y$$
$$c < 0 \Rightarrow L_{\max} \geqq C_{\max} - (A + 1)$$
$$\geqq (b + 1) + \sum_{i \in T - S} a_i - (A + 1) > y.$$

Thus, KNAPSACK has a solution *iff* there is a schedule with value $\leqq y$. The input string for the scheduling problem with respect to a binary encoding is clearly polynomial-bounded in $^2\log(A + b)$, *i.e.* in the length of the binary KNAPSACK input string. Thus we have found a polynomial-bounded reduction establishing the NP-completeness of the $n|1|r_n \geqq 0|L_{\max}$ problem.
(Q.E.D.)

Theorem 4.8 serves to justify the various implicit enumeration approaches to the $n|1|r_i \geqq 0|L_{max}$ problem [Dessouky and Margenthaler 1972; Bratley *et al.* 1973; Baker and Su 1974; McMahon and Florian 1975]. We shall describe and extend two branch-and-bound approaches to this problem below.

4.2.1.1. Lower bound by job splitting

A branching rule to enumerate all active schedules may be defined in the terminology of section 3.4 by letting subsets $Y \in \mathscr{X}$ correspond to partial schedules $(J_{v(1)}, \ldots, J_{v(s)})$ filling the first s positions in the schedule. Each $Y' \in b(Y)$ corresponds to an unscheduled job J_j ($j \in \bar{S} \triangleq \{1, \ldots, n\} - - \{v(1), \ldots, v(s)\}$) being scheduled in the $(s+1)$-st position under the restriction that $r_j < \min_{h \in \bar{S}} \{\max(C_{v(s)}, r_h) + p_h\}$; if $r_j \geqq \max(C_{v(s)}, r_h) + p_h$ for some $h \in \bar{S}$, then J_h could be inserted before J_j and the schedule would not be active.

A lower bound on the costs of all possible completions of $(J_{v(1)}, \ldots, J_{v(s)})$ can be obtained by the use of the procedure 'n1ri0pi1lmax' to schedule the remaining jobs from $C_{v(s)}$ onwards while allowing job splitting. If no job splitting occurs, this particular completion is feasible and optimal; the value of this complete solution is then an upper bound on the value of an optimal solution.

Extensive computational experiments with this approach have revealed that a newest active node search strategy produces the best results. We refer to appendix 1 for details.

4.2.1.2. The algorithm of McMahon and Florian

We shall now describe and refine a more sophisticated approach to the $n|1|r_i \geqq 0|L_{max}$ problem (cf. [McMahon and Florian 1975]). The algorithm is based on the following heuristic method for obtaining a feasible solution [Schrage 1971].

procedure *n1ri0lmaxinit* (n, r, p, q, π);
begin local S, Q, k, t, i;
    $S := \{1, \ldots, n\}$; $t := 0$; $k := 1$;
    while $S \neq \emptyset$ **do**
    begin $t := \max(t, \min_{j \in S} \{r_j\})$;
        $Q := \{j | j \in S, r_j \leqq t\}$;
        $i :\in \{j | j \in Q, p_j = \max\{p_h | h \in Q : q_h = \max_{g \in Q} \{q_g\}\}\}$;
        $\pi(k) := i$;

$$k := k+1;\ t := t+p_i;\ S := S-\{i\}$$

end

end *n1ri0lmaxinit*;

The initial schedule $(J_{\pi(1)}, \ldots, J_{\pi(n)})$ can be decomposed into *blocks*; $J_{\pi(h)}$ is the *last job in a block* if $C_{\pi(h)} \leqq r_{\pi(i)}$ for $i = h+1, \ldots, n$. It follows that $J_{\pi(g)}$ is the *first job in a block* if its starting time $S_{\pi(g)} = r_{\pi(g)} \leqq r_{\pi(i)}$ for $i = g+1, \ldots, n$.

For J_i in block $(J_{\pi(g)}, \ldots, J_{\pi(h)})$, we define $P_i \overset{\triangle}{=} \{j | S_{\pi(g)} \leqq S_j \leqq S_i\}$, $q_i^* \overset{\triangle}{=} \min_{j \in P_i} \{q_j\}$ and $Q_i \overset{\triangle}{=} \{j | j \in P_i, q_j = q_i^*\}$.

THEOREM 4.9. With respect to a schedule $(J_{\pi(1)}, \ldots, J_{\pi(n)})$ with starting times $S_{\pi(i)}$ and completion times $C_{\pi(i)}$ obtained by the procedure 'n1ri0lmaxinit', lower bounds on the value of an optimal schedule are given by

$$LB_i' \overset{\triangle}{=} r_i + p_i + q_i \qquad\qquad (i = 1, \ldots, n)$$

$$LB_i'' \overset{\triangle}{=} \begin{cases} C_i + q_i^* & \text{if } i \in Q_i \\ C_i + q_i^* + 1 & \text{if } i \notin Q_i \end{cases} \qquad (i = 1, \ldots, n)$$

PROOF. LB_i' requires no further comment. With respect to LB_i'', we define C_{ji} to be the minimum completion time of J_j if this job is scheduled last of $\{J_h | h \in P_i\}$. Note that $C_{ji} \geqq C_{ii} = C_i$ for all $j \in P_i$. A valid lower bound is now given by

$$(4\text{-}1) \quad \min_{j \in P_i} \{C_{ji} + q_j\}.$$

If $i \in Q_i$, we have that

$$(4\text{-}2) \quad C_{ji} + q_j \geqq C_{ii} + q_i = C_i + q_i^*.$$

Suppose that $i \notin Q_i$. If $j \in P_i - Q_i$, then

$$(4\text{-}3) \quad C_{ji} + q_j \geqq C_i + (q_i^* + 1).$$

We finally consider the case that $i \notin Q_i$ and $j \in Q_i$. If we move J_j to the last position of $\{J_h | h \in P_i\}$, we need J_k with $r_k \leqq S_j < S_k$ to take its place. From the procedure 'n1ri0lmaxinit' we know that, if such a J_k exists, we must have $k \in Q_i$ and $p_k \leqq p_j$. Thus, if J_k is moved forward to avoid machine idle time after S_j, a gap of at least one unit idle time now threatens to occur between S_k and $S_k + 1$. Repeating this argument as often as necessary, we conclude that:

(4-4) $C_{ji} + q_j \geqq (C_i + 1) + q_i^*.$

Together (4-1), (4-2), (4-3) and (4-4) establish the validity of LB_i''. (Q.E.D.)

At every node of the search tree, application of the procedure 'n1ri0lmaxinit' yields a complete solution $(J_{\pi(1)}, \ldots, J_{\pi(n)})$ with value L'_{max}, possibly leading to a decrease in the current upperbound UB. If $LB \overset{\triangle}{=} \max_i \{LB_i', LB_i''\} \geqq UB$, the node is eliminated; else we apply the branching rule described next.

Let the *critical job* J_i be the first job in the schedule with $C_i + q_i = L'_{max}$. The schedule can only be improved if C_i can somehow be reduced. The subset $Y \in \mathscr{X}$ of schedules corresponding to the current values of r_i and q_i can now be partitioned into disjoint subsets $Y' \in b(Y)$, each characterized by a particular J_j to be scheduled last of $\{J_h | h \in P_i\}$. However, we can immediately eliminate those J_j with $q_j \leqq q_i + UB - L'_{max}$ as candidates for the last position, since for those jobs $C_{ji} + q_j \geqq C_i + q_i + UB - L'_{max} = UB$.

With respect to the remaining J_j we can implement precedence constraints $J_h \prec J_j$ $(h \in P_i - \{j\})$ by suitably adjusting the r_i and q_i (see section 4.2.1.3). Maintaining these precedence constraints at deeper levels of the tree would require time-consuming administration of a continually changing precedence graph. We can instead realize a single precedence constraint $J_i \prec J_j$ by simply putting r_j equal to any lower bound on $C_{ji} - p_i$ not less than r_i. Each choice of J_j $(j \in P_i)$ corresponds to a particular subset $Y' \in b(Y)$; however, these subsets may be overlapping in this case.

We refer to appendix 1 for details on implementation, search strategy and computational experience with this algorithm. Within this approach, it turned out to be profitable under certain conditions to exploit the earlier mentioned equivalence relations by solving the inverse problem instead.

4.2.1.3. Precedence constraints

The results presented above can be easily extended to the $n|1|r_i \geqq 0, prec|L'_{max}$ problem. In this case, the inverse problem is characterized by triples (q_i, p_i, r_i) and precedence constraints $\prec'$ with $J_i \prec' J_j$ iff $J_j \prec J_i$.

As a general principle, note that we may always set

$$r_i := \max(r_i, \max_{J_i \prec J_j} \{r_j + p_j\})$$

$$q_i := \max(q_i, \max_{J_i \prec J_j} \{q_j + p_j\})$$

because in every feasible schedule $S_i \geq C_j \geq r_j + p_j$ if $J_j \prec J_i$ and $L'_j \geq C_i + p_j + q_j$ if $J_i \prec J_j$. Hence, if $J_i \prec J_j$, we may assume that $r_i < r_i + p_i \leq r_j$ and $q_i \geq q_j + p_j > q_j$.

It follows that theorem 4.6 also solves the $n|1|r_i \geq 0, prec|C_{\max}$ problem, and that application of theorem 4.6 to the inverse of a $n|1|prec|L_{\max}$ problem yields a special case of the general $n|1|prec|c_{\max}$ algorithm, to be discussed in section 4.2.3. For similar reasons, the procedure 'n1ri0pi1lmax' solves the $n|1|r_i \geq 0, p_i = 1, prec|L'_{\max}$ problem.

The algorithm described in section 4.2.1.1 can easily be adapted to solve the general $n|1|r_i \geq 0, prec|L_{\max}$ problem; this problem is of course NP-complete by theorem 3.4 (v). The precedence constraints are respected during the lower bound calculation of 4.2.1.1 and the only change required is that in selecting jobs for the $(s + 1)$-st position we should now restrict ourselves to jobs J_j with $j \in Q \overset{\triangle}{=} \{h|h \in \bar{S}: \{g|J_g \prec J_h\} \cap \bar{S} = \emptyset\}$ and such that $r_j < \min_{h \in Q}\{\max(C_{v(s)}, r_h) + p_h\}$.

With respect to section 4.2.1.2, it is easily verified that the procedure 'n1ri0lmaxinit' also yields an initial solution respecting the precedence constraints. LB'_i and LB''_i remain valid lower bounds. As to branching, we now only have to consider jobs J_j for the last position of $\{J_h|h \in P_i\}$ such that $q_j < q_i + UB - L'_{\max}$ and in addition $J_j \not\prec J_h$ for all $h \in P_i$. To maintain feasibility at deeper levels of the tree, it is sufficient to update r_j in the way indicated above and in addition to adjust r_h for all h such that $J_j \prec J_h$. More extensive adjustments only lead to additional computing time, as indicated by computational experiments with $n|1|r_i \geq 0, prec|L'_{\max}$ algorithms that are described in appendix 1.

We note finally that the $n|1|r_i \geq 0, p_i = 1|c_{\max}$ problem for arbitrary $c_i(t)$ can be solved by defining

$$c_{ij} \overset{\triangle}{=} \begin{cases} c_i(j) & \text{if } j > r_i \\ \infty & \text{if } j \leq r_i \end{cases} \qquad (i = 1, \ldots, n; j = 1, \ldots, C^*_{\max})$$

where $C^*_{\max}$ is the value of an optimal $n|1|r_i \geq 0, p_i = 1|C_{\max}$ schedule, as produced by theorem 4.6. The $n|1|r_i \geq 0, p_i = 1|c_{\max}$ problem is then equivalent to the following *bottleneck transportation problem*:

$$\text{minimize } \max_{i, j}\{c_{ij}X_{ij}\}$$

$$\text{subject to } \sum_{j=1}^{C^*_{\max}} X_{ij} = 1 \qquad\qquad (i = 1, \dots, n)$$

$$\sum_{i=1}^{n} X_{ij} \leqq 1 \qquad\qquad (j = 1, \dots, C^*_{\max})$$

$$X_{ij} \in \{0,1\} \qquad\qquad \begin{aligned} &(i = 1, \dots, n; \\ &\ j = 1, \dots, C^*_{\max}) \end{aligned}$$

Any active schedule for this problem is characterized by X_{ij} being 0 for $C^*_{\max} - n$ values of j, obtainable from the optimal $n|1|r_i \geqq 0, p_i = 1|C_{\max}$ schedule. Thus, the above problem reduces to a $n \times n$ bottleneck assignment problem, for which an $O(n^3)$ algorithm is available [Lawler 1976].*

The general $n|1|r_i \geqq 0|c_{\max}$ problem can now be solved by incorporating the above approach in a branch-and-bound algorithm analogously to section 4.2.1.1.

4.2.2. The $n|1|seq\ dep|c_{\max}$ problem

We shall restrict ourselves to the $C_{\max}$ criterion. If we have job dependent set-up times s_i and sequence dependent change-over times c_{ij} when J_j follows J_i, then $C_{\max}$ for a processing order $(J_{v(1)}, \dots, J_{v(n)})$ is given by

$$s_{v(1)} + \sum_{j=1}^{n-1} c_{v(j),\, v(j+1)} + \sum_{i=1}^{n} p_i$$

so that minimization of $C_{\max}$ is equivalent to solving a TRAVELLING SALESMAN problem on $n + 1$ cities $\{0, 1, \dots, n\}$ with distances c_{ij} $(i, j \neq 0)$, $c_{i0} = 0$, $c_{0i} = s_i$. We refer to [Bellmore and Nemhauser 1968; Isaac and Turban 1968] for extensive surveys on this NP-complete problem; more recent developments can be found in [Lenstra 1976].

4.2.3. The $n|1|prec|c_{\max}$ problem

Suppose that precedence constraints $J_i \prec J_j$ are given in the form of sets $A_i \overset{\triangle}{=} \{j|J_i \prec J_j\}$ and $B_i \overset{\triangle}{=} \{j|J_j \prec J_i\}$.

THEOREM 4.10 [Lawler 1973]. The following procedure generates a permutation π^* such that $(J_{\pi^*(1)}, \dots, J_{\pi^*(n)})$ is an optimal solution to the $n|1|prec|c_{\max}$ problem for arbitrary non-decreasing $c_i(t)$.

---

* We can do even better than that by performing an $O(\log n)$ binary search on the $O(n^2)$ thresholds [Lawler 1976]; for each threshold, we have to solve a matching problem that is *convex* in the sense of [Glover 1967] and can be solved in $O(n^2)$ steps, so that the total procedure takes $O(n^2 \log n)$ steps.

procedure *n1preccmax* (p, π^*);
begin local Q, S, k, i;
    $S := \{1, \ldots, n\}$; $k := n$;
    while $S \neq \emptyset$ **do**
    begin $Q := \{h | h \in S, A_h \cap S = \emptyset\}$;
        $i :\in \{j | j \in Q, c_j(\sum_{g \in S} p_g) = \min_{h \in Q}\{c_h(\sum_{g \in S} p_g)\}\}$;
        $\pi^*(k) := i$;
        $k := k - 1$; $S := S - \{i\}$
    end
end *n1preccmax*;

PROOF. Similar to the proof of theorem 4.5.   (Q.E.D.)

Remark 1. The $n|1|r_i \geqq 0, prec|L_{\max}$ problem has been discussed in section 4.2.1.3.

Remark 2. The procedure 'n1preccmax' again requires $O(n^2)$ steps.

4.3. $n|1||\sum c_i$ PROBLEMS

4.3.1. The $n|1||\sum w_i C_i$ problem

THEOREM 4.11 [Smith 1956]. The $n|1||\sum w_i C_i$ problem is solved in $O(n \log n)$ steps by ordering the jobs J_i according to increasing p_i/w_i ratio.

PROOF. Define $g(i, j) = p_i/w_i$. If in a schedule $(\pi(1), \ldots, \pi(n))$ adjacent jobs $J_{\pi(j)}$ and $J_{\pi(j+1)}$ are interchanged, the resulting schedule will be at least as good if

$$w_{\pi(j+1)}(\sum_{g=1}^{j-1} p_{\pi(g)} + p_{\pi(j+1)}) + w_{\pi(j)}(\sum_{g=1}^{j+1} p_{\pi(g)})$$
$$\leqq w_{\pi(j)}(\sum_{g=1}^{j} p_{\pi(g)}) + w_{\pi(j+1)}(\sum_{g=1}^{j+1} p_{\pi(g)})$$

which reduces to

$$w_{\pi(j)}p_{\pi(j+1)} \leqq w_{\pi(j+1)}p_{\pi(j)}$$

or

$$g(\pi(j+1), \pi(j)) \leqq g(\pi(j), \pi(j+1)).$$ (Q.E.D.)

By interpreting the $n|1||\sum C_i$ problem as a special case of the $n|1||\sum w_i C_i$ problem, we see that the SPT rule leads to an optimal schedule in this case. Several different proofs of this special result have been given (see [Conway et al. 1967]). The following proof is included because it illustrates a useful technique that we shall encounter again in lemma 5.4.

THEOREM 4.12. An $n|1||\sum C_i$ problem has the same optimal processing order as the problem obtained by replacing the processing times p_i by $p_i' = p_i + c \geq 0$ where c is a fixed constant.

PROOF. Consider the schedule given by a permutation $(v(1), \ldots, v(n))$ of $(1, \ldots, n)$; the completion time $C_{v(i)}$ is given by

$$C_{v(i)} = \sum_{j=1}^{i} p_{v(j)}.$$

Replacing $p_{v(j)}$ by $p_{v(j)} + c$, the completion time is given by

$$C'_{v(i)} = \sum_{j=1}^{i} (p_{v(j)} + c) = C_{v(i)} + ic.$$

Hence the new criterion value $\sum C_i'$ is related to the old one $\sum C_i$ by

$$\sum C_i' = \sum_{i=1}^{n} C'_{v(i)} = \sum C_i + \tfrac{1}{2} n(n+1)c. \qquad \text{(Q.E.D.)}$$

THEOREM 4.13. The $n|1||\sum C_i$ problem is solved in $O(n \log n)$ steps by the SPT rule, *i.e.* by ordering the jobs J_i according to increasing p_i.

PROOF. Apply theorem 4.12 with $c = -\min\{p_i\}$. If $p_j = 0$, there exists an optimal schedule with J_j in the first position. Repeat for the remaining jobs. $\qquad$ (Q.E.D.)

4.3.2. The $n|1||\sum w_i T_i$ problem

Efficient solution methods for the $n|1||\sum w_i T_i$ problem exist only for some special cases. For instance, if all w_i are equal, then:

(i) the SPT schedule is optimal if $d_i + p_i \leq C_{i+1}$ $(i = 1, \ldots, n-1)$ in this schedule;

(ii) the EDD schedule is optimal if $T_i \leq p_i$ $(i = 1, \ldots, n)$ in this schedule;

(iii) the SPT and EDD schedule are optimal if these schedules are identical (e.g., if all p_i or all d_i are equal) [Emmons 1969].

These results can be proved from corollaries 4.15, 4.17 and 4.19 in section 4.3.3.1.

For the general $n|1||\sum w_i T_i$ problem, we have the following complexity result.

THEOREM 4.14. The $n|1||\sum w_i T_i$ problem is NP-complete.

PROOF. We shall prove that KNAPSACK $\propto n|1||\sum w_i T_i$.

Given $a_1, \ldots, a_t, b, A = \sum_{i=1}^{t} a_i$, define:

$$n = t + 1$$

$$p_i = w_i = a_i, d_i = 0 \qquad\qquad (i = 1, \ldots, t)$$

$$p_n = 1, w_n = 2, d_n = b + 1$$

$$y = \sum_{\substack{i,j=1 \\ i \leq j}}^{t} a_i a_j + A - b.$$

Since $d_i = 0$ and $p_i/w_i = 1$ for $i = 1, \ldots, t$, the value of $\sum_{i=1}^{t} w_i T_i$ is not influenced by the processing order of these jobs (theorem 4.11). If $\sum_{i \in S} a_i = b$, $(\{J_i | i \in S\}, J_n, \{J_i | i \in T - S\})$ describes a processing order with value y. If $C_n \leq b$, then

$$\sum w_i T_i \geq \sum_{\substack{i,j=1 \\ i \leq j}}^{t} a_i a_j + A - b + 1 > y;$$

if $C_n \geq b + 2$, then $L_n > 0$ and

$$\sum w_i T_i = \sum_{\substack{i,j=1 \\ i \leq j}}^{t} a_i a_j + (A - b - L_n) + 2L_n > y.$$

It follows that KNAPSACK has a solution if and only if there is a schedule with value at most y. The NP-completeness of the $n|1||\sum w_i T_i$ problem again follows from theorem 3.3 (ii). (Q.E.D.)

Thus, for the general $n|1||\sum w_i T_i$ problem we can safely restrict ourselves to methods of implicit enumeration. The above result cannot be easily extended to the case that all weights w_i are equal; the complexity of the

$n|1||\sum T_i$ problem must remain an open question. In spite of extensive efforts, no efficient algorithm for this problem has been found yet and it seems safe to conjecture that the $n|1||\sum T_i$ problem is NP-complete as well.

It is none the less remarkable that very recently an efficient algorithm has been developed for the $n|1|p_i \leq p^*|\sum T_i$ problem [Lawler 1975a], requiring $O(n^5 p^*)$ steps. In order to view this result in a different light, let us define a *unary* encoding of the problem data to be an encoding of $O(\sum_{i=1}^{n} p_i)$ length.

In section 3.6, we have characterized the number of steps required by a good (efficient) algorithm as being polynomial in the length of the input string. Until now, we have assumed a binary encoding of the problem data. However, if we allow a unary encoding, then an $O(n^5 p^*)$ or $O(n^4 \sum_{i=1}^{n} p_i)$ algorithm is formally efficient with respect to this encoding. A similar result holds with respect to the $n|1|d_i = d^*|\sum w_i T_i$ problem: it can be solved in $O(n \sum_{i=1}^{n} p_i)$ steps by the dynamic programming approach of section 3.5.2. Such *unary efficient* algorithms need not necessarily be 'good' in the practical sense of the word, but it may pay none the less to distinguish between NP-completeness results with respect to unary and binary encoding (cf. [Garey *et al.* 1975]). NP-completeness with respect to unary encoding would then be the strongest possible result, and it is quite feasible for a problem to be both binary NP-complete and unary efficiently solvable. In this study we shall not explore this distinction any further; since the KNAPSACK problem is binary but not unary NP-complete, all our results hold only with respect to the standard binary encoding.*

All tested algorithms for the $n|1||\sum T_i$ and $n|1||\sum w_i T_i$ problems are of the implicit enumeration type. Especially with respect to the former problem, many elimination criteria have been developed [Emmons 1969] that lead to precedence constraints satisfied by at least one optimal schedule. All such elimination criteria, including those developed for the $n|1||\sum w_i T_i$ problem [Shwimer 1972], can be deduced from the elimination criteria for general non-decreasing cost functions $c_i(t)$ developed in section 4.3.3.1. Hence, we will not pursue this matter any further in this section.

---

* A comparable situation exists with respect to $n|1||\sum w_i U_i$ problems, *i.e.* $n|1||\sum c_i$ problems with $c_i(t) = $ if $t \leq d_i$ **then** 0 **else** w_i. If all w_i are equal, the problem can be solved efficiently by a 'greedy' algorithm [Moore 1968; Sturm 1970]; the general $n|1||\sum w_i U_i$ problem is NP-complete [Karp 1972], but there exists an algorithm requiring $O(n \sum_{i=1}^{n} p_i)$ steps [Lawler and Moore 1969]. (See also [Lawler 1975].)

Elimination criteria do not lead automatically to an optimal $n|1||\sum T_i$ or $n|1||\sum w_i T_i$ schedule. Thus, they have to be incorporated in some enumeration scheme, in combination with lower bounds, to yield implicit enumeration algorithms for these two problems. For instance, the elimination criteria from [Emmons 1969] combined with dynamic programming lead to an $n|1||\sum T_i$ algorithm [Srinivasan 1971] that turned out to be superior to other $n|1||\sum T_i$ algorithms surveyed in [Baker and Martin 1974]. With respect to the $n|1||\sum w_i T_i$ problem, a branch-and-bound algorithm was developed in [Shwimer 1972]. This latter algorithm is more easily discussed in the context of section 4.3.3.2. There, we shall describe a general $n|1||\sum c_i$ algorithm producing relatively superior results for the weighted tardiness case. However, even stronger bounds than the one presented in section 4.3.3.2 seem to be necessary to solve problems of reasonable size. The excellent results obtained by Fisher's $n|1||\sum T_i$ algorithm, of which the general $\sum c_i$ lower bound is based on the use of Lagrangian multipliers [Fisher 1974], may indicate a further step in the right direction.

4.3.3. The general $n|1||\sum c_i$ problem

Theorem 4.14 implies that the general $n|1||\sum c_i$ problem is *a fortiori* NP-complete. The dynamic programming approach outlined in section 3.5.1 requires $O(n2^n)$ steps; a similarly exponential approach can be found in [Schild and Fredman 1962]. None the less it is possible to derive some general elimination criteria in the form of dominance rules given below. Interpretation of these rules for the weighted tardiness case leads to simple proofs for a number of partly known tardiness results (cf. section 4.3.2).

As mentioned already, these elimination criteria do not necessarily produce an optimal schedule straightaway. Thus, it seems natural to combine the criteria with an enumeration scheme and a lower bounding rule to obtain an $n|1||\sum c_i$ branch-and-bound algorithm, to be described in section 4.3.3.2. First however, we will discuss the elimination criteria in more detail.

4.3.3.1. Elimination criteria

Suppose that we have found that there exists an optimal schedule whereby, for $i \in S$, the set $\{J_h | h \in B_i\}$ precedes J_i and the set $\{J_h | h \in A_i\}$ follows J_i. Any established relation 'J_i precedes J_j' implies that $i \in B_j$ and $j \in A_i$. In the following, we restrict ourselves to schedules which satisfy the precedence constraints, defined by B_i and A_i ($i \in S$). Throughout, $P(Q) \stackrel{\triangle}{=} \sum_{i \in Q} p_i$.

THEOREM 4.15. If for two jobs J_i and J_j $(i, j \in S)$ we have

(i) $c_i(t) - c_j(t)$ is a non-decreasing function of t on the interval $(P(B_j) + p_j, P(S - A_i))$, and

(ii) $p_i \leq p_j$,

then we only have to consider schedules in which J_i precedes J_j.

PROOF. Consider any schedule in which J_j precedes J_i. Denote by S the starting time of J_j and by C the finishing time of J_i. Compare this schedule with the schedule obtained by interchanging J_j and J_i (see figure 4.2).

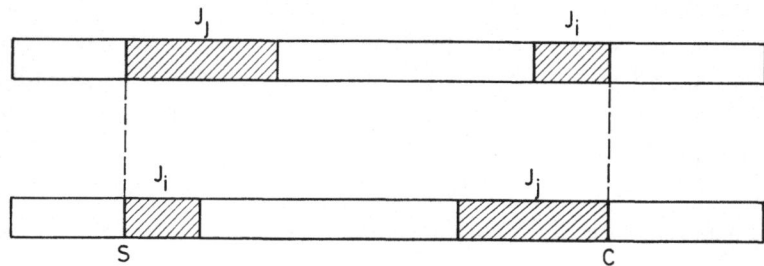

Figure 4.2.

The contribution to total costs by all jobs except J_j decreases or remains the same, as can be easily checked. As to J_j, it follows from

$$P(B_j) + p_j \leq S + p_j \leq C \leq P(S - A_i)$$

and condition (i) that

(4-5) $c_i(C) - c_j(C) \geq c_i(S + p_j) - c_j(S + p_j)$.

Because of condition (ii), we have

(4-6) $c_i(S + p_j) \geq c_i(S + p_i)$.

Together, (4-5) and (4-6) imply

$$c_i(C) + c_j(S + p_j) \geq c_i(S + p_i) + c_j(C),$$

which means that the joint contribution of J_i and J_j to total costs also decreases or remains the same.   (Q.E.D.)

COROLLARY 4.16. If $c_i(t) = w_i \max(0, t - d_i)$ for all i, and if for two jobs J_i and J_j $(i, j \in S)$ we have

   (i) $d_i \leqq d_j$,
   (ii) $w_i \geqq w_j$, and
   (iii) $p_i \leqq p_j$,

then we only have to consider schedules in which J_i precedes J_j.

PROOF. We can apply theorem 4.15 with $B_j = A_i = \emptyset$. Clearly, conditions (i) and (ii) imply that $c_i(t) - c_j(t)$ is non-decreasing on the interval $(0, P(S))$ (see figure 4.3).   (Q.E.D.)

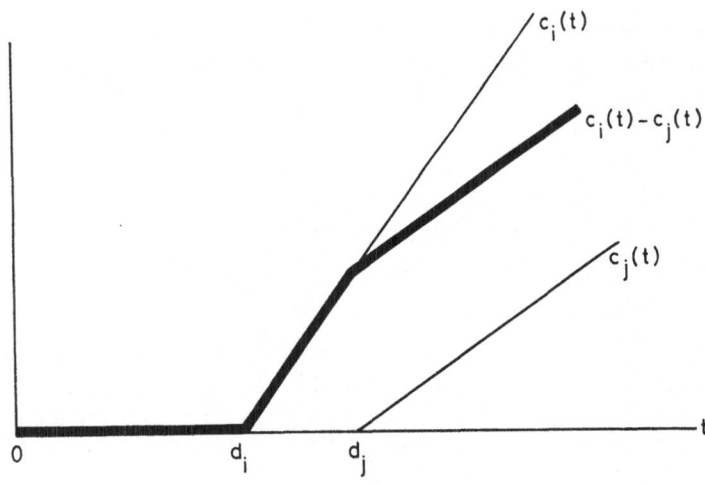

Figure 4.3.

COROLLARY 4.17. If $c_i(t) = w_i \max(0, t - d_i)$ for all i, and if for two jobs J_i and J_j $(i, j \in S)$ we have

   (i) $d_i \leqq P(B_j) + p_j$,
   (ii) $w_i \geqq w_j$, and
   (iii) $p_i \leqq p_j$,

then we only have to consider schedules in which J_i precedes J_j.

PROOF. Condition (i) implies that $c_i(t) > 0$ for $t > P(B_j) + p_j$, and it follows from condition (ii) that $c_i(t) - c_j(t)$ is non-decreasing on the required interval.   (Q.E.D.)

THEOREM 4.18. If for two jobs J_i and J_j $(i, j \in S)$ we have

   (i) $c_j(P(B_j) + p_j) = c_j(P(S - A_i) - p_j)$, and

(ii) $c_i(t) - c_j(t)$ is a non-decreasing function of t on the interval $(P(S - A_i) - p_j, P(S - A_i))$,

then we only have to consider schedules in which J_i precedes J_j.

PROOF. Clearly, conditions (i) and (ii) imply that $c_i(t) - c_j(t)$ is non-decreasing on the interval $(P(B_j) + p_j, P(S - A_i))$, so in the case that $p_i \leqq p_j$ we can apply theorem 4.15. Suppose now that $p_i > p_j$. Again, consider any schedule in which J_j precedes J_i, denote by S the starting time of J_j and by C the finishing time of J_i. Compare this schedule with the schedule obtained by putting J_j directly after J_i (see figure 4.4). The contribution to total costs by all jobs except J_j decreases or remains the same.

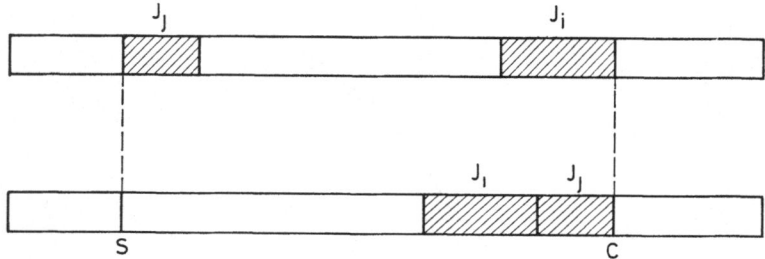

Figure 4.4.

As to J_j, it follows from

$$P(B_j) + p_j \leqq S + p_j < C - p_j \leqq P(S - A_i) - p_j$$

and condition (i) that

(4-7) $c_j(C - p_j) = c_j(S + p_j).$

Because of condition (ii), we have

(4-8) $c_i(C) - c_j(C) \geqq c_i(C - p_j) - c_j(C - p_j).$

Together, (4-7) and (4-8) imply

$$c_i(C) + c_j(S + p_j) \geqq c_i(C - p_j) + c_j(C),$$

which means that the joint contribution of J_i and J_j to total costs also decreases or remains the same.   (Q.E.D.)

The following corollaries and theorems are now easily proved [Rinnooy Kan *et al.* 1975].

COROLLARY 4.19. If $c_i(t) = w_i \max(0, t - d_i)$ for all i, and if for two jobs J_i and J_j $(i, j \in S)$ we have

    (i) $d_j \geqq P(S - A_i) - p_j$,
    (ii) $d_i \leqq d_j$, and
    (iii) $w_i \geqq w_j$,

then we only have to consider schedules in which J_i precedes J_j.

THEOREM 4.20. If for two jobs J_i and J_j $(i, j \in S)$ we have

$$c_j(P(B_j) + p_j) = c_j(P(S - A_i)),$$

then we only have to consider schedules in which J_i precedes J_j.

COROLLARY 4.21. If $c_i(t) = w_i \max(0, t - d_i)$ for all i, and if for two jobs J_i and J_j $(i, j \in S)$ we have

$$d_j \geqq P(S - A_i),$$

then we only have to consider schedules in which J_i precedes J_j.

THEOREM 4.22. If for a job J_j $(j \in S)$ we have

$$c_j(p_j) = c_j(P(S)),$$

then we only have to consider schedules in which J_j comes last among $\{J_i | i \in S\}$.

COROLLARY 4.23. If $c_i(t) = w_i \max(0, t - d_i)$ for all i, and if for a job J_j $(j \in S)$ we have

$$d_j \geqq P(S),$$

then we only have to consider schedules in which J_j comes last among $\{J_i | i \in S\}$.

Corollaries 4.16 and 4.23 were used in [Shwimer 1972]. Corollaries 4.16, 4.17 and 4.19 reduce to theorems to be found in [Emmons 1969] for the special case that $w_j = 1$ for all j. The above proofs are considerably simpler than the original ones. Corollary 4.23 is known as *Elmaghraby's Lemma* [Elmaghraby 1968].

    Repeated application of the above elimination criteria could lead to the creation of *precedence cycles*. If, however, we update all sets

A_h ($h \in \{i\} \cup B_i$) and B_g ($g \in \{j\} \cup A_j$) in the obvious way as soon as we have found that $i \in B_j$, $j \in A_i$, we can avoid such cycles by only examining hitherto unrelated pairs (i, j) (i.e., $i \notin B_j \cup A_j$). Suppose that we found that 'J_i precedes J_j'. If it then turned out that for some $g \in A_j$, $h \in B_i$ we have $g \in B_h$, then we would have set $i \in A_j$ in a previous stage; hence we would not have examined this pair anew.

4.3.3.2. A branch-and-bound algorithm

A branching rule for the $n|1||\sum c_i$ problem can be defined in the notation of section 3.4 in the following way. Nodes in the search tree that are defined by subsets $Y \in \mathcal{X}$ correspond to a set $\{J_i | i \in \bar{S}\}$ to be scheduled from 0 to $P(\bar{S})$ and a set $\{J_i | i \in S \triangleq \{1, \ldots, n\} - \bar{S}\}$ filling the last $|S|$ positions of the schedule in a given order (if $Y = X$, $S = \emptyset$). Each $Y' \in b(Y)$ corresponds to a particular J_j ($j \in \bar{S}$) being scheduled in the $|\bar{S}|$-th position, leaving $\{J_i | i \in \bar{S} - \{j\}\}$ to be scheduled from 0 to $P(\bar{S} - \{j\})$. Thus, schedules are filled from back to front.

A lower bound $LB(S)$ on all possible completions of the partial schedule defined by S is given by

$$LB(S) = c(S) + LB^*(\bar{S})$$

where $c(S)$ denotes the known costs incurred by scheduling $\{J_i | i \in S\}$ in the given order and $LB^*(\bar{S})$ is a lower bound on the costs c^* of an optimal schedule $(J_{\pi^*(1)}, \ldots, J_{\pi^*(\bar{s})})$ for the jobs in $\{J_i | i \in \bar{S}\}$, renumbered from 1 to $\bar{s} \triangleq |\bar{S}|$.

Now, if $p_i = p^*$ ($i = 1, \ldots, \bar{s}$), the costs of putting J_i in the j-th position are given by $c_{ij} \triangleq c_i(jp^*)$; a schedule with minimum total cost is then given in $O(\bar{s}^3)$ steps by the solution to the *linear assignment problem*:

$$(4\text{-}9) \quad \min_{\pi} \sum_{j=1}^{\bar{s}} c_{\pi(j)j}$$

where π runs over all permutations of $\{1, \ldots, \bar{s}\}$.

If not all p_i are equal, the above idea can be used to compute lower bounds in two ways.

First, each job can be treated as a sequence of p_i/g jobs of identical length $g = \text{g.c.d.} \{p_1, \ldots, p_{\bar{s}}\}$, in which case (4-9) becomes a $(P(\bar{S})/g) \times \bar{s}$ linear transportation problem. Suitable cost coefficients for the case that $c_i(t) = = w_i' t + w_i'' \max(0, t - d_i)$ can be found in [Gelders and Kleindorfer 1974, 1975].

Instead of this linear transportation problem, we can also work with the following $(P(\bar{S})/g) \times (P(\bar{S})/g)$ linear assignment problem. For the sake of an easy notation, we assume that $g = 1$. Then $c_{(i,j)k}$ ($i = 1, \ldots, \bar{s}; j = 1, \ldots, p_i;$ $k = 1, \ldots, P(\bar{S})$) is equal to $(1/p_i)$-th of the costs incurred if J_i would be finished at time $k + p_i - j$: $c_{(i,j)k} = c_i(k + p_i - j)/p_i$. We can take $c_{(i,j)k} = \infty$ if $k + p_i - j > P(\bar{S})$ or if $k - j < 0$.

If, however, one wants to avoid such a large scale assignment problem, a second approach seems preferable [Rinnooy Kan *et al.* 1975]. Here, c_{ij} becomes a lower bound on the cost of putting J_i in the j-th position, while precedence constraints as given by A_i and B_i are taken into account. Defining

$$R_i(k) \triangleq \min_Q \{P(Q) | Q \subset \{1, \ldots, \bar{s}\} - (B_i \cup \{i\} \cup A_i), |Q| = k\}$$

$$t_{ij} \triangleq P(B_i) + p_i + R_i(j - |B_i| - 1)$$

we obtain such c_{ij} by putting

$$c_{ij} = \begin{cases} c_i(t_{ij}) & \text{for } |B_i| < j \le |\{1, \ldots, \bar{s}\} - A_i| \\ \infty & \text{otherwise.} \end{cases}$$

Using these c_{ij} in (4-9) given the desired lower bound $LB^*(\bar{S})$: if $(J_{\pi^*(1)}, \ldots, J_{\pi^*(\bar{s})})$ is the optimal schedule, we have that $\sum_{i=1}^{\bar{s}} c_{\pi^*(i)}(C_{\pi^*(i)}) \ge \sum_{i=1}^{\bar{s}} c_{\pi^*(i)i}$ because the c_{ij} are underestimates, and $\sum_{i=1}^{\bar{s}} c_{\pi^*(i)i} \ge LB^*(\bar{S})$ by (4-9).

In every node of the search tree, the solution to (4-9) can also be evaluated as a schedule; this may lead to a decrease in the current upper bound UB. If $LB(S) \ge UB$, the node can be eliminated; otherwise, $\{J_r | r \in \bar{S}, \bar{S} \cap A_r = \emptyset\}$ are candidates for the $\bar{s}$-th position. A complete solution $LB^*(\bar{S} - \{r\})$ of the assignment problem in a descendant node may still be avoided by calculating an initial lower bound $LB'(S \cup \{r\})$. This lower bound is based on the optimal solution to (4-9), as obtained during the calculation of $LB^*(\bar{S})$. (4-9) may be reformulated as

$$\text{minimize} \quad \sum_{i=1}^{\bar{s}} \sum_{j=1}^{\bar{s}} c_{ij} X_{ij}$$

$$\text{subject to} \quad \sum_{i=1}^{\bar{s}} X_{ij} = 1 \qquad\qquad (j = 1, \ldots, \bar{s})$$

$$\sum_{j=1}^{\bar{s}} X_{ij} = 1 \qquad\qquad (i = 1, \ldots, \bar{s})$$

$$X_{ij} \ge 0 \qquad\qquad (i, j = 1, \ldots, \bar{s})$$

or as the dual problem

$$\text{maximize } \sum_{i=1}^{\bar{s}} U_i + \sum_{j=1}^{\bar{s}} V_j$$

$$\text{subject to } U_i + V_j \leqq c_{ij} \qquad\qquad (i, j = 1, \dots, \bar{s})$$

and we have $LB^*(\bar{S}) = \sum_{i=1}^{\bar{s}} \sum_{j=1}^{\bar{s}} c_{ij} x_{ij}^* = \sum_{i=1}^{\bar{s}} u_i^* + \sum_{i=1}^{\bar{s}} v_j^*$. Now, $(u_i^*, v_j^*)_{i \neq r, j \neq \bar{s}}$
provides a feasible dual solution to the assignment problem obtained by
removing the r-th row and the $\bar{s}$-th column; it follows that

$$\sum_{i \neq r} u_i^* + \sum_{j \neq \bar{s}} v_j^* = LB^*(\bar{S}) - u_r^* - v_{\bar{s}}^* \leqq LB^*(\bar{S} - \{r\}).$$

Combining this with $c(S \cup \{r\}) = c(S) + c_{r\bar{s}}$, we obtain an initial lower
bound

$$LB'(S \cup \{r\}) \overset{\triangle}{=} (c(S) + c_{r\bar{s}}) + (LB^*(\bar{S}) - u_r^* - v_{\bar{s}}^*)$$

$$= LB(S) + c_{r\bar{s}} - u_r^* - v_{\bar{s}}^* \geqq LB(S).$$

$LB'(S \cup \{r\})$ can be quickly calculated, may lead to early elimination of
the node in the search tree corresponding to $S \cup \{r\}$ and provides a satisfactory heuristic ordering to use in a newest active node search procedure.

If the node corresponding to $S \cup \{r\}$ cannot be eliminated by means of
LB' or elimination criteria, $LB^*(\bar{S} - \{r\})$ has to be calculated. In that case,
(u_i^*, v_j^*) still provides a feasible dual solution to the new $(\bar{s}-1) \times (\bar{s}-1)$
linear assignment problem, and (x_{ij}^*) provides a partial primal solution;
orthogonality can be arranged by simply resetting $x_{ij}^* = 0$ whenever
$u_i + v_j < c_{ij}$ and $x_{ij}^* = 1$. The dual assignment algorithm developed by B.
Dorhout [Dorhout 1975] allows full exploitation of all available data and
seems a natural choice for the calculation of $LB^*(\bar{S})$.

Availability of feasible dual solutions suggests an alternative lower
bounding rule whereby only one $n \times n$ linear assignment problem is solved
with $S = \emptyset$, and lower bounds throughout the search tree are provided by
sums of appropriate dual variables (cf. [Gelders and Kleindorfer 1974]).
Reasonably good results were obtained using this variation (see [Rinnooy
Kan et al. 1975]).

The algorithm, summarily described above, has been the subject of
extensive experimentation for the weighted tardiness case. We refer to
appendix 2 for details on implementation and on the generation of test data.
The algorithm was found to perform satisfactorily relative to the previously
best $n|1||\sum w_i T_i$ algorithm [Shwimer 1972] that incorporates a similar

branching rule and a lower bound given by

$$LB''(S \cup \{r\}) \overset{\triangle}{=} c(S \cup \{r\}) +$$

$$+ \min_{i \in \bar{S} - \{r\}} \{w_i \max (0, P(\bar{S} - \{r\}) - d_i) +$$

$$\min_{h \in \bar{S} - \{r, i\}} \{w_h\} \cdot T^*_{\max}(\bar{S} - \{r, i\})\},$$

where $T^*_{\max}(Q)$, *i.e.* the minimal maximal tardiness of Q, is given by theorem 4.3. A similar bound for a general cost function $c_i(t)$ could be found by means of theorem 4.5. Sometimes, on simple problems, Shwimer's algorithm was somewhat faster than the algorithm described above, but on these occasions it was in turn outperformed by a simple lexicographic enumeration algorithm (cf. [Lenstra and Rinnooy Kan 1975]) with a crude lower bound $LB''(S \cup \{r\}) = c(S \cup \{r\})$.

Generally speaking, even stronger lower bounds seem to be required to reduce the size of the $n|1||\sum c_i$ search tree. Fisher's bound [Fisher 1974] may be suitable for this purpose, although it did not produce significantly superior results in some preliminary experiments. Stronger elimination criteria, taken into account to the fullest possible extent during the lower bound calculation, may also lead to better algorithms for this complicated scheduling problem.

4.4. $n|1|\Gamma|\sum c_i$ PROBLEMS

4.4.1. The $n|1|r_i \geq 0|\sum c_i$ problem

As in section 4.2.1, we first consider some special cases. If $p_i = p^*$ $(i = 1, \ldots, n)$, then, if $p^* = 1$, we define analogously to sections 4.2.1 and 4.3.3.2:

$$c_{ij} \overset{\triangle}{=} \begin{cases} c_i(j) & \text{if } j > r_i \\ \infty & \text{if } j \leq r_i \end{cases} \qquad (i = 1, \ldots, n; j = 1, \ldots, C^*_{\max})$$

where $C^*_{\max}$ denotes the minimum time needed to process all jobs that can be found by ordering the jobs according to increasing r_i (theorem 4.6). The $n|1|r_i \geq 0, p_i = 1|\sum c_i$ problem is then equivalent to the following *linear transportation problem*:

$$\text{minimize } \sum_{i=1}^{n} \sum_{j=1}^{C^*_{\max}} c_{ij} X_{ij}$$

$$\text{subject to} \sum_{j=1}^{C^*_{max}} X_{ij} = 1 \qquad\qquad (i = 1, \ldots, n)$$

$$\sum_{i=1}^{n} X_{ij} \leq 1 \qquad\qquad (j = 1, \ldots, C^*_{max})$$

$$X_{ij} \in \{0, 1\} \qquad\qquad (i = 1, \ldots, n;$$
$$j = 1, \ldots, C^*_{max})$$

As in section 4.2.1, any active schedule for this problem will have $x_{ij} = 0$ for $(C^*_{max} - n)$ values of j, obtainable from the schedule producing C^*_{max}. Thus, we can effectively reduce the problem to an $n \times n$ linear assignment problem.

Counterexamples similar to the one provided in section 4.2.1 indicate that this approach cannot be generalized to the case that $p^* > 1$, unless p^* divides $g = $ g.c.d. $\{r_1, \ldots, r_n\}$ (this contradicts remarks in [Tremolières 1973]). For some cost functions $c_i(t)$, however, we actually need less than the $O(n^3)$ steps required to solve the assignment problem.

THEOREM 4.24. The following $O(n \log n)$ procedure generates a permutation π^* such that $(J_{\pi^*(1)}, \ldots, J_{\pi^*(n)})$ is an optimal solution to the $n|1|r_i \geq 0$, $p_i = 1|\sum w_i C_i$ problem with $\eta_i := -w_i$ and to the $n|1|r_i \geq 0, p_i = 1|\sum T_i$ problem with $\eta_i := d_i$.

procedure *n1ri0pi1wiciti* (η, π^*);
begin local S, Q, k, t, i;
$\quad S := \{1, \ldots, n\}; t := 0; k := 1;$
$\quad$ **while** $S \neq \emptyset$ **do**
$\quad$ **begin** $t := \max\{t, \min_{j \in S}\{r_j\}\};$
$\quad\quad\quad Q := \{j | j \in S, r_j \leq t\};$
$\quad\quad\quad i :\in \{j | j \in Q, \eta_j = \min_{h \in Q}\{\eta_h\}\};$
$\quad\quad\quad \pi^*(k) := i;$
$\quad\quad\quad k := k+1; t := t+1; S := S - \{i\}$
$\quad$ **end**
end *n1ri0pi1wiciti*;

PROOF. Trivial; cf. theorem 4.7.   (Q.E.D.)

It follows from theorem 4.6 and from results obtained in section 4.2.1 that there is one schedule minimizing C_{max} and $\sum w_i C_i$, and one schedule minimizing L_{max}, T_{max} and $\sum T_i$.

No similar single pass dispatching rule can be devised to solve the $n|1|r_i \geq 0, p_i = 1|\sum w_i T_i$ problem: any single pass procedure to solve this problem would have to consider jobs not yet available, as shown by the following example. (Note that it does remain true that idle time on the machine can never be advantageous.) Consider the $3|1|r_i \geq 0, p_i = 1|\sum w_i T_i$ problem with $r_1 = r_2 = d_1 = 0$, $w_1 = 1$, $d_2 = 2$, $w_2 = 3$, $r_3 = 1$, $w_3 = 5$. If $d_3 = 1$, the optimal schedule is (J_2, J_3, J_1) with value 8. If $d_3 = 3$, the optimal schedule is (J_1, J_2, J_3) with value 1. Hence d_3 influences the choice at $t = 0$, although $r_3 = 1 > 0$.

As before, the above approaches with $p_i = 1$ can be extended to solve various $n|1|r_i \geq 0, job\ spl|\sum c_i$ problems. The subsequent incorporation of these solution methods in a branch-and-bound approach to $n|1|r_i \geq 0|\sum c_i$ problems will now be justified by theorems 4.25 and 4.26 below. Let us define an *id-encoding* of scheduling problem data to be the encoding whereby subsets of identical jobs are represented by a number indicating their cardinality and a single copy of the data. With respect to such an encoding, we can prove the following strong result.

THEOREM 4.25. The $n|1|r_n \geq 0|\sum C_i$ problem is NP-complete with respect to the id-encoding.

PROOF. Given $a_1, \ldots, a_t, b, A = \sum_{i=1}^{t} a_i, a_* = \max_i \{a_i\}$, we prove:

KNAPSACK $\propto n|1|r_n \geq 0|\sum C_i$

$$n = t + t' + u + 1$$
$$r_i = 0, p_i = \tau + a_j \qquad (i \in T = \{1, \ldots, t\})$$
$$r_i = 0, p_i = \tau \qquad (i \in T' = \{t+1, \ldots, t+t'\})$$
$$r_i = 0, p_i = v \qquad (i \in U = \{t+t'+1, \ldots, t+t'+u\})$$
$$r_n = t\tau + b, p_n = 1$$
$$y = v + \tfrac{1}{2}u(u+1)v$$

where

$$t' = t(t+1)a_*$$
$$\tau = (t'+1)(b+1) + t'$$
$$u = \tfrac{1}{2}(t+t')(t+t'+1)\tau + (t+1)\tau$$
$$v = u(\sigma + 1)$$
$$\sigma = \sum_{j \notin U} p_j = (t+t')\tau + A + 1.$$

If KNAPSACK has a solution, then $\sum_{i \in S} a_i = b$ for some $S \subset T$. Defining
$S' = \{t + i | i \in T - S\} \subset T'$, we have for a processing order ($\{J_i | i \in S'\}$,
$\{J_i | i \in S\}, J_n, \{J_i | i \in T' - S'\}, \{J_i | i \in T - S\}, \{J_i | i \in U\}$) that

$$\sum_{i \notin U} C_i = \sum_{i \in S' \cup S} C_i + C_n + \sum_{i \in (T' - S') \cup (T - S)} C_i \leq$$

$$\leq \sum_{i=1}^{t} i(\tau + a_*) + t\tau + b + 1 + \sum_{i=t+1}^{t+t'} (i\tau + b + 1) + \sum_{i=1}^{t} ia_* =$$

$$= \tfrac{1}{2}(t + t')(t + t' + 1)\tau + t\tau + (t' + 1)(b + 1) + t(t + 1)a_* = u$$

and

$$\sum_{i \in U} C_i = \sum_{i=1}^{u} (\sigma + iv) = u\sigma + \tfrac{1}{2}u(u + 1)v.$$

Hence,

$$\sum_i C_i \leq u + u\sigma + \tfrac{1}{2}u(u + 1)v = y.$$

Conversely, if $\sum_i C_i \leq y$ for some schedule, we claim that

(i) $\{J_j | j \notin U\}$ precedes $\{J_i | i \in U\}$;
(ii) $S_i \leq \sigma$ for some $i \in U$;
(iii) exactly t jobs precede J_n;
(iv) $S_n = t\tau + b$.

It follows from (i) and (ii) that $\{J_j | j \notin U\}$ is scheduled without interruption
from 0 to σ. By (iii) and (iv), exactly t jobs from $\{J_i | i \in T \cup T'\}$ occupy a
period of length $t\tau + b$. This implies that KNAPSACK has a solution, as is
easily seen.

We now turn to the proofs of (i), (ii), (iii) and (iv).

(i) If J_j, $j \notin U$, follows some J_i, $i \in U$, then we have

$$\sum_i C_i \geq C_j + \sum_{i \in U} C_i > v + \tfrac{1}{2}u(u + 1)v = y.$$

(ii) If $S_i > \sigma$ for all $i \in U$, then we have

$$\sum_i C_i > \sum_{i \in U} C_i \geq u(\sigma + 1) + \tfrac{1}{2}u(u + 1)v = y.$$

Since $\sum_i C_i \leq y$ and, by (i) and (ii), $\sum_{i \in U} C_i \geq u\sigma + \tfrac{1}{2}u(u + 1)v$, we now know
that $\sum_{j \notin U} C_j \leq u$.

(iii) Let exactly s jobs from $\{J_i | i \in T \cup T'\}$ precede J_n.

If $0 \leq s \leq t-1$, then we have

$$\sum_{j \notin U} C_j \geq \sum_{j=1}^{s} j\tau + t\tau + b + 1 + \sum_{j=s+1}^{t+t'} (j\tau + (t-s)\tau + b + 1) =$$

$$= u - t' + (t + t' - s)(t-s)\tau + (t-s)(b+1) >$$

$$> u - t' + (t' + 1)\tau > u.$$

If $t + 1 \leq s \leq t + t'$, then we have

$$\sum_{j \notin U} C_j \geq \sum_{j=1}^{s} j\tau + s\tau + 1 + \sum_{j=s+1}^{t+t'} (j\tau + 1) =$$

$$= u + (s - t - 1)\tau + t + t' - s + 1 \geq$$

$$\geq u + 1 > u.$$

(iv) Note that $S_n \geq r_n = t\tau + b$. If $S_n > t\tau + b$, then we have

$$\sum_{j \notin U} C_j \geq \sum_{j=1}^{t} j\tau + t\tau + b + 2 + \sum_{j=t+1}^{t+t'} (j\tau + b + 2) =$$

$$= u + 1 > u.$$

The id-encoding is essential for the above reduction to be polynomial-bounded. In this encoding, the problem data given above require an amount of space that is only linear in $\log A$. Note that this special encoding would not be necessary if KNAPSACK were NP-complete with respect to a unary encoding; this, however, is not the case. (Q.E.D.)

Inspection of the intricate NP-completeness proof for the $n|2|F|\sum C_i$ problem given in [Garey *et al.* 1975] reveals that this proof can be adapted to provide an NP-completeness proof for the $n|1|r_i \geq 0|\sum C_i$ problem that does not critically depend on the use of the id-encoding. In view of these complications we give the relatively easy proofs for two slightly weaker results, valid with respect to the ordinary $O(\log \sum_{i=1}^{n} p_i)$ encoding.*

---

* Similar results hold with respect to the $\sum w_i U_i$ problems: the $n|1|r_i \geq 0, p_i = 1|\sum w_i U_i$ problem can be solved efficiently [Lawler 1976; Lageweg 1975] and the $n|1|r_n \geq 0|\sum U_i$ problem is NP-complete [Lenstra *et al.* 1975].

THEOREM 4.26. The following problems are NP-complete:

    (i) $n|1|r_n \geq 0|\sum w_i C_i$

    (ii) $n|1|r_n \geq 0|\sum T_i$.

PROOF. Given $a_1, \ldots, a_t, b, A = \sum_{i=1}^{t} a_i$, we prove:

    (i) KNAPSACK $\propto n|1|r_n \geq 0|\sum w_i C_i$

$n = t + 1$

$r_i = 0, p_i = w_i = a_i$ $(i = 1, \ldots, t)$

$r_n = b, p_n = 1, w_n = 2$

$y = \sum_{\substack{i, j = 1 \\ i \leq j}}^{t} a_i a_j + A + b + 2.$

If $\sum_{i \in S} a_i = b$, the schedule described by $(\{J_i | i \in S\}, J_n, \{J_i | i \in T - S\})$ has value y.

    If $C_n \geq b + 2$,

$$\sum w_i C_i \geq \sum_{\substack{i, j = 1 \\ i \leq j}}^{n} a_i a_j + (A - b - 1) + 2(b + 2) > y.$$

    (ii) KNAPSACK $\propto n|1|r_n \geq 0|\sum T_i$

$n = t + 1$

$r_i = 0, p_i = a_i, d_i = A + 1$ $(i = 1, \ldots, t)$

$r_n = b, p_n = 1, d_n = b + 1$

$y = 0.$ (Q.E.D.)

Branch-and-bound algorithms for these problems can be organized along the lines of section 4.2.1.1.

4.4.2. The $n|1|seq\ dep|\sum c_i$ problem

We shall restrict our attention to $c_i(t) = t$, i.e. to the $n|1|seq\ dep|\sum C_i$ problem. With sequence dependent change-over times c_{ij} and job dependent set-up times s_i the value of the objective function corresponding to a permutation of job indices $(v(1), \ldots, v(n))$ is equal to

(4-10) $\sum\limits_{j=1}^{n} [s_{v(1)} + \sum\limits_{i=1}^{j} p_{v(1)} + \sum\limits_{i=1}^{j-1} c_{v(i),\,v(i+1)}] =$

$= \sum\limits_{j=1}^{n} (n-j+1)p_{v(j)} + \sum\limits_{j=1}^{n-1} (n-j)c_{v(j),\,v(j+1)} + ns_{v(1)}.$

The first component of the objective function can be easily minimized by means of theorem 4.11. However, the existence of sequence dependent change-over times increases the complexity of the problem as indicated by the following theorem.

THEOREM 4.27. The $n|1|seq\ dep|\sum C_i$ problem is NP-complete.

PROOF. We shall show that DIRECTED HAMILTONIAN PATH $\propto n|1|seq\ dep|\sum C_i$. For a graph G with n vertices, define c_{ij} to be equal to 0 if (i,j) is an arc in G and 1 otherwise. Taking all p_i equal to 1 and $s_i = 0$, G contains a hamiltonian path if and only if there exists a permutation v such that $\sum C_i \leq$ $\leq \frac{1}{2}n(n+1)$, since the latter inequality is equivalent to $c_{v(j),\,v(j+1)} = 0$ for $j = 1, \ldots, n-1$.   (Q.E.D.)

To solve the $n|1|seq\ dep|\sum C_i$ problem, first note the following formulation. If we put $c_{0i} = s_i$, $c_{i0} = \infty$, $p_0 = 0$, minimization of (4-10) is equivalent to a *quadratic assignment problem*:

$$\text{minimize} \sum\limits_{i=0}^{n} \sum\limits_{j=0}^{n} \sum\limits_{k=0}^{n} \sum\limits_{l=0}^{n} d_{ij} f_{kl} X_{ik} X_{jl}$$

$$\text{subject to} \sum\limits_{i=0}^{n} X_{ij} = 1 \qquad\qquad (j = 0, \ldots, n)$$

$$\sum\limits_{j=0}^{n} X_{ij} = 1 \qquad\qquad (i = 0, \ldots, n)$$

$$X_{ij} \in \{0, 1\} \qquad\qquad (i, j = 0, \ldots, n)$$

with

$$d_{ij} \overset{\triangle}{=} p_j + c_{ij}$$

$$f_{kl} \overset{\triangle}{=} \begin{cases} n - k & \text{if } k = l - 1 \\ 0 & \text{otherwise.} \end{cases}$$

The choice of c_{i0} guarantees that the optimal solution will have $x_{00}^* = 1$. A quadratic assignment algorithm (e.g. [Lawler 1963]) could now be used to solve the $n|1|seq\ dep|\sum C_i$ problem. However, the form of (4-10) suggests the following special branch-and-bound algorithm.

All possible permutation schedules can be enumerated by successively choosing one out of all n jobs for the first position in the schedule, one out of the $(n-1)$ remaining jobs for the second position, etc. etc. Suppose that J_i $(i \in S)$ fill the first $|S|$ positions in the schedule. We want to find a lower bound on the costs of scheduling the $\bar{s}$ remaining jobs $\{J_i | i \in \bar{S}\}$. Suppose that the last job J_r of $\{J_i | i \in S\}$ has completion time T. We then want to find $LB^*(\bar{S})$ such that

$$(4\text{-}11) \quad LB^*(\bar{S}) \leqq \sum_{l=1}^{\bar{s}} (T + \sum_{k=0}^{l-1} (c_{\pi(k), \pi(k+1)} + p_{\pi(k+1)}))$$

for all assignments $\pi: \{0, \ldots, \bar{s}\} \to \bar{S} \cup \{r\}$ such that $\pi(0) = r$. If we have $2\bar{s} + 2$ constants u_i, v_i $(i \in \bar{S} \cup \{r\})$ such that

$$\bar{c}_{ij} = c_{ij} - u_i - v_j \geqq 0 \qquad\qquad (i, j \in \bar{S} \cup \{r\})$$

then (4-11) can be rewritten as follows

$$(4\text{-}12) \quad LB^*(\bar{S}) \leqq \bar{s}T + \sum_{l=1}^{\bar{s}} \sum_{k=0}^{l-1} \bar{c}_{\pi(k), \pi(k+1)} + \sum_{l=1}^{\bar{s}} \sum_{k=0}^{l-1} u_{\pi(k)}$$

$$+ \sum_{l=1}^{\bar{s}} \sum_{k=0}^{l-1} (v_{\pi(k+1)} + p_{\pi(k+1)}).$$

Rewriting the last two terms in (4-12) respectively as

$$\sum_{l=0}^{\bar{s}-1} (\bar{s} - l) u_{\pi(l)} = \bar{s}u_r + \sum_{l=1}^{\bar{s}-1} (\bar{s} - l) u_{\pi(l)}$$

and as

$$\sum_{l=1}^{\bar{s}} (\bar{s} - l + 1)(v_{\pi(l)} + p_{\pi(l)}),$$

we find permutations π_u^* and π_v^* such that

$$u_{\pi_u^*(l)} \leqq u_{\pi_u^*(l+1)} \qquad\qquad (l = 1, \ldots, \bar{s} - 2)$$

$$v_{\pi_v^*(l)} + p_{\pi_v^*(l)} \leqq v_{\pi_v^*(l+1)} + p_{\pi_v^*(l+1)} \qquad\qquad (l = 1, \ldots, \bar{s} - 1)$$

By virtue of theorem 4.13, we can then take

$$LB^*(\bar{S}) = \bar{s}(T + u_r) + \sum_{l=1}^{\bar{s}-1} (\bar{s} - l) u_{\pi_u^*(l)} + \sum_{l=1}^{\bar{s}} (\bar{s} - l + 1)(v_{\pi_v^*(l)} + p_{\pi_v^*(l)}).$$

The u_i and v_j can be obtained from the solution to the dual of the linear assignment problem with cost coefficients c_{ij} (cf. section 4.3.3.2). Although no computational experience has been obtained, the lower bound $LB^*(\bar{S})$ is certainly stronger than any of the simple lower bounds proposed in [Van Deman and Baker 1974].

4.4.3. The $n|1|prec|\sum c_i$ problem

We first consider the $n|1|prec|\sum w_i C_i$ problem. In this case, the optimal schedule without precedence constraints can be easily obtained through theorem 4.11, and difficulties only arise when the ordering according to increasing p_i/w_i ratio is not compatible with the given precedence constraints. In general, if J_i has to precede J_j $(i \in B_j)$ and $p_i/w_i > p_j/w_j$, J_i and J_j will be adjacent in an optimal schedule unless J_h exists such that $i \in B_h$, $h \in B_j$, or $h \in B_j$ and $p_i/w_i < p_h/w_h$, or $i \in B_h$ and $p_h/w_h < p_j/w_j$. This observation does not lead to a generally efficient algorithm (cf. [Gapp et al. 1965]) and in fact, polynomial algorithms are known only for the case that the precedence graph $H = (V, A)$ is a branching (i.e., the case characterized by tree in section 2.2). Efficient procedures for the $n|1|tree|\sum w_i C_i$ problem requiring $O(n \log n)$ steps can be found in [Horn 1972] and [Sidney 1975]. The latter algorithm can be extended to slightly more general precedence constraints [Lawler 1975b]. However, we conjecture that both the $n|1|prec|\sum C_i$ and the $n|1|p_i = 1, prec|\sum w_i C_i$ problem are NP-complete.

For a general non-decreasing cost function $c_i(t)$ NP-completeness of the $n|1|prec|\sum c_i$ problem is a direct consequence of the NP-completeness of the general $n|1||\sum c_i$ problem (theorem 3.4 (v)). The following theorem contains the strongest NP-completeness result obtained so far; the proof involves the CLIQUE problem introduced in theorem 3.3.*

THEOREM 4.28. The $n|1|p_i = 1, prec|\sum T_i$ problem is NP-complete.

PROOF. CLIQUE $\propto n|1|p_i = 1, prec|\sum T_i$.

Given $G = (N, E)$ and an integer k, we define $n_0 \triangleq |N|$, $e_0 \triangleq |E|$, $n_1 \triangleq n_0 - k$, $f \triangleq \frac{1}{2}k(k-1)$, $e_1 \triangleq e_0 - f$, and consider the $n|1|p_i = 1, prec|\sum T_i$ problem defined by

$$n = n_0 + n_0 e_0$$

$$d_i = n_0 + fn_0 \qquad\qquad (i = 1, ..., n_0)$$

$$d_{(j+1)n_0} = k + fn_0 \qquad\qquad (j = 1, ..., e_0)$$

---

* By means of a similar reduction the $n|1|p_i = 1, prec|\sum U_i$ problem can be proved to be NP-complete [Garey and Johnson 1975].

$$d_{jn_0+h} = n_0 + n_0 e_0 \qquad\qquad (j = 1, \ldots, e_0;$$
$$h = 1, \ldots, n_0 - 1)$$

$$J_i \prec J_{jn_0+1} \text{ if node } i \text{ lies on edge } j \qquad (i = 1, \ldots, n_0;$$
$$j = 1, \ldots, e_0)$$

$$J_{jn_0+h} \prec J_{jn_0+h+1} \qquad\qquad (j = 1, \ldots, e_0;$$
$$h = 1, \ldots, n_0 - 1)$$

$$y = n_1 e_1 + \tfrac{1}{2} n_0 e_1 (e_1 + 1).$$

Job J_i $(1 \leq i \leq n_0)$ represents node i of G; the chain of n_0 jobs $J_{jn_0+1} \prec \ldots \prec \prec J_{(j+1)n_0}$ $(1 \leq j \leq e_0)$ represents edge j. From the choice of due dates for J_{jn_0+h} $(h = 1, \ldots, n_0 - 1)$ it follows easily that we may restrict ourselves to schedules whereby the jobs in an edge chain are performed consecutively. At most f of these chains can be on time and thus at least e_1 of these chains will be late. The earliest possible completion time of a late $J_{(j+1)n_0}$ is greater than $(f+1)n_0 = d_i$ $(1 \leq i \leq n_0)$, and we may therefore assume that e_1 late chains $J_{jn_0+1} \prec \ldots \prec J_{(j+1)n_0}$ fill the last $n_0 e_1$ positions in the schedule (cf. corollary 4.17). Hence, for any schedule we have that

$$\sum T_i \geq \sum_{j=1}^{e_1} [(fn_0 + (j+1)n_0) - (k + fn_0)] = y.$$

If G has a k-clique, this bound can be achieved (figure 4.5). Conversely, if G has no k-clique, then at least $e_1 + 1$ jobs $J_{(j+1)n_0}$ are late and

$$\sum T_i \geq y + 1 > y. \qquad\qquad\qquad \text{(Q.E.D.)}$$

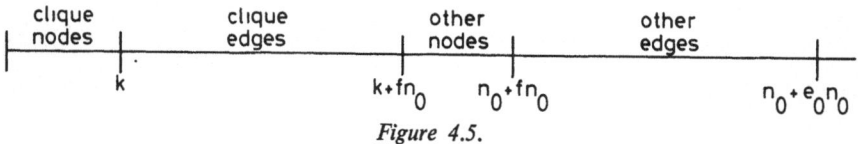

Figure 4.5.

5

Two-machine and three-machine problems

In this chapter we discuss problems involving two or three machines. We shall be mainly interested in a further exploration of the borderline between 'easy' and 'hard' problems as discussed in section 3.6. The crucial result here is Johnson's efficient algorithm for the $n|2|F|C_{max}$ problem. In section 5.1 we try to extend Johnson's approach to solve other $n|2|\gamma, \Gamma|c_{max}$ or $n|3|\gamma, \Gamma|c_{max}$ problems; with a few exceptions, many of these turn out to be NP-complete. A similar situation exists with respect to the $n|2|F|\sum c_i$ problem discussed in section 5.2. In both sections, we shall occasionally suggest implicit enumeration approaches to solve NP-complete problems. Finally, in section 5.3 we show that Johnson's approach can be used to solve a variety of two-machine problems involving time lags, whereby jobs do not have to be finished on M_1 before starting on M_2.

5.1. THE $n|2|\gamma, \Gamma|c_{max}$ AND $n|3|\gamma, \Gamma|c_{max}$ PROBLEM

The following two theorems will be applied throughout sections 5.1 and 5.2.

THEOREM 5.1 [Conway *et al.* 1967]. There exists an optimal solution to an $n|m|F|\delta$ problem with the same processing order on M_1 and M_2.

PROOF. Trivial.   (Q.E.D.)

THEOREM 5.2 [Johnson 1954]. There exists an optimal solution to an $n|m|F|C_{max}$ problem with the same processing order on M_{m-1} and M_m.

PROOF. Trivial.   (Q.E.D.)

Thus the $n|2|F|\delta$ and $n|2|P|\delta$ problems, and the $n|3|F|C_{max}$ and $n|3|P|C_{max}$ problems are essentially equivalent. The optimal schedule with respect to

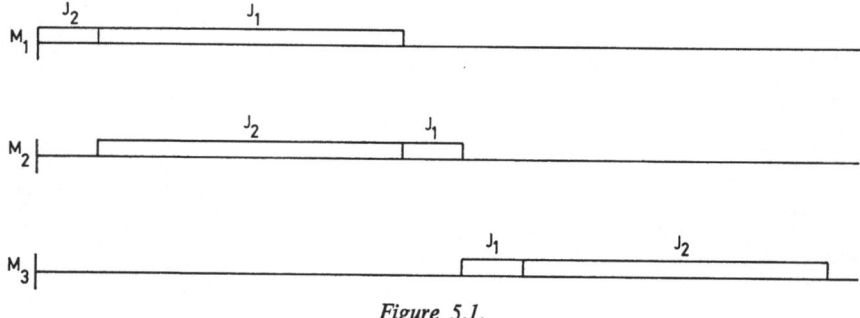

Figure 5.1.

the $2|3|F|\sum C_i$ problem with $p_{11}=p_{22}=p_{23}=5$ and $p_{12}=p_{13}=p_{21}=1$ illustrated in figure 5.1 indicates that theorem 5.2 does not hold for all regular measures.

We shall now describe an efficient algorithm to solve the $n|2|F|C_{max}$ problem.

THEOREM 5.3 [Johnson 1954]. The following procedure generates an optimal solution $(J_{\pi^*(1)}, \ldots, J_{\pi^*(n)})$ to the $n|2|F|C_{max}$ problem.

```
procedure n2fcmax (p₁, p₂, π*);
begin local S, k, l, pmin, i;
      S := {1, ..., n}; k := 1; l := n;
      while S ≠ ∅ do
      begin pmin := min {pₕ₁, pₕ₂};
                   h∈S
             i :∈ {j | j ∈ S, pⱼ₁ = pmin ∨ pⱼ₂ = pmin};
             if pᵢ₁ = pmin then
             begin π*(k) := i;
                     k := k+1; S := S−{i}
             end
             else
             begin π*(l) := i;
                     l := l−1; S := S−{i}
             end
      end
end n2fcmax;
```

Remark. By an appropriate preconditioning of S, this algorithm can be executed in $O(n \log n)$ steps.

PROOF. Our proof differs from the original one; it is based on the following two lemmas.

LEMMA 5.4. The $n|2|F|C_{max}$ problem with $p_{i1} = a_i$, $p_{i2} = b_i$ has the same optimal processing order as the $n|2|F|C_{max}$ problem with $p_{i1} = a_i + c$, $p_{i2} = b_i + c$.

PROOF. Consider the schedule defined by a permutation $(\pi(1), \ldots, \pi(n))$, leading to starting times $S_{\pi(i)1}$ and $S_{\pi(i)2}$ for the problem defined by (a_i, b_i) and $S'_{\pi(i)1}$ and $S'_{\pi(i)2}$ for the problem defined by $(a_i + c, b_i + c)$. We have obviously:

$$S'_{\pi(i)1} = S_{\pi(i)1} + (i-1)c.$$

We claim that

$$S'_{\pi(i)2} = S_{\pi(i)2} + ic.$$

This is obviously true for $i = 1$. Assuming the formula correct for $i = j - 1$, we have

$$S'_{\pi(j)2} = \max(S'_{\pi(j)1} + (a_{\pi(j)} + c), S'_{\pi(j-1)2} + (b_{\pi(j-1)} + c))$$

$$= \max((S_{\pi(j)1} + (j-1)c) + (a_{\pi(j)} + c),$$

$$(S_{\pi(j-1)2} + (j-1)c) + (b_{\pi(j-1)} + c))$$

$$= S_{\pi(j)2} + jc.$$

The lemma now follows from the fact that $C'_{\pi(n)}$ and $C_{\pi(n)}$ differ by the sequence independent term $(n+1)c$.   (Q.E.D.)

LEMMA 5.5. Consider an $n|2|F|C_{max}$ problem with $p_{i1} = a_i$, $p_{i2} = b_i$, in which M_1 is available at τ_1 and M_2 at τ_2.

  (i) If $a_i = 0$, there exists an optimal schedule with J_i in the first position.
  (ii) If $b_i = 0$, there exists an optimal schedule with J_i in the last position.

PROOF. (i) Consider any schedule whereby J_i is not in the first position (figure 5.2). Put $S \overset{\triangle}{=} S_{i1}$, $T \overset{\triangle}{=} C_i$ and let M_2 become available for job J_j on time R.

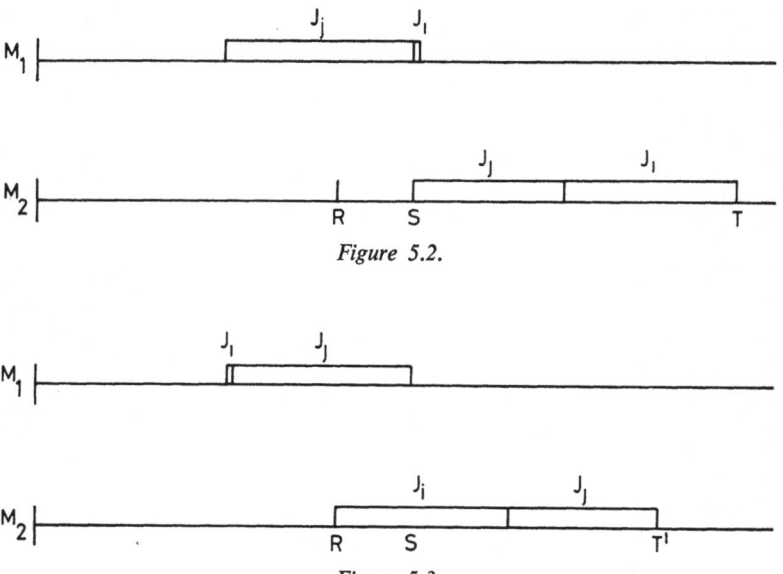

Figure 5.2.

Figure 5.3.

Compare this schedule to the schedule obtained by interchanging J_j and J_i, with C_j now becoming equal to T' (figure 5.3).

We have

(5-1) $T = \max(R, S) + b_j + b_i$

(5-2) $T' = \max(\max(R, S - a_j) + b_i, S) + b_j.$

Now,

(5-3) $\max(R, S) + b_i \geqq S$

and

(5-4) $\max(R, S) \geqq \max(R, S - a_j).$

It follows from (5-1), (5-2), (5-3) and (5-4) that $T' \leqq T$. Hence the new schedule cannot be worse than the old one, which proves (i).

   (ii) The proof is immediately obtained by applying (i) to the inverse problem.   (Q.E.D.)

The correctness of the above $n|2|F|C_{\max}$ algorithm is now obvious: it is justified by taking $c := -\text{pmin}$, applying lemma 5.4 and then lemma 5.5.

                                                                          (Q.E.D.)

Let us now try to extend the above approach to the $n|2|G|C_{\max}$ problem.

Define $\mathscr{J}_{12} \triangleq \{J_i|n_i = 2, \ \mu(O_{i1}) = 1, \ \mu(O_{i2}) = 2\}, \ \mathscr{J}_{21} \triangleq \{J_i|n_i = 2, \ \mu(O_{i1}) = 2, \ \mu(O_{i2}) = 1\}, \ \mathscr{J}_1 \triangleq \{J_i|n_i = 1, \ \mu(O_{i1}) = 1\}, \ \mathscr{J}_2 \triangleq \{J_i|n_i = 1, \ \mu(O_{i1}) = 2\}$, where O_{ir} is the r-th operation of J_i. If $\mathscr{J} = \mathscr{J}_{12} \cup \mathscr{J}_{21} \cup \ \cup \mathscr{J}_1 \cup \mathscr{J}_2$, then $n_i \leqq 2$ for all i and we have the following theorem.

THEOREM 5.6 [Jackson 1956]. The $n|2|G, n_i \leqq 2|C_{\max}$ problem is solved by choosing the following processing order:

- on M_1: $\mathscr{J}_{12} - \mathscr{J}_1 - \mathscr{J}_{21}$
- on M_2: $\mathscr{J}_{21} - \mathscr{J}_2 - \mathscr{J}_{12}$

where $\mathscr{J}_{12}$ and $\mathscr{J}_{21}$ are ordered by Johnson's algorithm, and $\mathscr{J}_1$ and $\mathscr{J}_2$ are ordered arbitrarily.

PROOF. Trivial. (Q.E.D.)

This result is essentially the strongest possible one, as demonstrated by the following theorems.

THEOREM 5.7. The $n|2|G, n_i \leqq 3|C_{\max}$ problem is NP-complete.

PROOF. KNAPSACK $\propto n|2|G, n_i \leqq 3|C_{\max}$

Given $a_i, \ldots, a_t, b, A = \sum_{i=1}^{t} a_i$, define

$$n = t + 1$$
$$p_{i1} = a_i, \mu(O_{i1}) = 1 \qquad\qquad (i \in T = \{1, \ldots, t\})$$
$$p_{n1} = b, \mu(O_{n1}) = 2, p_{n2} = 1, \mu(O_{n2}) = 1, p_{n3} = A - b, \mu(O_{n3}) = 2$$
$$y = A + 1$$

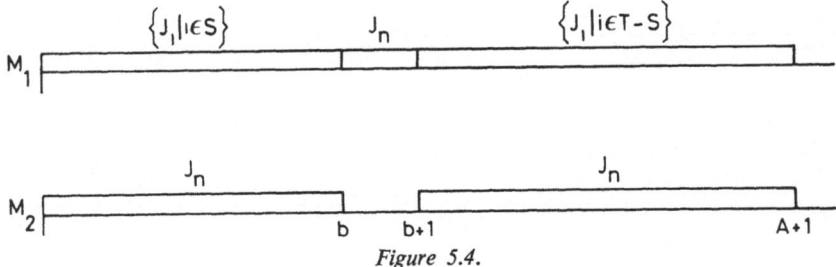

Figure 5.4.

If $\sum_{i \in S} a_i = b$ for some $S \subset T$, there exists a schedule with value $C_{max} = y$ (figure 5.4).

If KNAPSACK has no solution, then $\sum_{i \in S} a_i - b = c \neq 0$ for all $S \subset T$, and we have for a processing order $(\{J_i | i \in S\}, J_n, \{J_i | i \in T - S\})$ on M_1 that

$$c > 0 \Rightarrow C_{max} = \sum_{i \in S} p_{i1} + p_{n2} + p_{n3} = A + c + 1 > y$$

$$c < 0 \Rightarrow C_{max} = p_{n1} + p_{n2} + \sum_{i \in T - S} p_{i1} = A - c + 1 > y. \qquad \text{(Q.E.D.)}$$

THEOREM 5.8. The $n|3|G, n_i \leq 2|C_{max}$ problem is NP-complete.

PROOF. KNAPSACK $\propto n|3|G, n_i \leq 2|C_{max}$

Given $a_1, \ldots, a_t, b, A = \sum_{i=1}^{t} a_i$, define

$n = t + 2$

$p_{i1} = p_{i2} = a_i, \mu(O_{i1}) = 1, \mu(O_{i2}) = 3 \qquad\qquad (i \in T = \{1, \ldots, t\})$

$p_{n-1,1} = b, \mu(O_{n-1,1}) = 1, p_{n-1,2} = 2A - 2b, \mu(O_{n-1,2}) = 2$

$p_{n1} = 2b, \mu(O_{n1}) = 2, p_{n2} = A - b, \mu(O_{n2}) = 3$

$y = 2A.$

If $\sum_{i \in S} a_i = b$ for some $S \subset T$, there exists a schedule with value $C_{max} = y$ (figure 5.5).

If $\sum_{i \in S} a_i - b = c \neq 0$ for all $S \subset T$, we have for a processing order $(\{J_i | i \in S\}, J_{n-1}, \{J_i | i \in T - S\})$ on M_1 that

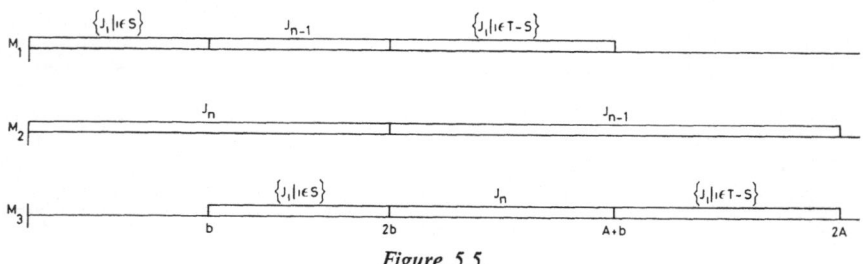

Figure 5.5.

$$c > 0 \Rightarrow C_{\max} \geqq \sum_{i \in S} p_{i1} + p_{n-1,1} + p_{n-1,2} = 2A + c > y$$

$$c < 0 \Rightarrow C_{\max} \geqq \min(\sum_{i \in S} p_{i1} + p_{n-1,1} + 1, p_{n1}) + p_{n2} + \sum_{i \in T-S} p_{i2}$$

$$= 2A + 1 > y. \tag{Q.E.D.}$$

Thus, only a very limited class of $n|m|G|C_{\max}$ problems can be solved efficiently. A branch-and-bound approach to the $n|2|G|C_{\max}$ problem could employ the algorithm described in theorem 5.6 within a lower bound calculation in an obvious way; for implicit enumeration approaches to the general $n|m|G|C_{\max}$ problem, see section 6.3.

Let us now investigate possible extensions of theorem 5.3 to $n|3|F$, $\Gamma|C_{\max}$ problems.

THEOREM 5.9 (cf. [Johnson 1954]). If in an $n|3|F|C_{\max}$ problem with $p_{i1} = a_i$, $p_{i2} = b_i$, $p_{i3} = c_i$, we have that either

   (i) $b_i \leqq a_j$ for all i, j,

or

   (ii) $b_i \leqq c_j$ for all i, j,

then the problem has the same optimal processing order as the $n|2|F|C_{\max}$ problem with $p_{i1} = a_i + b_i$, $p_{i2} = b_i + c_i$.

PROOF. (i) A permutation $(\pi(1), \ldots, \pi(n))$ defines starting times $S_{\pi(i)1}$, $S_{\pi(i)2}$, $S_{\pi(i)3}$ for the problem defined by (a_i, b_i, c_i) and $S'_{\pi(i)1}$, $S'_{\pi(i)2}$ for the problem defined by $(a_i + b_i, b_i + c_i)$. We have that

$$S_{\pi(i)1} = S_{\pi(i-1)1} + a_{\pi(i-1)}.$$

We claim that

$$S_{\pi(i)2} = S_{\pi(i)1} + a_{\pi(i)}.$$

This is obvious for $i = 1$. Assuming the formula correct for $i = j - 1$, we have that

$$S_{\pi(j)2} = \max(S_{\pi(j-1)2} + b_{\pi(j-1)}, S_{\pi(j)1} + a_{\pi(j)})$$

$$= \max(S_{\pi(j-1)1} + a_{\pi(j-1)} + b_{\pi(j-1)}, S_{\pi(j)1} + a_{\pi(j)})$$

$$= \max(S_{\pi(j)1} + b_{\pi(j-1)}, S_{\pi(j)1} + a_{\pi(j)})$$

$$= S_{\pi(j)1} + a_{\pi(j)}.$$

Therefore

(5-5) $S_{\pi(i)3} = \max(S_{\pi(i-1)3} + c_{\pi(i-1)}, S_{\pi(i)1} + a_{\pi(i)} + b_{\pi(i)})$

For the $n|2|F|C_{\max}$ problem, we have:

$$S'_{\pi(i)1} = S'_{\pi(i-1)1} + a_{\pi(i-1)} + b_{\pi(i-1)}$$

$$= S_{\pi(i)1} + \sum_{h=1}^{i-1} b_{\pi(h)}$$

as can be easily proved by induction. We claim that

(5-6) $S'_{\pi(i)2} = S_{\pi(i)3} + \sum_{h=1}^{i-1} b_{\pi(h)}.$

If $i = 1$, then obviously:

$$S'_{\pi(1)2} = S'_{\pi(1)1} + a_{\pi(1)} + b_{\pi(1)}$$

$$= a_{\pi(1)} + b_{\pi(1)}$$

$$= S_{\pi(1)3}.$$

Assuming (5-6) correct for $i = j - 1$, we find:

(5-7) $S'_{\pi(j)2} = \max(S'_{\pi(j)1} + a_{\pi(j)} + b_{\pi(j)}, S'_{\pi(j-1)2} + b_{\pi(j-1)} + c_{\pi(j-1)})$

$$= \max(S_{\pi(j)1} + \sum_{h=1}^{j-1} b_{\pi(h)} + a_{\pi(j)} + b_{\pi(j)},$$

$$S_{\pi(j-1)3} + \sum_{h=1}^{j-2} b_{\pi(h)} + b_{\pi(j-1)} + c_{\pi(j-1)})$$

$$= \max(S_{\pi(j)1} + a_{\pi(j)} + b_{\pi(j)}, S_{\pi(j-1)3} + c_{\pi(j-1)}) + \sum_{h=1}^{j-1} b_{\pi(h)}.$$

From (5-5) and (5-7), we see that (5-6) is correct for $i = j$. The proof with respect to (i) is now obvious from (5-6), since $S_{\pi(n)3} + c_{\pi(n)}$ and $S'_{\pi(n)2} + b_{\pi(n)} + c_{\pi(n)}$ differ by the sequence independent term $\sum_{h=1}^{n} b_{\pi(h)}$.

    (ii) Again we can prove (ii) by applying (i) to the inverse problem.

                                        (Q.E.D.)

A minor variation on the approach of theorem 5.9 is formulated in the next theorem.

THEOREM 5.10 [Arthanari and Mukhopadhyay 1971]. If in an $n|3|F|C_{\max}$ problem with $p_{i1} = a_i$, $p_{i2} = b_i$, $p_{i3} = c_i$, we have that either

(i) $a_i \leqq b_j$ for all i, j;

or that:

(ii) $c_i \leqq b_j$ for all i, j,

the problem can be solved by solving n $n|2|F|C_{\max}$ problems, corresponding to the n possible choices of first jobs or last jobs respectively.

PROOF. (i) We have:

(5-8) $\quad S_{\pi(i)2} = \max(S_{\pi(i)1} + a_{\pi(i)}, S_{\pi(i-1)2} + b_{\pi(i-1)})$

$\qquad\qquad = S_{\pi(i-1)2} + b_{\pi(i-1)}$

(5-9) $\quad S_{\pi(i)3} = \max(S_{\pi(i)2} + b_{\pi(i)}, S_{\pi(i-1)3} + c_{\pi(i-1)}).$

Together, (5-8) and (5-9) define an $n|2|F|C_{\max}$ problem whose solution value depends on $a_{\pi(1)}$ and $\{b_i, c_i\}$. Minimizing this value over all possible choices of $a_{\pi(1)}$ will produce an optimal schedule.

(ii) Apply (i) to the inverse problem. $\qquad\qquad$ (Q.E.D.)

The following extension of theorem 5.9 will find application in section 6.1.

THEOREM 5.11. The $n|3|F, M_2$ *non-bott*$|C_{\max}$ problem with $p_{i1} = a_i$, $p_{i2} = b_i$, $p_{i3} = c_i$ has the same optimal processing order as the $n|2|F|C_{\max}$ problem with $p_{i1} = a_i + b_i$, $p_{i2} = b_i + c_i$.

PROOF. Formula (5-5) again holds with respect to the problem defined by (a_i, b_i, c_i). $\qquad\qquad$ (Q.E.D.)

By now, we have all but exhausted the class of $n|2|\gamma, \Gamma|c_{\max}$ problems and $n|3|\gamma, \Gamma|c_{\max}$ problems that can be solved efficiently, as demonstrated by the next theorem.*

THEOREM 5.12. The following problems are NP-complete:

(i) $\quad n|2|F|L_{\max}$
(ii) $\quad n|2|F, tree|C_{\max}$

---

* See section 6.4 for an efficient solution method for the $n|2|F$, *no wait*$|C_{\max}$ problem.

(iii) $n|2|F, r_n \geqq 0|C_{max}$
(iv) $n|3|F|C_{max}$.

PROOF.

(i) From theorem 3.4 (xiv) and theorem 4.8.
(ii) KNAPSACK $\propto n|2|F, tree|C_{max}$

Given $a_1, \ldots, a_t, b, A = \sum_{i=1}^{t} a_i$, define:

$$n = t + 2$$
$$p_{i1} = ta_i, p_{i2} = 1 \qquad\qquad (i \in T = \{1, \ldots, t\})$$
$$p_{n-1,1} = 1, p_{n-1,2} = tb$$
$$p_{n1} = 1, p_{n2} = t(A - b)$$
$$J_{n-1} \prec J_n$$
$$y = t(A + 1) + 1.$$

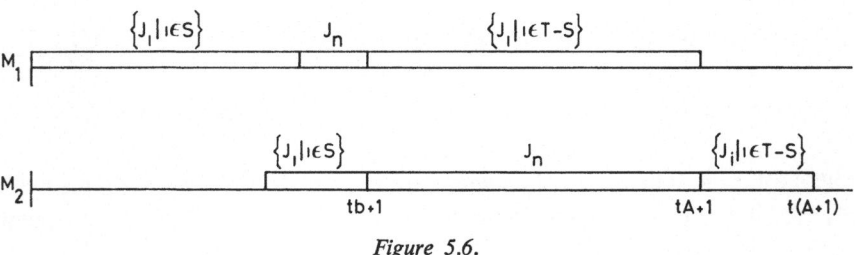

Figure 5.6.

See figure 5.6. We have for a processing order $(\{J_i|i \in R\}, J_{n-1}, \{J_i|i \in S\},$ $J_n, \{J_i|i \in T - (R \cup S)\})$ on M_1 and M_2 that

$$R \neq \emptyset \Rightarrow C_{max} \geqq t + p_{n-1,1} + p_{n-1,2} + p_{n1} + p_{n2} =$$
$$= t(A + 1) + 2 > y.$$

Hence $R = \emptyset$, and the schedule defines a partition $(S, T - S)$.
If $\sum_{i \in S} a_i - b = c \neq 0$ for all $S \subset T$, we have that

$$c > 0 \Rightarrow C_{max} \geqq p_{n-1,1} + \sum_{i \in S} p_{i1} + \sum_{i \in S} p_{i2} + p_{n2} + \sum_{i \in T-S} p_{i2}$$
$$= t(A + 1 + c) + 1 > y$$

$$c < 0 \Rightarrow C_{max} \geqq p_{n-1,1} + p_{n-1,2} + p_{n1} + \sum_{i \in T-S} p_{i1}$$
$$= t(A - c) + 2 > y.$$

(iii) KNAPSACK $\propto n|2|F, r_n \geqq 0|C_{max}$

Given $a_1, \ldots, a_t, b, A = \sum_{i=1}^{t} a_i$, define:

$n = t + 1$

$r_i = 0, p_{i1} = ta_i, p_{i2} = 1$ $\qquad (i \in T = \{1, \ldots, t\})$

$r_n = tb, p_{n1} = 1, p_{n2} = t(A - b)$

$y = t(A + 1).$

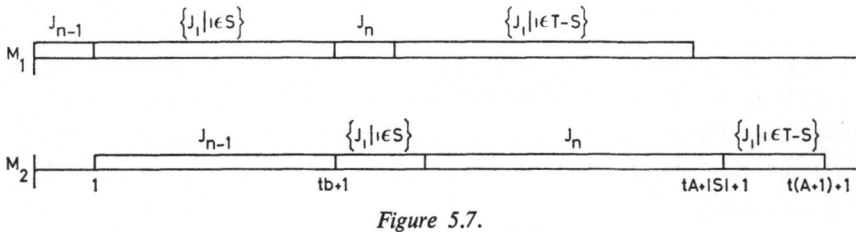

Figure 5.7.

See figure 5.7. If $\sum_{i \in S} a_i - b = c \neq 0$ for all $S \subset T$, we have for a processing order $(\{J_i | i \in S\}, J_n, \{J_i | i \in T - S\})$ on M_1 that:

$$c > 0 \Rightarrow C_{max} \geqq \sum_{i \in S} p_{i1} + p_{n1} + p_{n2} = t(A + c) + 1 > y$$

$$c < 0 \Rightarrow C_{max} \geqq r_n + p_{n1} + \sum_{i \in T-S} p_{i1} = t(A - c) + 1 > y.$$

(iv) From theorem 3.4 (xv) and (iii) above. (Q.E.D.)

Branch-and-bound methods for the $n|3|F|C_{max}$ problem have been mainly studied in the more general context of the $n|m|P|C_{max}$ problem; we refer to section 6.1 for a discussion. To solve the $n|2|F|L_{max}$ problem or, equivalently by inversion, the $n|2|F, r_i \geqq 0|C_{max}$ problem, one might try to use theorem 5.3 in the way suggested in section 4.2.1.2.

5.2. THE $n|2|F|\sum c_i$ PROBLEM

Theorem 5.1 implies that the $n|2|F|\sum c_i$ and $n|2|P|\sum c_i$ problems are equivalent for any non-decreasing $c_i(t)$. Theorem 4.25 may be combined with theorem 3.4 (xiv) to prove the NP-completeness of the $n|2|P|\sum C_i$ problem with respect to the id-encoding. A complicated NP-completeness proof avoiding this dependency can be found in [Garey *et al.* 1975].

We can provide simple proofs for two slightly weaker results.*

THEOREM 5.13. The following problems are NP-complete:

    (i) $n|2|F|\sum w_i C_i$
    (ii) $n|2|F|\sum T_i$.

PROOF. (i, ii) From theorem 3.4 (xiv) and theorem 4.26.   (Q.E.D.)

A branch-and-bound approach to the $n|2|F|\sum c_i$ problem is justified by the complexity results. Here we are hampered by the fact that, even in the simple case that $c_i(t) = t$ for all i, no elimination criteria have been developed so far: the rule suggested in [Conway *et al.* 1967] that J_i precedes J_j if $p_{i1} \leqq p_{j1}$ and $p_{i2} \leqq p_{j2}$, is incorrect as demonstrated by the optimal schedule for the $3|2|F|\sum C_i$ problem with $p_{11} = 9$, $p_{12} = 5$, $p_{21} = 8$, $p_{22} = 2$, $p_{31} = 1$, $p_{32} = 12$ (figure 5.8).

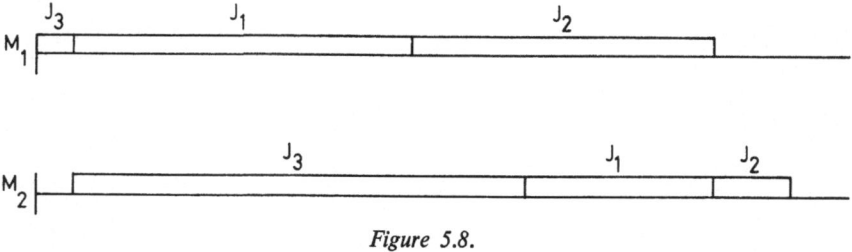

Figure 5.8.

An obvious enumeration scheme for the $n|2|F|\sum c_i$ problem is the following. Suppose that $\{J_i | i \in S\}$ have been scheduled on M_1 and M_2 in the order defined by $\sigma: \{1, ..., s\} \to S$, where $s \stackrel{\triangle}{=} |S|$. We branch by next scheduling successively all J_r $(r \in \bar{S} \stackrel{\triangle}{=} \{1, ..., n\} - S)$ in the $(s + 1)$-th position. Starting times S_{r1} and S_{r2} are then given by

---

* Since $n|1|r_n \geqq 0|\sum U_i$ is NP-complete (section 4.3.2), the $n|2|F|\sum U_i$ problem is NP-complete by theorem 3.4 (xiv) [Lenstra *et al.* 1975].

$$S_{r1} = C(\sigma, 1) \triangleq \sum_{h \in S} a_h$$

$$S_{r2} = \max(C(\sigma, 2), S_{r1} + a_r)$$

where $C(\sigma, 2) \triangleq C_{\sigma(s)}$.

Thus, $\bar{s} = |\bar{S}|$ new nodes in the search tree are created, each one corresponding to a specific subset $\{J_i | i \in \bar{S} - \{r\}\}$ of unscheduled jobs.

Analogously to section 4.3.3.2, we now seek to find a lower bound $LB(S)$ on the cost of all possible completions of the partial schedule defined by σ. We have:

$$LB(S) = c(S) + LB^*(\bar{S})$$

where

$$c(S) = \sum_{h=1}^{s} c_{\sigma(h)}(C_{\sigma(h)})$$

and $LB^*(\bar{S})$ is a lower bound on the costs of scheduling $\{J_i | i \in \bar{S}\}$ if M_1 becomes available on $C(\sigma, 1)$ and M_2 becomes available on $C(\sigma, 2)$.

We can now extend the idea of a linear assignment lower bound (section 4.3.3.2) to this more general case. Again, renumber $\{J_i | i \in \bar{S}\}$ from 1 to $\bar{s}$. Let

$$R_i(k) \triangleq \min_{Q} \{\sum_{l \in Q} a_l | Q \subset \bar{S} - \{i\}, |Q| = k\};$$

$$S_i(k) \triangleq \min_{Q} \{\sum_{l \in Q} b_l | Q \subset \bar{S} - \{i\}, |Q| = k\}.$$

If we define

$$t_{ij} \triangleq \max(C(\sigma, 1) + a_i + R_i(j-1),$$
$$\max(C(\sigma, 1) + R_i(1), C(\sigma, 2)) + S_i(j-1)) + b_i$$
$$(i = 1, \ldots, \bar{s}; j = 2, \ldots, \bar{s})$$

$$t_{i1} \triangleq \max(C(\sigma, 1) + a_i, C(\sigma, 2)) + b_i \qquad (i = 1, \ldots, \bar{s})$$

then t_{ij} is a lower bound on the completion time of J_i if it is scheduled in the j-th position among $\{J_h | h \in \bar{S}\}$. Possibly stronger t_{ij} can be obtained in a way to be indicated below.

If we define $c_{ij} \triangleq c_i(t_{ij})$, then $LB^*(\bar{S})$ can be obtained by solving the linear assignment problem

$$\min_{\pi} \sum_{i \in S} c_{i\pi(i)}$$

where π runs over all permutations of $\{1, \ldots, \bar{s}\}$.

The proof of the correctness of this lower bound is similar to the one given in section 4.3.3.2.

Having found $LB^*(\bar{S}) = \sum\limits_{i=1}^{\bar{s}} \sum\limits_{j=1}^{\bar{s}} c_{ij}x_{ij}^* = \sum\limits_{i=1}^{\bar{s}} u_i^* + \sum\limits_{j=1}^{\bar{s}} v_j^*$, we can obtain an initial lower bound $LB'(S \cup \{r\})$ on the costs of scheduling J_r in the $(n - \bar{s} + 1)$-th position by using the fact that the (i,j)-th cost coefficient used to find $LB^*(\bar{S})$ cannot be greater than the $(i, j-1)$-th one in the node that corresponds to J_r being scheduled in the $(n - \bar{s} + 1)$-th position. Hence $(u_i^*, v_j^*)_{i \neq r, j \neq 1}$ remains dual feasible and we obtain

$$LB'(S \cup \{r\}) \overset{\triangle}{=} c(S) + c_r(C_r) + \sum\limits_{\substack{i=1 \\ i \neq r}}^{\bar{s}} u_i^* + \sum\limits_{j=2}^{\bar{s}} v_j^*$$

$$= LB(S) + (c_{r1} - u_r^* - v_1^*) \geqq LB(S).$$

The initial lower bound can be used in a newest active node branch-and-bound algorithm in the way described in section 4.3.3.2. Dorhout's dual algorithm again seems the most suitable linear assignment algorithm. Generally, the algorithm could be expected to be less efficient than the one presented in section 4.3.3.2 due to the absence of elimination criteria.

Taking $c_i(t) = t$ for all i, we could use the above lower bound in an $n|2|F|\sum C_i$ algorithm. Extensive computational experiments have been carried out with respect to this problem [Kohler and Steiglitz 1975] using a lower bound developed in [Ignall and Schrage 1965]. We shall now show that this lower bound $LB_1^*(\bar{S})$ is never stronger than $LB^*(\bar{S})$ developed above.

$LB_1^*(\bar{S})$ is defined by

$$(5\text{-}10) \quad LB_1^*(\bar{S}) \overset{\triangle}{=} \max(\sum\limits_{i=1}^{\bar{s}} (K + (\bar{s} - i + 1)a_{\rho^*(i)} + b_{\rho^*(i)}),$$

$$\sum\limits_{i=1}^{\bar{s}} (L + (\bar{s} - i + 1)b_{\sigma^*(i)}))$$

where

$$a_{\rho^*(1)} \leqq a_{\rho^*(2)} \leqq \cdots \leqq a_{\rho^*(\bar{s})}, \, b_{\sigma^*(1)} \leqq b_{\sigma^*(2)} \leqq \cdots \leqq b_{\sigma^*(\bar{s})},$$

$$K \overset{\triangle}{=} C(\sigma, 1),$$

$$L \overset{\triangle}{=} \max(C(\sigma, 2), C(\sigma, 1) + \min\limits_{l \in S}\{a_l\}).$$

$LB_1^*(\bar{S})$ can be easily justified by application of theorem 4.13.

We can rewrite (5-10) as follows

$$LB_1^*(\bar{S}) = \max(\sum_{i=1}^{\bar{s}}(K + \sum_{l=1}^{i}a_{\rho^*(l)} + b_{\rho^*(i)}),$$

$$\sum_{i=1}^{\bar{s}}(L + \sum_{l=1}^{i}b_{\sigma^*(l)})).$$

It is clear from the definition that

$$R_i(k) = \begin{cases} \sum_{l=1}^{k}a_{\rho^*(l)} & \text{if } i \notin \{\rho^*(1), \ldots, \rho^*(k)\} \\ \sum_{\substack{l=1 \\ \rho^*(l) \neq i}}^{k+1} a_{\rho^*(l)} & \text{otherwise.} \end{cases}$$

This implies that

$$R_i(k) \geq \sum_{l=1}^{k}a_{\rho^*(l)}.$$

Hence for all permutations π of $\{1, \ldots, \bar{s}\}$

$$\sum_{i=1}^{\bar{s}}(\sum_{l=1}^{i}a_{\rho^*(l)}) \leq \sum_{i=1}^{\bar{s}}a_i + \sum_{i=1}^{\bar{s}}R_i(\pi(i) - 1),$$

since $R_i(\pi(i) - 1)$ corresponds to exactly one $R_i(k)$ for some $k \in \{0, \ldots, \bar{s}-1\}$, and $\sum_{l=1}^{\bar{s}}a_{\rho^*(l)} = \sum_{i=1}^{\bar{s}}a_i$.

It follows that

$$\sum_{i=1}^{\bar{s}}(K + \sum_{l=1}^{i}a_{\rho^*(l)} + b_{\rho^*(i)})$$

$$\leq \sum_{i=1}^{\bar{s}}(K + a_i + R_i(\pi(i) - 1) + b_i)$$

for all π, and similarly (for all π)

$$\sum_{i=1}^{\bar{s}}(L + \sum_{l=1}^{i}b_{\sigma^*(l)}) \leq \sum_{i=1}^{\bar{s}}(L + b_i + S_i(\pi(i) - 1)).$$

Hence, (5-10) is not greater than

$$\max(\sum_{i=1}^{\bar{s}}(K + a_i + R_i(\pi(i) - 1) + b_i),$$

$$\sum_{i=1}^{\bar{s}}(L + b_i + S_i(\pi(i) - 1)))$$

for all π, hence also not greater than

$$(5\text{-}11) \quad \sum_{i=1}^{\bar{s}} \max(K + a_i + R_i(\pi(i) - 1) + b_i, L + b_i + S_i(\pi(i) - 1)))$$

for any π, and therefore also not greater than the minimum of (5-11) taken over all π. It follows that $LB_1^*(\bar{S}) \leqq LB^*(\bar{S})$, since

$$L \leqq \max(C(\sigma, 2), C(\sigma, 1) + \min(a_i, R_i(1)))$$

for all i.

The t_{ij} as defined above are apparently strong enough to obtain the dominance result $LB^*(\bar{S}) \geqq LB_1^*(\bar{S})$. Stronger t_{ij} can be obtained at the expense of more computation. For instance, if we define

$$t_{ijh}'' \overset{\triangle}{=} C(\sigma, 1) + R_i(h) + S_i(j - h) + b_i \qquad (h = 2, \dots, j-1)$$

and take

$$t_{ij}' \overset{\triangle}{=} \max(t_{ij}, \max_h\{t_{ijh}''\}),$$

we obtain possibly stronger lower bounds on the earliest possible finishing time of J_i when put in the j-th position.

There is a natural way to strengthen t_{ij} further if $j = \bar{s}$. In that case, $\{J_h | h \in \bar{S} - \{i\}\}$ have to precede J_i and a lower bound on its completion time is given by

$$\max(\sum_{i=1}^n a_h, C_{\max}^*(C(\sigma, 1), C(\sigma, 2), \bar{S} - \{i\})) + b_i$$

where $C_{\max}^*(\tau_1, \tau_2, Q)$ is the minimum $C_{\max}$ of $\{J_h | h \in Q\}$ when M_1 becomes available at τ_1 and M_2 becomes available at τ_2. $C_{\max}^*(\tau_1, \tau_2, Q)$ can be easily obtained for any $Q \subset \bar{S}$ by transferring the optimal ordering of $\{J_j | j \in \bar{S}\}$, as found by the algorithm of theorem 5.3, to $\{J_h | h \in Q\}$. The resulting ordering of Q is optimal because J_g precedes J_h in the optimal ordering of any Q iff $\min(p_{g1}, p_{h2}) \leqq \min(p_{h1}, p_{g2})$.

Extension of the above approach to smaller values of j is computationally expensive. To calculate $t_{i, \bar{s}-1}$ in this way, we would want to find

$$\min_g \{\max(\sum_{\substack{h=1 \\ h \neq g}}^n a_h, C_{\max}^*(C(\sigma, 1), C(\sigma, 2), \bar{S} - \{i, g\}))\} + b_i$$

corresponding to all possible choices of a $\bar{s}$-th job J_g. It is doubtful if these and similar calculations for other t_{ij} would increase the overall computational efficiency of the $n|2|P|\sum c_i$ algorithm.

5.3. THE $n|2|P|C_{max}$ PROBLEM WITH TIME LAGS

We conclude chapter 5 by a brief discussion of two-machine problems involving *time lags* that reflect the situation in which jobs can start on M_2 before being completely finished on M_1. Our main purpose is to point out that a number of special cases [Mitten 1958; Johnson 1958; Szwarc 1968; Nabeshima 1963] can be deduced from a simple general principle formulated in theorem 5.14 below.

Let us suppose that constants l_i and l_i' $(i = 1, \ldots, n)$ are given such that J_i may start on M_2 l_i time units after J_i started on M_1, but J_i cannot finish on M_2 until l_i' time units have elapsed after its completion time on M_1.

THEOREM 5.14. The $n|2|P|C_{max}$ problem with time lags (l_i, l_i') and processing times $p_{i1} = a_i$, $p_{i2} = b_i$ has the same optimal processing order as the $n|2|F|C_{max}$ problem with processing times

$$p_{i1} = a_i + \max(l_i - a_i, l_i' - b_i),$$

$$p_{i2} = b_i + \max(l_i - a_i, l_i' - b_i).$$

PROOF. A permutation $(\pi(1), \ldots, \pi(n))$ defines starting times $S_{\pi(i)1}, S_{\pi(i)2}$ for the problem defined by (l_i, l_i', a_i, b_i) as follows:

$$S_{\pi(i)1} = S_{\pi(i-1)1} + a_{\pi(i-1)}$$

$$S_{\pi(i)2} = \max(S_{\pi(i-1)2} + b_{\pi(i-1)}, S_{\pi(i)1} + l_{\pi(i)},$$
$$\qquad\qquad S_{\pi(i)1} + a_{\pi(i)} + l_{\pi(i)}' - b_{\pi(i)})$$

$$\quad = \max(S_{\pi(i-1)2} + b_{\pi(i-1)},$$
$$\qquad\qquad S_{\pi(i)1} + a_{\pi(i)} + \max(l_{\pi(i)} - a_{\pi(i)}, l_{\pi(i)}' - b_{\pi(i)})).$$

The proof can now be completed by an argument similar to the one following (5-5). (Q.E.D.)

Theorem 5.14 covers the special cases treated at great length in [Mitten 1958; Johnson 1958] where $l_i' = l_i$ and hence $p_{i1} = a_i + l_i - \min(a_i, b_i)$, $p_{i2} = b_i + l_i + \min(a_i, b_i)$, in [Szwarc 1968] where $l_i = a_i$ and in [Nabeshima 1963] where $a_i = a_i' + a_i''$ and $l_i' = l_i'' - a_i''$.

6

General flow-shop and job-shop problems

In this chapter we consider general flow-shop and job-shop problems for which the number m of machines is variable. All these problems can be proved to be NP-complete from results in previous chapters; consequently the algorithms discussed in this chapter are mainly of the branch-and-bound type. We begin by discussing the general $n|m|P|\delta$ problem in section 6.1. Section 6.2 contains a brief discussion of the $n|m|F|\delta$ problem. In section 6.3 we turn to the general $n|m|G|\delta$ problem, concentrating on the classification and extension of possible approaches to the $n|m|G|C_{max}$ problem. Chapter 6 concludes with section 6.4 on the $n|m|\gamma, no\ wait|\delta$ problem.

6.1. THE $n|m|P|\delta$ PROBLEM

In this section we consider the general permutation flow-shop problem; each job J_i consists of m operations O_{ik} $(k = 1, \ldots, m)$, the machine orders per job as given by the v_i $(i = 1, \ldots, n)$ are all equal to $(1, 2, \ldots, m)$ and we consider only schedules defined by a single permutation $\pi = (\pi(1), \ldots, \pi(n))$ of $\{1, \ldots, n\}$, giving the processing order on each machine.

We shall consider only the $n|m|P|c_{max}$ problem, concentrating on the C_{max} criterion. With respect to $n|m|P|\sum c_i$ problems, there is an obvious, but possibly not very powerful generalization of the $n|2|P|\sum c_i$ algorithm sketched in section 5.2; details are left to the reader.

Complexity results obtained in chapter 5 establish NP-completeness of the $n|m|P|C_{max}$ problem for $m \geq 3$ and of the $n|m|P|L_{max}$ problem for $m \geq 2$. Thus, we will restrict ourselves in this section to implicit enumeration approaches of the branch-and-bound type. An obvious branching rule is defined by letting $Y \in \mathscr{X}$ correspond to a partial schedule $(J_{\sigma(1)}, \ldots, J_{\sigma(s)})$, whereby jobs J_i $(i \in S \triangleq \{\sigma(1), \ldots, \sigma(s)\})$ occupy the first s positions on each machine in the order given by σ. Any permutation $\bar{\sigma}$ of the remaining job-indices $i \in \bar{S} \triangleq \{1, \ldots, n\} - S$ defines a *completion* of σ, i.e. a permutation schedule $\sigma \bar{\sigma} \overset{\triangle}{=} (\sigma(1), \ldots, \sigma(s), \bar{\sigma}(1), \ldots, \sigma(\bar{s}))$, where $\bar{s} \overset{\triangle}{=} |\bar{S}|$. Subsets $Y' \in b(Y)$ correspond to the $\bar{s}$ possible choices for the $(s+1)$-st job or, equivalently, to the $\bar{s}$ permutations $\sigma i \overset{\triangle}{=} (\sigma(1), \ldots, \sigma(s), i)$.

In section 6.1.1 we consider some elimination criteria whereby subsets corresponding to a partial schedule σ' can be eliminated because a schedule at least as good exists among the completions of another partial schedule σ''. These elimination criteria have turned out to be of little algorithmic value and thus we shall pay relatively more attention to the development of strong lower bounds. These are analyzed and discussed in section 6.1.2.

6.1.1. Elimination criteria for the $n|m|P|C_{\max}$ problem

In this section, we deal only with the $C_{\max}$ criterion. We shall be interested in finding conditions under which all completions of a partial schedule $\sigma' = (\sigma'(1), \ldots, \sigma'(s'))$ can be eliminated because a schedule at least as good exists among the completions of $\sigma'' = (\sigma''(1), \ldots, \sigma''(s''))$. Defining $C(\sigma, k)$ for any partial schedule σ to be the completion time of its last job $J_{\sigma(s)}$ on M_k, we will say that σ'' *dominates* σ' if for any permutation π' of the complement $\bar{S}'$ of $S' \overset{\triangle}{=} \{\sigma'(1), \ldots, \sigma'(s')\}$, we can find a permutation π'' of the complement $\bar{S}''$ of $S'' \overset{\triangle}{=} \{\sigma''(1), \ldots, \sigma''(s'')\}$, such that $C(\sigma''\pi'', m) \leqq C(\sigma'\pi', m)$.

THEOREM 6.1 [Ignall and Schrage 1965; McMahon 1969; Smith and Dudek 1967]. If $S' = S''$, then σ'' dominates σ' if $C(\sigma'', k) \leqq C(\sigma', k)$ for all $k \in \{1, \ldots, m\}$.

PROOF. Trivial.   (Q.E.D.)

The above criterion is the strongest possible one if $S' = S''$ in the following sense: if $C(\sigma'', k_0) > C(\sigma', k_0)$ for some k_0, processing times p_{ik} ($i \in \bar{S}'$) can be chosen in such a way that $C(\sigma''\bar{\sigma}, m) > C(\sigma'\bar{\sigma}, m)$ for every completion [McMahon 1969].

For the case that $S' \subset S''$ and $|S'' - S'| = 1$, several elimination criteria have been developed that give conditions for the dominance of $\sigma' = \sigma i$ by $\sigma'' = \sigma ji$. Under these circumstances, dominance is implied by

$$C(\sigma jiv'v'', m) \leqq C(\sigma iv'jv'', m)$$

for all permutations $v'v''$ of $\bar{S}''$. We define $\Delta_k \overset{\triangle}{=} C(\sigma ji, k) - C(\sigma i, k)$ and can now formulate the following conditions, each of which has been claimed to imply dominance of σi by σji:

(i)   [Smith and Dudek 1967]

$$\Delta_{k-1} \leqq p_{jk} \qquad\qquad (k = 2, ..., m)$$

(ii) [Smith and Dudek 1969]

$$\begin{cases} \Delta_{k-1} \leqq p_{jk} \\ C(\sigma j, k-1) \leqq C(\sigma i, k-1) \end{cases} \qquad\qquad (k = 2, ..., m)$$

(iii) [Bagga and Chakravarti 1968]

$$\Delta_k \leqq p_{jk} \qquad\qquad (k = 2, ..., m)$$

(iv) [McMahon 1969; Szwarc 1973]

$$\begin{cases} \Delta_{k-1} \leqq p_{j,k-1} \\ \Delta_{k-1} \leqq p_{jk} \end{cases} \qquad\qquad (k = 2, ..., m)$$

(v)   [Szwarc 1971]

$$\Delta_{k-1} \leqq \Delta_k \leqq p_{jk} \qquad\qquad (k = 2, ..., m)$$

(vi) [Szwarc 1973]

$$\max_{u=1,...,k} \{\Delta_u\} \leqq p_{jk} \qquad\qquad (k = 1, ..., m)$$

(vii) [Szwarc 1973]

$$\Delta_k \leqq \min_{u=k,...,m} \{p_{ju}\} \qquad\qquad (k = 1, ..., m)$$

Elimination criteria (i) and (iii) have been proved incorrect through counter-examples in [McMahon 1969; Szwarc 1971]; with respect to the remaining ones we have the following theorems.

THEOREM 6.2. Condition (ii) implies conditions (iv), (v), (vi) and (vii); the latter four conditions are equivalent.

PROOF. The equivalence of (iv), (v), (vi) and (vii) is easily established (cf. [Szwarc 1973]).
(ii) $\Rightarrow$ (iv): trivial if $k = 2$. If $k \geqq 3$, then

$$C(\sigma i, k-1) = \max(C(\sigma i, k-2), C(\sigma, k-1)) + p_{i,k-1}$$

$$\geqq \max(C(\sigma j, k-2), C(\sigma, k-1)) + p_{i,k-1}$$

$$= C(\sigma j, k-1) - p_{j,k-1} + p_{i,k-1}.$$

Hence,

(6-1) $C(\sigma j, k-1) + p_{i,k-1} \leqq C(\sigma i, k-1) + p_{j,k-1}.$

Moreover,

$$C(\sigma i, k-1) + p_{j,k-1} \geqq C(\sigma i, k-2) + p_{i,k-1} + p_{j,k-1}$$

and since $\Delta_{k-2} = C(\sigma ji, k-2) - C(\sigma i, k-2) \leqq p_{j,k-1}$, we have

(6-2) $C(\sigma ji, k-2) + p_{i,k-1} \leqq C(\sigma i, k-1) + p_{j,k-1}.$

Together, (6-1) and (6-2) imply that $\Delta_{k-1} \leqq p_{j,k-1}.$ (Q.E.D.)

THEOREM 6.3 [McMahon 1969; Szwarc 1973]. The partial schedule σji dominates the partial schedule σi if (iv), (v), (vi) or (vii) holds.

PROOF. We easily prove by induction on k and the number of elements of v'
that (v) implies

$$C(\sigma jiv', k) - C(\sigma iv', k) \leqq C(\sigma ji, k) - C(\sigma i, k).$$

Thus, in particular $\Delta_m \leqq p_{jm}$ implies

$$C(\sigma jiv', m) \leqq C(\sigma iv', m) + p_{jm} \leqq C(\sigma iv'j, m).$$

It follows (cf. theorem 6.1) that

$$C(\sigma jiv'v'', m) \leqq C(\sigma iv'jv'', m).$$ (Q.E.D.)

We refer to [McMahon 1969] for a systematic counterexample showing that
(iv), (v), (vi) and (vii) are the strongest possible conditions for elimination
in the previously mentioned sense.

The above analysis can be extended to the case that $S' \subset S''$ with $S'' - S'$
of arbitrary cardinality [McMahon 1969]; this leads to very stringent conditions, and the disappointing performance on all but the smallest problems
of the simpler criteria mentioned above [McMahon 1971] suggests that such
extensions would be of little algorithmic value.

6.1.2. Lower bounds for the $n|m|P|c_{max}$ problem

Given a partial schedule defined by σ, we now want to find a lower bound
on the costs of all possible completions $\sigma \bar{\sigma}$. Again, we mainly restrict
ourselves to the C_{max} criterion. We shall be particularly concerned with the
trade-off between the sharpness of the lower bound and its computational
requirements: a stronger bound eliminates relatively more nodes of the

search tree, but if its computational requirements become excessively large it may become advantageous to search through larger parts of the tree, using a weaker, but more quickly computable lower bound.

We generally shall obtain lower bounds for the $n|m|P|C_{max}$ problem by relaxing the capacity constraints on some machines, *i.e.* by treating bottleneck machines of capacity one as non-bottleneck machines of infinite capacity.

From the complexity results in chapter 5 we know that any problem involving three or more bottleneck machines is likely to be NP-complete. Let us therefore restrict ourselves to choosing two machines M_u and M_v ($1 \leq u \leq v \leq m$) to be bottleneck machines. It follows that each partial schedule σ then essentially defines a problem involving at most five machines, of which at most two are bottleneck ones:

(i) a sequence of non-bottleneck machines $M_g, M_{g+1}, \ldots, M_h$ ((g, h) is $(u + 1, v - 1)$ or $(v + 1, m)$) can be treated as one non-bottleneck machine $M_{(g,h)}$ with processing times $p_{i(g,h)} \triangleq \sum_{k=g}^{h} p_{ik}$;

(ii) the partial schedule σ defines release dates r_{iu} of J_i on M_u:

$$r_{iu} = \max_{1 \leq l \leq u-1} \{C(\sigma, l) + \sum_{k=l}^{u-1} p_{ik}\}$$

and the r_{iu} may be interpreted as processing times $p_{i(0,u-1)}$ on a non-bottleneck machine to be indicated by $M_{(0,u-1)}$.

Note that if $u = v$, at most three machines are involved of which at most one is a bottleneck one.

Any lower bound on the costs of scheduling

$$\{J_i | i \in \bar{S} \triangleq \{1, \ldots, n\} - \{\sigma(1), \ldots, \sigma(s)\}\}$$

on $M_{(0,u-1)}, M_u, M_{(u+1,v-1)}, M_v, M_{(v+1,m)}$ in that order provides a valid lower bound; in fact, all previously presented lower bounds can be interpreted in this context. To arrive at a further classification of possible approaches to this lower bound calculation, note that we may eliminate non-bottleneck machines $M_{(g,h)}$ from the problem and compensate for this by adding terms $l_{(g,h)} \triangleq \min_{i \in S} \{p_{i(g,h)}\}$ to the lower bound based on the remaining problem; the lower bound that we shall use here is obtained by finding the optimal schedule with respect to this remaining problem. (Note that if $u = 1$, $v = m$ or $v = u + 1$, we have $l_{(0,u-1)} = C(\sigma, 1)$, $l_{(v+1,m)} = 0$ or $l_{(u+1,v-1)} = 0$ respectively.)

Any such approach to the calculation of a lower bound can be represented by a string Ω of at most five symbols from $\{\Box, \triangle, *\}$ where
- $\Box$ indicates a bottleneck machine;
- $\triangle$ indicates a non-bottleneck machine on which the various given processing times are taken into account;
- $*$ indicates a non-bottleneck machine that is to be ignored through the device introduced above.

A lower bound $LB(u, v, \Omega)$ is calculated by finding the value $LB^*(u, v, \Omega)$ of the optimal $C_{\max}$ solution to the problem that remains after elimination of the non-bottleneck machines indicated by $*$, and by adding to $LB^*(u, v, \Omega)$ possible terms $l_{(g, h)}$. Note that this lower bound may be further strengthened by exploiting the fact that M_v is not available before $C(\sigma, v)$. $LB(W, \Omega) \triangleq \max_{(u, v) \in W} \{LB(u, v, \Omega)\}$ is now a valid lower bound for every $W \subset Z \triangleq \{(k, l) | 1 \leq k \leq l \leq m\}$.

The weakest of all these lower bounds, for which $\Omega = (*\Box*)$, is clearly dominated by the strongest possible approach with $\Omega' = (\triangle\Box\triangle\Box\triangle)$ in the general sense that for every choice of u and v we can always find values u' and v' such that $LB(u', v', \Omega') \geq LB(u, v, \Omega)$. Similar dominance rules are indicated by a directed arc (Ω, Ω') in the directed graph drawn in figure 6.1. We have not distinguished between symmetric pairs such as $(\triangle\Box*)$ and $(*\Box\triangle)$ or $(\triangle\Box\triangle\Box*)$ and $(*\Box\triangle\Box\triangle)$ (cf. the remark following theorem 2.3)

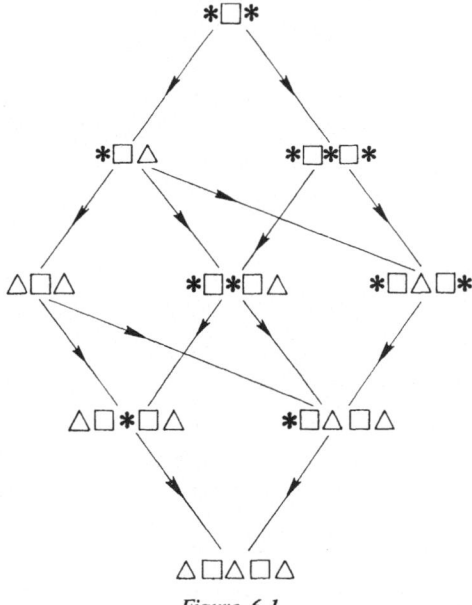

Figure 6.1.

and thus we retain nine different strings that together constitute the vertex set of the graph.

Apart from the relations deducible from the graph by transitivity considerations, no further relations hold; thus, for example, $LB(Z, (\triangle\square\triangle))$ can be larger or smaller than $LB(Z, (*\square\triangle\square*))$, depending on the processing times (an example appears below). The correctness of the relations given in figure 6.1 is easily proved; in fact, in all cases that $u \neq v$ we can take $u' = u$ and $v' = v$ and in the remaining cases we can usually take $u' = u$ and $v' = u + 1$ or $v' = m$.

As stated before, the lower bound $LB(Z, (\triangle\square\triangle\square\triangle))$ is the strongest possible one in this scheme, but its calculation may require a disproportionate amount of time. In order to examine this aspect we shall now discuss the computational complexity of each lower bound and compare it to bounds appearing in the literature.

(i) $(*\square*)$

Ignoring the first and last non-bottleneck machine, we have to minimize $C_{\max}$ on one machine $M_u = M_v$; clearly $LB^*(u, u, (*\square*)) = \sum_{i\in S} p_{iu}$ and

$$LB(u, u, (*\square*)) = \min_{i\in S}\{r_{iu}\} + \sum_{i\in S} p_{iu} + \min_{i\in S}\{q_{iu}\}$$

where $q_{iu} \triangleq p_{i(u+1,m)}$.

Note as a general principle that we may replace $\min_{i\in S}\{r_{iu}\} + \min_{i\in S}\{q_{iv}\}$ by $\min_{i,j\in S, i\neq j}\{r_{iu} + q_{jv}\}$, leading to a possibly sharper bound.

Taking $W_1 \triangleq \{(u, u)|u \in \{1, \ldots, m\}\}$, we find that $LB(W_1, (*\square*))$ is the lower bound used in [Ignall and Schrage 1965; McMahon 1971]; through its use of r_{iu} instead of $C(\sigma, u)$ this bound is slightly stronger than the bounds used in [Brown and Lomnicki 1966; Lomnicki 1965; McMahon and Burton 1967].

(ii) $(*\square\triangle)$

Ignoring the first non-bottleneck machine, we have to minimize the maximum lateness with respect to due-dates $c - q_{iu}$ on M_u (cf. section 4.2.1). $LB^*(u, u, (*\square\triangle))$ and $LB^*(u, u, (\triangle\square*))$ are found by means of theorems 4.3 and 4.6. Adding $l_{(0,u-1)}$ or $l_{(u+1,m)}$ respectively, we obtain $LB(u, u, (*\square\triangle))$ and $LB(u, u, (\triangle\square*))$. If $W_2 \triangleq \{(m, m)\}$, we find that $LB(W_2, (\triangle\square*))$ through its use of r_{im} instead of $C(\sigma, 1) + \sum_{k=1}^{m-1} p_{ik}$ is slightly stronger than the lower bound proposed in [Ashour 1970].

(iii) $(*\square*\square*)$

Ignoring $M_{(0,u-1)}$, $M_{(u+1,v-1)}$ and $M_{(v+1,m)}$, we obtain $LB^*(u, v, \Omega)$ by solving the $n|2|P|C_{\max}$ problem on M_u and M_v by means of theorem 5.3.

These problems can be solved in advance for all $(u, v) \in W$; the optimal relative order of the jobs does not change if some of them are removed, nor is it influenced by availability of M_v from $C(\sigma, v)$ onwards. We find that

$$LB(u, v, (*\square*\square*)) = LB^*(u, v, (*\square*\square*))$$

$$+ \min_{i,j,h \in S, i \neq h} \{r_{iu} + p_{j(u+1,v-1)} + q_{hv}\}.$$

(iv) $(*\square\triangle\square*)$

$LB^*(u, v, (*\square\triangle\square*))$ is found by solving the $n|3|P, M_2 \text{ non-bott}|C_{\max}$ problem on M_u, $M_{(u+1,v-1)}$ and M_v by means of the algorithm indicated in theorem 5.11; availability of M_v on $C(\sigma, v)$ again does not change the optimal processing order. The so-called job-based bound from [McMahon and Burton 1967] and extended in [McMahon 1971] to

$$\min_{i \in S} \{r_{iu}\} + \max_{i \in \bar{S}} \{p_{i(u,m)} + \sum_{j \in S, j \neq i} \min(p_{ju}, p_{jm})\}$$

is easily seen to be an underestimate of $LB(u, m, (*\square\triangle\square*))$.

(v) $(\triangle\square\triangle)$

Calculation of $LB(u, u, (\triangle\square\triangle))$ corresponds to solving an $n|1|r_i \geq 0|L'_{\max}$ problem on M_u defined by triples (r_{iu}, p_{iu}, q_{iu}) (cf. section 4.2.1). We have found this problem to be NP-complete (theorem 4.8) and finding $LB(u, u, (\triangle\square\triangle))$ thus seems to imply the use of a branch-and-bound method such as the algorithms described in sections 4.2.1.1 and 4.2.1.2. The excellent computational result obtained with these algorithms, as reported in appendix 1, justifies serious consideration of this lower bound approach.

(vi) $(*\square*\square\triangle), (\triangle\square*\square\triangle), (*\square\triangle\square\triangle), (\triangle\square\triangle\square\triangle)$

The $n|2|P|L_{\max}$ problem on M_u and M_v corresponding to $LB^*(u, v, (*\square*\square\triangle))$ has been shown to be NP-complete (theorem 5.12 (i)), as has the $n|2|P, r_i \geq 0|C_{\max}$ problem corresponding to $LB^*(u, v, (\triangle\square*\square*))$. Essentially, we have replaced a non-bottleneck machine in $(\triangle\square\triangle)$ by a bottleneck one. No specific algorithms have been developed for these problems as yet. Similar remarks apply to the NP-complete problems corresponding to the remaining lower bound approaches.

In view of the above discussion, the lower bounds under (iv) and (v) are obvious candidates for further investigation. Bound $LB(Z, (*\square\triangle\square*))$ dominates all previously developed bounds and can be calculated efficiently. There are, however, occasions on which $LB(Z, (\triangle\square\triangle))$ may produce a stronger result than $LB(Z, (*\square\triangle\square*))$ and *vice versa*.

Example. Take $n = m = p_{12} = p_{13} = p_{22} = p_{31} = p_{32} = 3$, $p_{11} = p_{33} = 2$, $p_{21} = p_{23} = 1$; then

$$LB(2, 2, (\triangle\square\triangle)) = 12 > LB(Z, (*\square\triangle\square*)) = \max(11, 11, 11) = 11.$$

If we change p_{i2} to 1 ($i = 1, 2, 3$), we have that

$$LB(1, 3, (*\square\triangle\square*)) = 9 > LB(Z, (\triangle\square\triangle)) = \max(8, 6, 8) = 8.$$

The above example shows that the relative strength of the two bounds depends on the processing times of the problem. Similar examples can be constructed for every pair (Ω, Ω') not linked by a directed path in figure 6.1.

Lower bounds $LB(u, v, (*\square\triangle\square*))$ and $LB(u, u, (\triangle\square\triangle))$ have been tested and compared with previous bounds with mixed results. We refer to appendix 3 for details.

We note finally that the bounds introduced in this section can be easily adapted to solve the $n|m|P, r_i \geq 0|C_{\max}$ and $n|m|P|L_{\max}$ problems: this just involves adding one more non-bottleneck machine (cf. section 4.2.1). Generalization to the general $n|m|P|c_{\max}$ problem is not obvious.

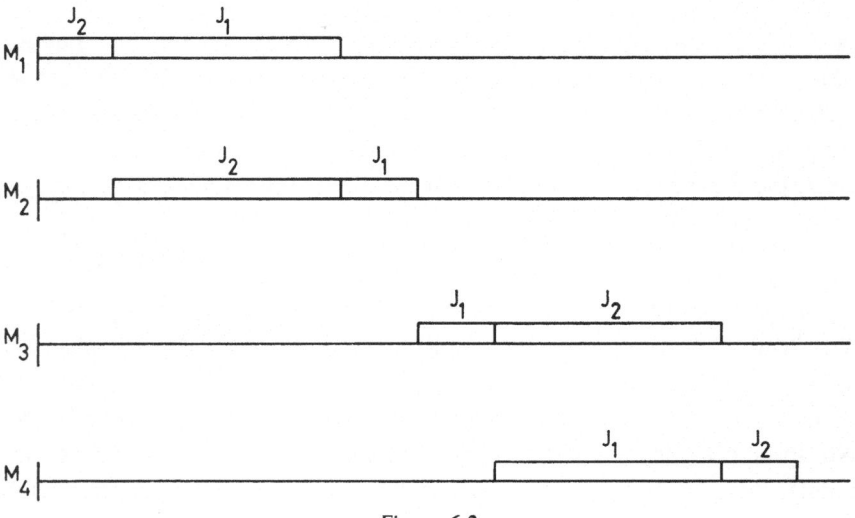

Figure 6.2.

6.2. THE $n|m|F|\delta$ PROBLEM

From theorems 5.1 and 5.2 we know that there exists an optimal $n|m|F|\delta$ schedule with the same processing order on M_1 and M_2; if $\delta = C_{\max}$, we can similarly assume identical processing orders on M_{m-1} and M_m. The optimal schedule for the $2|4|F|C_{\max}$ problem with $p_{11} = p_{22} = p_{23} = p_{14} = 3$, $p_{21} = p_{12} = p_{13} = p_{24} = 1$ illustrated in figure 6.2 indicates that this result cannot be extended any further.

It follows that we may either settle for a suboptimal solution by solving the corresponding $n|m|P|\delta$ problem (section 6.1) or attack the problem by means of methods developed for the $n|m|G|\delta$ problem, to be discussed in the next section.

6.3. THE $n|m|G|\delta$ PROBLEM

Several simple cases of the $n|m|G|\delta$ problem have been proved to be NP-complete in chapter 5 (cf. theorems 5.7 and 5.8). Even within the class of NP-complete problems though, the general $n|m|G|\delta$ problem appears to be a relatively difficult one. Note, for instance, that various mostly complicating assumptions such as $r_i \geqq 0$, *prec*, *tree* and M_k *non-bott* can be easily incorporated in the disjunctive graph model. A traditional and by now classical quotation from [Conway et al. 1967] asserts pessimistically that 'many proficient people have considered this problem, and all have come away essentially empty-handed. Since this frustration is not reported in the literature, the problem continues to attract investigators who just cannot believe that a problem so simply structured can be so difficult until they have tried it.'

The complexity results indicate that our quest for reasonable solution methods can be restricted to branch-and-bound approaches. The disjunctive graph model provides a convenient framework in which to describe such algorithms. In terms of a disjunctive graph $\mathscr{G} = (\mathscr{V}, \mathscr{C}, \mathscr{D})$, the $n|m|G|C_{\max}$ problem consists of settling each pair of disjunctive arcs in such a way that the resulting directed graph is acyclic and has a critical path of minimum weight. Accordingly, subsets $Y \in \mathscr{X}$ will correspond to partial schedules defined by a subset $D \subset \mathscr{D}$ of chosen disjunctive arcs; the augmentation of D in a branching step is determined by the branching rule. Concentrating on the case that $\delta = C_{\max}$, we discuss in section 6.3.1 how to calculate lower bounds on all possible completions of the partial schedule defined by D. In section 6.3.2 we examine how a strong lower bound appearing from the discussion in section 6.3.1 can be combined with several branching rules to yield branch-and-bound algorithms of reasonable quality.

6.3.1. Lower bounds

Let $D \subset \mathcal{D}$ be a subset of chosen disjunctive arcs and let $D' = \{(r, s)|(s, r) \in D\}$ contain the rejected disjunctive arcs. Feasible job-shop schedules correspond to subsets D_0 such that:

   (i) $D_0 \cup D_0' = \mathcal{D}$;
   (ii) $\mathcal{G}(D_0)$ is an acyclic directed graph.

Thus, we seek to find a lower bound $LB(D)$ on the weight $C_{max}(D_0)$ of the critical path in $\mathcal{G}(D_0)$ with respect to every $D_0 \supseteq D$ that satisfies properties (i) and (ii) above.

We obtain such a lower bound $LB_k^*(D)$ $(1 \leq k \leq m)$ by relaxing the capacity constraints on all machines except M_k. This relaxation corresponds to disregarding all disjunctive arcs in $\mathcal{D} - (D \cup D')$ except those on M_k. Accordingly, on each M_k earliest possible starting times t_r for O_r are determined by

$$\begin{cases} t_0 = 0 \\ t_r = \max_{(s,r) \in \mathscr{C} \cup D} \{t_s + p_s\} \end{cases}$$

and similarly tails q_r for O_r can be calculated by

$$\begin{cases} q_* = 0 \\ q_r = \max_{(r,s) \in \mathscr{C} \cup D} \{p_s + q_s\} \end{cases}$$

(cf. $LB(k, k, (\triangle \square \triangle))$ in section 6.2.1). We note that the tails q_r are related to the latest possible starting times T_r with

$$\begin{cases} T_* = t_* \\ T_r = \min_{(r,s) \in \mathscr{C} \cup D} \{T_s - p_r\} \end{cases}$$

by $q_r = t_* - T_r - p_r$. Clearly,

$$t_r \leq S_r$$

$$S_r + p_r + q_r \leq C_{max}(D_0)$$

with respect to every completion $D_0 \supseteq D$.

It follows immediately that a valid lower bound $LB_k^*(D)$ is provided by the value of the optimal schedule for the $n|1|r_i \geq 0, prec|L'_{max}$ problem, defined by $|M_k|$ triples (t_r, p_r, q_r) $(O_r \in M_k)$ and precedence constraints $\prec$ with $O_r \prec O_s$ if there is a path in $\mathcal{G}(D)$ from r to s. This observation extends to every lower bound $LB_k(D)$ on $LB_k^*(D)$; if $LB_k(D) \leq LB_k^*(D)$ we may take

$$LB(D) = \max(\max_{M_k \in \mathcal{M}_0} \{LB_k(D)\}, \max_{J_i \in \mathcal{J}_0} \{C_i\})$$

where $\mathcal{M}_0$ is the set of machines on which there are still unsettled pairs of disjunctive arcs, and $\mathcal{J}_0 \triangleq \{J_i | \{M_{\mu(O_r)} | O_r \in J_i\} \subseteq \mathcal{M} - \mathcal{M}_0\}$ is the set of jobs whose completion time is fixed by previous settlement decisions.

It turns out that all lower bounds presented in the literature correspond to special choices for $LB_k(D) \leq LB_k^*(D)$, as indicated by the following survey.

(i) (cf. [Ashour et al. 1973; Ashour et al. 1974; Ashour and Hiremath 1973; Ashour and Parker 1971; Charlton and Death 1970a; Schrage 1970])

$$LB_k(D) = \min_{O_r \in M_k} \{t_r\} + \sum_{O_r \in M_k} p_r.$$

(ii) (cf. [Ashour and Parker 1971; Ashour et al. 1974; Charlton and Death 1970; Greenberg 1968; Nabeshima 1971; Nemeti 1964; Schrage 1970a; Sussmann 1972])

$$LB_k(D) = \max_{O_r \in M_k} \{t_r + p_r + q_r\}$$

(cf. LB_i' in section 4.2.1.2).

(iii) [Ashour et al. 1974; Brooks and White 1965; Sang and Florian 1970; Florian et al. 1971]

$$LB_k(D) = LB_k'(D) + \min_{O_r \in M_k} \{q_r\},$$

where $LB_k'(D)$ is the value of the optimal $n|1|r_i \geq 0|C_{max}$ schedule defined by (t_r, p_r) for $O_r \in M_k$ as obtained by theorem 4.6.

(iv) [Schrage 1970a]

$$LB_k(D) = \min_{O_r \in M_k} \{t_r\} + LB_k''(D),$$

where $LB_k''(D)$ is the value of the optimal $n|1||L'_{max}$ problem defined by (p_r, q_r) for $O_r \in M_k$, as obtained by theorem 4.3.

(v) [Bratley *et al.* 1973; McMahon and Florian 1975]

$$LB_k(D) = LB_k'''(D),$$

where $LB_k'''(D)$ is the value of the optimal $n|1|r_i \geq 0|L'_{max}$ schedule defined by (t_r, p_r, q_r) $(O_r \in M_k)$, obtainable by branch-and-bound algorithms such as those described in sections 4.2.1.1 and 4.2.1.2.

All bounds $LB_k(D)$ except $LB_k'''(D)$ can be calculated efficiently; it is easy to construct examples in which these bounds are strictly exceeded by $LB_k^*(D)$. With respect to $LB_k'''(D)$ such an example is less obvious. Note, as in section 4.2.1.3, that if we have a precedence constraint on M_k:

(6-3) $O_r \prec O_s$

then

(6-4) $\begin{cases} t_s \geq t_r + p_r > t_r \\ q_r \geq p_s + q_s > q_s. \end{cases}$

Given (6-4), the question is now if explicit consideration of precedence constraints (6-3) can ever lead to a lower bound $LB_k^*(D)$ strictly greater than $LB_k'''(D)$. An affirmative answer to this question is provided by the

Table 6.1.

r	t_r	p_r	q_r
1	0	2	3
2	2	1	2
3	0	2	5
4	3	2	6
5	7	2	2

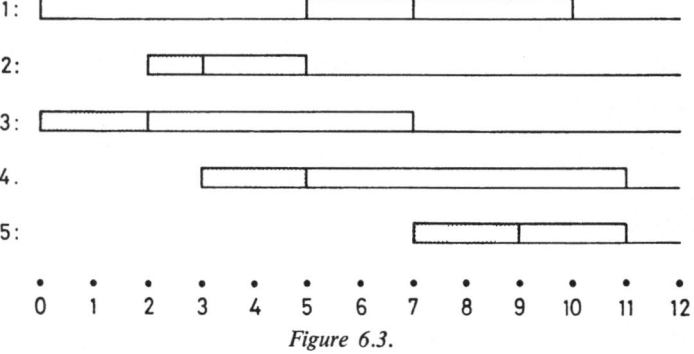

Figure 6.3.

$5|1|r_i \geqq 0|L'_{max}$ problem defined by the data in table 6.1 (cf. [Lenstra and Rinnooy Kan 1973]). Suppose that $(1, 2) \in D$; note that $t_2 \geqq t_1 + p_1$ and $q_1 \geqq p_2 + q_2$. If we ignore the precedence constraint $O_1 \prec O_2$, we find a unique optimal schedule $(3, 2, 4, 1, 5)$ with value $LB'''_k(D) = 11$ (cf. figure 6.3). Explicit inclusion of this precedence constraint leads to $LB^*_k(D) = = 12 > LB'''_k(D)$.

The relatively small increase in computer running times caused by the incorporation of precedence constraints in the algorithms of section 4.2.1.1 and 4.2.1.2 (cf. appendix 1) seems to justify serious consideration of $LB^*_k(D)$ as a lower bound. In the following section we shall see how this bound can be combined with two branching rules to yield $n|m|G|C_{max}$ branch-and-bound algorithms. Note that we may stop calculating $LB^*_{k_0}(D)$ as soon as an upper bound on $LB^*_{k_0}(D)$ is not greater than the largest $LB^*_k(D)$ found so far. Also, the node can be eliminated if any lower bound on $LB^*_k(D)$ appearing during its calculation reaches the current upper bound on the optimal $n|m|G|C_{max}$ schedule.

It is worth noting that within this bounding approach the solution of several $n|1|r_i \geqq 0, prec|L'_{max}$ problems is necessary to obtain just one lower bound for the $n|m|G|C_{max}$ problem, although both problems are NP-complete and thus equivalent up to a polynomial-bounded reduction! The computational success of this approach clearly points to variations in problem complexity that are insufficiently expressed by the current complexity measures.

We note finally that lower bounds for the $n|m|G|L'_{max}$ problem can be obtained in a completely analogous way by replacing q_r by $q_r + c - d_{i(O_r)}$. Sequence dependent change-over times can be added as weights on arcs (r, s) without invalidating the lower bound approach. With respect to general regular measures $f(C_1, \ldots, C_n)$, an obvious lower bound is given by $f(t_{N_1} + p_{N_1}, \ldots, t_{N_n} + p_{N_n})$.

6.3.2. Branching rules

Suppose that in the current node of the $n|m|G|C_{max}$ search tree calculation of $LB^*_k(D)$ does not lead to immediate elimination (*i.e.*, $LB^*_k(D)$ is smaller than the value UB of the currently best schedule). In that case, we will usually attempt to find a completion $D_0 \supseteq D$ such that $C_{max}(D_0) = LB(D)$, e.g. by evaluating the overall schedule defined by the one-machine schedules producing $LB^*_k(D)$, or by some other heuristic. If again we are unsuccessful, further branching according to some branching rule is inevitable. In this section we present two such rules for the $n|m|G|C_{max}$ problem; a third one, presented in [Balas 1969] and extended in [Agarwal 1975] has turned out to produce disappointing computational results and will not be considered here (cf. [Florian *et al.* 1971]).

6.3.2.1. The procedure 'actsched'

A frequently used branching rule is based on the procedure 'actsched' introduced in section 3.1. In each node corresponding to $D \subset \mathcal{D}$, we have a set S of scheduleable operations O_s: all predecessors $O_q \lll O_s$ have been scheduled, *i.e.* pairs $\{(q, q'), (q', q)\}$ have been settled for all $O_{q'} \in M_{\mu(O_q)}$. If $O_r \in M_k$ is chosen for the next position on M_k, the corresponding subset $Y' \in b(Y)$ is obtained by adding to D disjunctive arcs (r, r') for all unscheduled operations $O_{r'} \in M_k$. Indeed, all pairs $\{(r, r'), (r', r)\}$ $(O_{r'} \in M_k)$ have then been settled.

To combine this enumeration scheme with $LB_k^*(D)$, we consider the structure of the precedence constraints $\prec$ on M_k. If $O_q \in M_k$ has been scheduled already, then O_q precedes all unscheduled operations on M_k; the precedence constraints determine a processing order for these operations O_q and a starting time S_q for each of them. It follows that finding $LB_k^*(D)$ in this case boils down to solving the $n|1|r_i \geq 0, prec|L'_{max}$ problem only with respect to the set M_k' of unscheduled operations; we obtain a value $LB_k^{**}(D)$, and take

$$LB_k^*(D) = \max(LB_k^{**}(D), \max_{O_r \in M_k - M_{k'}} \{S_r + p_r + q_r\}).$$

With respect to $LB_k^{**}(D)$, we finally note that precedence constraints $\prec$ on M_k' are of a special type: they can occur only between operations $O_r, O_s \in M_k'$ if $\iota(O_r) = \iota(O_s)$, in which case $O_r \prec O_s$ if $r < s$.

Hence, if $|J_i \cap M_k| \leq 1$ for all (i, k), $LB_k'''(D) = LB_k^*(D)$ and thus provides an equally strong lower bound.

6.3.2.2. Branching on disjunctive arcs

A second branching rule is obtained by defining $b(Y)$ for Y corresponding to $D \subset \mathcal{D}$ as containing two subsets Y' corresponding to $D_{rs} \triangleq D \cup \{(r, s)\}$ and $D_{sr} \triangleq D \cup \{(s, r)\}$ respectively (cf. [Charlton and Death 1970]). Here, $\{(r, s), (s, r)\}$ is a pair of previously unsettled disjunctive arcs, chosen in a way to be discussed below. An advantage of such a scheme might be that it allows early settlement of particularly crucial disjunctive pairs $\{(r, s), (s, r)\}$, after which all other settlement decisions may follow more or less automatically.

In some respects the above branching rule compares unfavorably to the one outlined in section 6.3.2.1. Precedence constraints $\prec$ on M_k can now have an arbitrary structure and must be taken into account explicitly during the solution of the $n|1|r_i \geq 0, prec|L'_{max}$ problem on M_k. Furthermore, the search tree defined by this procedure is binary ($|b(Y)| = 2$ for all $Y \in \mathcal{X}$), but its maximum depth is now $\sum_{k=1}^{m} \frac{1}{2}|M_k| (|M_k| - 1)$ as compared to $N_n = \sum_{k=1}^{m} |M_k|$ for the previous approach. It seems that the above rule can be competitive only if

(i) we succeed in identifying essential branching decisions in the upper levels of the search tree;

(ii) we can choose a branching pair $\{r, s\}$ in such a way that $\mathcal{G}(D_{rs})$ and $\mathcal{G}(D_{sr})$ do not contain cycles.

With respect to (ii) we note that a cycle in $\mathcal{G}(D_{rs})$ or $\mathcal{G}(D_{sr})$ can only occur if there exists a path from s to r or from r to s in $\mathcal{G}(D)$.

In that case, r and s are linked by an arc in the *transitive closure* of $\mathcal{G}(D)$. Explicit construction of this transitive closure would therefore solve problem (ii).

It turns out, however, that certain indicators calculated to solve problem (i) often allow solution of problem (ii) at the same time. In fact, cycles will be avoided altogether if we restrict the choice of a branching pair $\{r, s\}$ to the set $E(D)$ of all *conflicts*, i.e. pairs $\{r, s\}$ for which both

(6-5) $t_r + p_r > t_s$

and

(6-6) $t_s + p_s > t_r$.

THEOREM 6.4. If $\{r, s\} \in E(D)$, $\mathcal{G}(D_{rs})$ and $\mathcal{G}(D_{sr})$ do not contain cycles.

PROOF. The existence of paths from s to r or from r to s in $\mathcal{G}(D)$ implies that either $t_r \geq t_s + p_s$ or $t_s \geq t_r + p_r$, which contradicts (6-5) and (6-6).

(Q.E.D.)

We claim that there always exists a conflict on at least one M_k. For if there is no conflict on M_k, an optimal schedule with value $LB_k^*(D)$ can be obtained by setting $S_r := t_r$. In that case

$$LB_k^*(D) = \max_{O_r \in M_k} \{S_r + p_r + q_r\}$$

$$= \max_{O_r \in M_k} \{t_r + p_r + (t_* - T_r - p_r)\}$$

so that

(6-7) $LB_k^*(D) \leqq t_*$

and moreover

(6-8) $S_r + p_r = t_r + p_r \leqq t_{r+1}.$

It follows that $S_r := t_r$ $(O_r \in \mathcal{O})$ would define an overall feasible schedule with value $LB(D) = t_* = \max_r \{t_r + p_r + q_r\}$; in that case, there would be no need to branch at all.

Consider now the machines M_k in order of non-increasing $LB_k^*(D)$. If $LB_k(D) > t_*$, then there is a conflict on M_k because of (6-7). If $LB_k(D) = t_*$ and if $S_r + p_r > t_{r+1}$ for $O_r \in M_k$, this may again indicate the presence of a conflict because of (6-8). We can also try to locate the machine on which a conflict exists by explicit construction of $E(D)$. We know that the latter set is not empty and eventually we should find a machine M_k on which at least one conflict can be found.

A way to find a suitable branching pair on this M_k is now provided by the introduction of *penalties*

$$P_{rs} \triangleq t_r + p_r - T_s.$$

The usefulness of these penalties as branching indicators is illustrated by the following theorem and its corollary.

THEOREM 6.5. If $P_{rs} \geqq 0$, then $\mathcal{G}(D_{rs})$ contains a path of weight $t_* + P_{rs}$.

PROOF. A path with the required weight is given by the longest paths from 0 to r and from s to $*$, joined by arc (r, s):

$$t_r + p_r + (t_* - T_s) = t_* + P_{rs}. \tag{Q.E.D.}$$

COROLLARY 6.6.

   (i)   If $P_{rs} \geqq UB - t_*$, we may eliminate the subset Y' corresponding to D_{rs}.
   (ii) If $LB(D) - t_* < P_{rs} < UB - t_*$, then $LB(D_{rs}) > LB(D)$.
   (iii) If $0 < P_{rs} \leqq LB(D) - t_*$, then the critical path in $\mathcal{G}(D_{rs})$ exceeds t_* by at least P_{rs}.

PROOF. Immediate from theorem 6.5.   (Q.E.D.)

Theorem 6.5 suggests that a reasonable indicator of the 'cruciality' of $\{r, s\}$ is given by

$$P_{rs}^* \triangleq \min(P_{rs}, P_{sr});$$

a plausible candidate for branching is the unsettled pair of disjunctive arcs $\{(r_0, s_0), (s_0, r_0)\}$ such that

$$P_{r_0 s_0}^* = \max_{(r, s) \notin D \cup D'} \{P_{rs}^*\}.$$

Unfortunately, however, a complicated example shows that sometimes $\{r_0, s_0\} \notin E(D)$ and that $\mathscr{G}(D_{r_0 s_0})$ or $\mathscr{G}(D_{s_0 r_0})$ may contain a cycle (see [Lageweg *et al.* 1976]). If we have constructed $E(D)$ in a previous stage, $\{r_0, s_0\} \in E(D)$ can be checked immediately. A theoretical alternative is indicated by the following theorem.

THEOREM 6.7. $\mathscr{G}(D_{r_0 s_0})$ and $\mathscr{G}(D_{s_0 r_0})$ do not contain a cycle if any of the four following conditions holds:

  (i) $P_{r_0 s_0}^* > 0$;

  (ii) $P_{r_0 s_0}^* \leq 0$ and $|P_{r_0 s_0} - P_{s_0 r_0}| < p_{r_0} + p_{s_0}$;

  (iii) $P_{r_0 s_0}^* \leq 0$ and $P_{s_0 r_0} > P_{r_0 s_0} = P_{r_0 s_0}^* > t_{s_0} - T_{s_0}$;

  (iv) $P_{r_0 s_0}^* \leq 0$ and $P_{r_0 s_0} > P_{s_0 r_0} = P_{r_0 s_0}^* > t_{r_0} - T_{r_0}$.

PROOF. (i) If $P_{r_0 s_0}^* > 0$, then $\{r_0, s_0\} \in E(D)$ since

$$t_{r_0} + p_{r_0} - t_{s_0} \geq t_{r_0} + p_{r_0} - T_{s_0}$$
$$= P_{r_0 s_0}$$
$$\geq P_{r_0 s_0}^*$$
$$> 0$$

and similarly

$$t_{s_0} + p_{s_0} - t_{r_0} > 0.$$

  (ii) If a path exists in $\mathscr{G}(D)$ from r_0 to s_0, then we have that

(6-9) $t_{s_0} + p_{s_0} \geq (t_{r_0} + p_{r_0}) + p_{s_0}$

and

$$t_* - T_{r_0} \geqq p_{r_0} + t_* - T_{s_0}$$

(6-10) $T_{s_0} \geqq T_{r_0} + p_{r_0}.$

Together, (6-9) and (6-10) imply that:

$$t_{r_0} + p_{r_0} - T_{s_0} + p_{s_0} \leqq t_{s_0} + p_{s_0} - T_{r_0} - p_{r_0}$$

$$P_{r_0s_0} + p_{s_0} + p_{r_0} \leqq P_{s_0r_0}.$$

Similarly, if a path exists from s_0 to r_0, we find that

(6-11) $P_{s_0r_0} + p_{r_0} + p_{s_0} \leqq P_{r_0s_0}.$

Hence, a path from r_0 to s_0 or from s_0 to r_0 cannot exist if

$$|P_{r_0s_0} - P_{s_0r_0}| < p_{r_0} + p_{s_0}.$$

(iii) If $P_{s_0r_0} > P_{r_0s_0}$, then it follows from (6-11) that in $\mathscr{G}(D)$ no path exists from s_0 to r_0. It follows from $P_{r_0s_0} > t_{s_0} - T_{s_0}$ that

$$t_{r_0} + p_{r_0} - T_{s_0} > t_{s_0} - T_{s_0}$$

$$t_{r_0} + p_{r_0} > t_{s_0}$$

and hence no path exists from r_0 to s_0 either.

(iv) Similar to (iii).   (Q.E.D.)

If, finally, the conditions of theorem 6.7 do not apply, then explicit identification of the non-empty set of conflicts on M_k is definitely necessary and $\{r_0, s_0\}$ is then chosen by maximization of P_{rs}^* over this set. This completes our discussion of the second branching rule, the main steps of which are summarized on page 125.

The two $n|m|G|C_{\max}$ algorithms described in sections 6.3.2.1 and 6.3.2.2 have been computationally tested and compared. We refer to appendix 4 for details. Roughly speaking, it appears that the P_{rs}^*, although useful, are not sufficiently good branching indicators to compensate for the more intricate lower bound calculations and the increased depth of the search tree, inherent to the approach of section 6.3.2.2. The approach of section 6.3.2.1 seems to represent the best available $n|m|G|C_{\max}$ algorithm. However, the lower bound $LB_k^*(D)$, though the strongest one available, is still too weak to prune large parts of the search tree in an early stage. This points to a number of $n|2|G, \Gamma|C_{\max}$ problems (e.g., those corresponding to $(\triangle\square*\square*)$, $(\triangle\square*\square\triangle)$, $(\triangle\square\triangle\square*)$ and $(\triangle\square\triangle\square\triangle)$) as interesting topics for future research. Continuing efforts in this area seem to be required.

---

1   Order machines by non-increasing $LB_k^*(D)$.

---

2   Find machine M_k with at least one conflict by checking if

      (i) $LB_k^*(D) > t_*$, or
      (ii) $\{r, s\} \in E(D)$ for some $O_r, O_s \in M_k$.

---

3   Calculate $P_{rs} = t_r + p_r - T_s$ for all $O_r, O_s \in M_k$ and find $\{r_0, s_0\}$ such that $P_{r_0 s_0}^* = \min(P_{r_0 s_0}, P_{s_0 r_0})$ is maximal.

---

4   Branch on $\{r_0, s_0\}$ if $\{r_0, s_0\} \in E(D)$ or if

      (i) $P_{r_0 s_0}^* > 0$, or
      (ii) $P_{r_0 s_0}^* \leqq 0$ and $|P_{r_0 s_0} - P_{s_0 r_0}| < p_{r_0} + p_{s_0}$, or
      (iii) $P_{r_0 s_0}^* \leqq 0$ and $P_{s_0 r_0} > P_{r_0 s_0} = P_{r_0 s_0}^* > t_{s_0} - T_{s_0}$, or
      (iv) $P_{r_0 s_0}^* \leqq 0$ and $P_{r_0 s_0} > P_{s_0 r_0} = P_{r_0 s_0}^* > t_{r_0} - T_{r_0}$.

---

5   If none of the four conditions in step 4 apply, then branch on the conflict on M_k that maximizes $P_{r_0 s_0}^*$.

6.4. THE $n|m|\gamma$, *no wait*$|\delta$ PROBLEM

In this section we shall discuss the implications of the *no wait* assumption whereby no intermediate storage is allowed: $S_{r+1} = S_r + p_r$ for all $O_r \in \mathcal{O} - B_*$. We shall examine only the criteria $\delta = C_{\max}$ and $\delta = \sum C_i$. Let us consider the former case first under the additional assumption that passing is not permitted and that $M_k \cap J_i \neq \emptyset$ for all (k, i), so that in fact we restrict ourselves to schedules whereby the processing orders of the jobs are identical on each machine (*i.e.*, $\gamma = G, P$; cf. [Piehler 1960; Reddi and Ramamoorthy 1972; Wismer 1972; Grabowski and Syslo 1973; Syslo 1974]). Most previous research has been concentrated on the $n|m|F$, *no wait*$|C_{\max}$ problem; allowing different processing orders on each machine while maintaining the *no wait* assumption necessitates an elaborate branching scheme [Reddi and Ramamoorthy 1973; Goyal 1975]. This is why we have opted for the intermediary course sketched above. Another desirable extension to the case of non-zero but limited intermediate storage has been considered briefly only for the case that $m = 2$ [Dutta and Cunningham 1975].

To study the $n|m|G, P, no \ wait|C_{max}$ problem, let us define partial sums of processing times as follows:

$$Q_i(k_1, k_2) \triangleq \sum_{k=k_1}^{k_2} p_{ik} \quad \text{for } 1 \leq i \leq n, 1 \leq k_1 \leq k_2 \leq n_i$$

and

$$\left.\begin{aligned} k_i'(l) &\triangleq \min \{k|\mu(O_{ik}) = l, \ 1 \leq k \leq n_i\} \\ k_i''(l) &\triangleq \max \{k|\mu(O_{ik}) = l, \ 1 \leq k \leq n_i\} \end{aligned}\right\} \text{for } 1 \leq i \leq n, 1 \leq l \leq m.$$

$O_{ik_i'(l)}$ and $O_{ik_i''(l)}$ are the first and last operations of J_i on M_l.

For each pair of jobs (J_i, J_j), we will calculate a coefficient c_{ij}, representing the minimum difference between the starting times of O_{i1} and O_{j1} if J_j is scheduled directly after J_i, knowing that $O_{ik_i''(l)}$ has to precede $O_{jk_j'(l)}$ on M_l, for $1 \leq l \leq m$. We introduce a directed graph G_{ij} with vertex set N_{ij} and arc set A_{ij}, defined by

$$N_{ij} \triangleq \{O_{hk}|h = i, j, 1 \leq k \leq n_h\}$$

$$A_{ij} \triangleq \{(O_{hk}, O_{h,k+1})|h = i, j, 1 \leq k \leq n_h - 1\} \cup$$

$$\cup \{(O_{ik_i''(l)}, O_{jk_j'(l)})|1 \leq l \leq m\};$$

a weight p_{hk} is attached to each vertex $O_{hk} \in N_{ij}$. For an example with $m = 3$ and machine orders $(2, 1, 2, 3, 2)$ and $(1, 2, 3, 1)$, the graph G_{ij} is given in figure 6.4.

As to the critical path in G_{ij}, it is clear that

(i) it starts from O_{i1} and ends in O_{jn_j};

(ii) it contains exactly one arc $(O_{ik_i''(l)}, O_{jk_j'(l)})$.

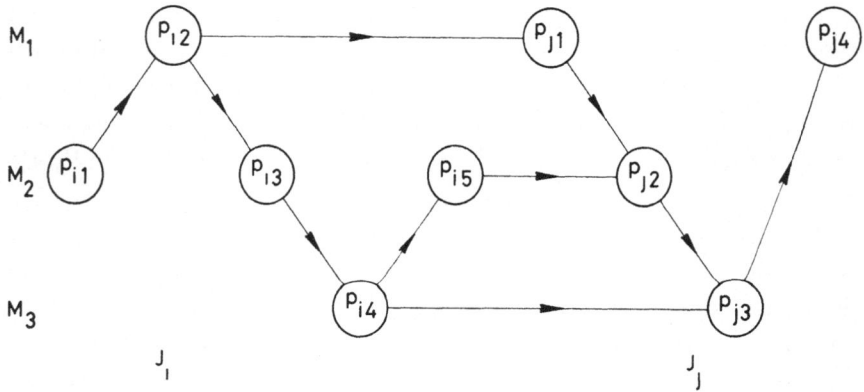

Figure 6.4.

Now c_{ij} is equal to the latest possible starting time of O_{j1} in G_{ij} if O_{i1} starts at time zero and O_{jn_j} finishes as early as possible. It follows from (i) and (ii) that

(6-12) $\quad c_{ij} = \max_{l} \{Q_i(1, k_i''(l)) + Q_j(k_j'(l), n_j)\} - Q_j(1, n_j) =$

$$= \max_{l} \{Q_i(1, k_i''(l)) - Q_j(1, k_j'(l) - 1)\}.$$

The minimum total processing time is now given by

(6-13) $\quad \min_{v} \{ \sum_{i=1}^{n-1} c_{v(i), v(i+1)} + Q_{v(n)}(1, n_{v(n)}) \}$

where v runs over all permutations of $\{1, \ldots, n\}$; $v(i)$ is the i-th job in a processing schedule.

We add a dummy job J_0 with $n_0 = m$, $\mu(O_{ik}) = k$ and $p_{0k} = 0$ for $1 \leq k \leq m$. According to (6-12) its coefficients are given by $c_{0i} = 0$, $c_{i0} = Q_i(1, n_i)$ for $1 \leq i \leq n$. Determination of (6-13) now corresponds to a TRAVELLING SALESMAN problem on a complete directed graph with $n + 1$ vertices $0, 1, \ldots, n$ and weights c_{ij}.

This particular TRAVELLING SALESMAN problem is *euclidean* (i.e., $c_{ij} + c_{jk} \geq c_{ik}$ for all $i, j, k \in N$):

$$\max_{l} \{Q_i(1, k_i''(l)) + Q_j(k_j'(l), n_j)\} +$$

$$+ \max_{l} \{Q_j(1, k_j''(l)) + Q_k(k_k'(l), n_k)\} \geq$$

$$\geq \max_{l} \{Q_i(1, k_i''(l)) + Q_k(k_k'(l), n_k)\} + Q_j(1, n_j),$$

and this is true, since for any $l \in \{1, \ldots, m\}$

$$[Q_i(1, k_i''(l)) + Q_j(k_j'(l), n_j)] + [Q_j(1, k_j''(l)) + Q_k(k_k'(l), n_k)] \geq$$

$$\geq [Q_i(1, k_i''(l)) + Q_k(k_k'(l), n_k)] + Q_j(1, n_j).$$

We make two final remarks on this formulation.

Remark 1. In a flow-shop we know that $\mu(O_{ik}) = k$ for $1 \leq k \leq m$, and (6-12) simplifies to $c_{ij} = \max_{l} \{Q_i(1, l) - Q_j(1, l - 1)\}$, which corresponds to the results given in [Piehler 1960; Reddi and Ramamoorthy 1972].

Remark 2. So far, distances have been defined as differences between the starting times of the first operations of jobs. More generally, one might arbitrarily select any two operations O_{ik_i*} and O_{ik_i**} for each job J_i and define c_{ij} as the minimum difference between the starting times of O_{ik_i*} and O_{jk_j**} if J_i precedes J_j directly. This will lead to modifications in (6-12) and (6-13), but to the same TRAVELLING SALESMAN problem (cf. [Goyal 1973; Reddi and Ramamoorthy 1973a]).

We have now seen that the $n|m|G$, P, no $wait|C_{\max}$ problem can be solved as a TRAVELLING SALESMAN problem (cf. section 4.2.2). This need not necessarily be the simplest way to solve such a problem. For instance, if $m = 2$, we may rewrite (6-13) as follows:

$$\min_v \{p_{v(1)1} + \max(p_{v(2)1}, p_{v(1)2}) + \ldots +$$

$$+ \max(p_{v(n)1}, p_{v(n-1)2}) + p_{v(n)2}\} =$$

$$= \min_v \{ \sum_{j=1}^{n-1} \max(p_{v(j+1)1} - p_{v(j)2}, 0) + p_{v(1)1} + \sum_{j=1}^{n} p_{v(j)2}\}.$$

$\sum_{j=1}^{n} p_{v(j)2}$ is a sequence independent term. It follows that the cost coefficients c_{ij} for this particular TRAVELLING SALESMAN problem are given by

$$\begin{cases} c_{ij} = \max(p_j - p_i, 0) \\ c_{i0} = 0, \, c_{0i} = p_{i1}. \end{cases} \qquad (i, j = 1, \ldots, n)$$

Note that this is equivalent to

$$(6\text{-}14) \quad c_{ij} = \begin{cases} \int_{B_i}^{A_j} f(x)\,dx & \text{if } A_j \geqq B_i \\ \int_{A_j}^{B_i} g(x)\,dx & \text{if } A_j < B_i \end{cases} \qquad (i, j = 0, \ldots, n)$$

with $A_i = p_{i1}$, $B_i = p_{i2}$ $(i = 1, \ldots, n)$, $A_0 = -\infty$, $B_0 = 0$, $f(x) \equiv 1$, $g(x) \equiv 0$. However, TRAVELLING SALESMAN problems whose cost coefficients can be described by equations of type (6-14) with $f(x) + g(x) \geqq 0$ for all x can be solved by a polynomial-bounded $O(n^2)$ algorithm given in [Gilmore and Gomory 1964].

No such results are known for other fixed values of m, but we have the following complexity result for a variable m.

THEOREM 6.8. The $n|m|F$, no $wait|C_{\max}$ problem is NP-complete.

PROOF. DIRECTED HAMILTONIAN PATH $\propto n|m|F$, no wait$|C_{max}$.

Given $G' = (V', A')$, we define

$$n = |V'|$$

$$m = n(n-1) + 2.$$

All jobs have the same machine order $(M_1, M_2, \ldots, M_{m-1}, M_m)$. To each pair of jobs (J_i, J_j) $(i, j = 1, \ldots, n, j \neq i)$ there corresponds one machine $M_k = M_{\kappa(i,j)}$ $(k = 2, \ldots, m-1)$, such that for no J_h some $M_{\kappa(i,h)}$ directly follows an $M_{\kappa(h,j)}$. Such an ordering of the pairs (i, j) can easily be constructed if $n \geq 3$.* Due to this property of the ordering, partial sums $Q_h(k)$ of the processing times (corresponding to $Q_h(1, k)$ in remark 1 above) can be defined unambiguously by

$$Q_h(k) \triangleq \begin{cases} k\mu + \lambda & \text{if } k \quad = \kappa(h, j) \text{ and } (h, j) \in A' \\ k\mu + \lambda + 1 & \text{if } k \quad = \kappa(h, j) \text{ and } (h, j) \notin A' \\ k\mu - \lambda & \text{if } k + 1 = \kappa(i, h) \text{ and } (i, h) \in A' \\ k\mu - \lambda - 1 & \text{if } k + 1 = \kappa(i, h) \text{ and } (i, h) \notin A' \\ k\mu & \text{otherwise} \end{cases}$$

for $k = 1, \ldots, m$, $h = 1, \ldots, n$, where

$$\lambda \geq 1$$

$$\mu \geq 2\lambda + 3.$$

The processing times are given by (cf. remark 1 above)

$$p_{h1} \triangleq Q_h(1)$$

$$p_{hk} \triangleq Q_h(k) - Q_h(k-1) \qquad\qquad (k = 2, \ldots, m)$$

Due to the choice of μ, these processing times are all strictly positive integers.

We can now compute the c_{ij}, as defined in remark 1. Due to the choice of λ, it is immediate that $Q_i(l) - Q_i(l-1)$ is maximal for $l = \kappa(i, j)$.

Hence,

$$c_{ij} = \begin{cases} \mu + 2\lambda & \text{if } (i, j) \in A' \\ \mu + 2\lambda + 2 & \text{if } (i, j) \notin A' \end{cases}$$

* For instance: $(1, 2), (1, 3), \ldots, (1, n), (2, n), \ldots, (2, 1), (3, n), \ldots, (3, 1), \ldots, (n-1, n), \ldots, (n-1, 1), (n, n-1), \ldots, (n, 1)$.

Since $Q_i(m) = m\mu$ for all J_i, it now follows that G' has a hamiltonian path *iff* this $n|m|F, no\ wait|C_{max}$ problem has a solution with value

$$C_{max} \leqq (n - 1)(\mu + 2\lambda) + m\mu. \qquad\qquad \text{(Q.E.D.)}$$

The $n|m|G, P, no\ wait|\sum C_i$ problem can be studied along the same lines; calculation of the c_{ij} in this case leads to a problem of the type discussed in section 4.4.2 (cf. [Van Deman and Baker 1974]). No specific results for fixed m are known in this case, but it is easily seen that the graph G' from the proof of theorem 6.8 has a directed hamiltonian path *iff* the $n|m|F, no\ wait|\sum C_i$ problem constructed in that proof has a solution with value

$$\sum C_i \leqq \tfrac{1}{2}n(n - 1)(\mu + 2\lambda) + nm\mu.$$

Thus, the $n|m|F, no\ wait|\sum C_i$ problem is also NP-complete.

7

Concluding remarks

In this final chapter we summarize our results with respect to the complexity of scheduling problems in section 7.1. In section 7.2 we shall indicate how theory and algorithms developed in the previous chapters might be applicable in solving practical scheduling problems.

7.1. COMPLEXITY OF SCHEDULING PROBLEMS

In chapters 3, 4, 5 and 6 we have on various occasions examined the complexity of $\alpha|\beta|\gamma, \Gamma|\delta$ scheduling problems for various values of the parameters α, β, γ, Γ and δ. Throughout, our objective has been to locate as precisely as possible the borderline between 'easy' problems (in $\mathcal{P}$) and 'hard' (NP-complete) problems. In this section we shall summarize the complexity results to obtain an overall view of this borderline.

The complexity results are surveyed in table 7.1. Problems marked by an asterisk (*) in this table can be solved in polynomial-bounded time; in table 7.2 we provide a reference to the section where the good algorithm in question is discussed. The problems marked by a note of exclamation (!) are, roughly speaking, the easiest problems known to be NP-complete. Question-marks (?) indicate open problems that will be briefly recalled below. Table 7.3 summarizes the reductions that have been used establish NP-completeness in chapters 3, 4, 5 and 6. NP-completeness is a consequence of these problem reductions and the NP-completeness results given in theorem 3.3.

We now comment briefly on the open problems mentioned in table 7.1.

(i) $n|1|prec|\sum w_i C_i$

We conjecture the $n|1|prec|\sum w_i C_i$ problem to be NP-complete in view of the fruitless attempts to extend the $O(n \log n)$ algorithms for the $n|1|tree|\sum w_i C_i$ problem to the case of general precedence constraints

Table 7.1. Complexity of machine scheduling problems.

n jobs	1 machine	2 machines	m machines
C_{max}	* $prec, r_i \geqq 0$	* F * $F, no\ wait$! $F, tree$! $F, r_n \geqq 0$	! $\underline{m=3}:F$? $\underline{m=3}:F, no\ wait$! $F, no\ wait$
		* $G, n_i \leqq 2$! $G, n_i \leqq 3$	* $\underline{n=2}:G$! $\underline{m=3}:G, n_i \leqq 2$
$\sum w_i C_i$	* $tree$? $prec$! $r_n \geqq 0, w_i = 1$ † ! $r_n \geqq 0$	! $F, w_i = 1$? $F, no\ wait, w_i = 1$	! $F, no\ wait, w_i = 1$
L_{max}	* $prec$ * $prec, r_i \geqq 0, p_i = 1$! $r_n \geqq 0$	! F	
$\sum w_i T_i$	* $r_i \geqq 0, p_i = 1$ * $p_i \leqq p^*, w_i = 1$? $w_i = 1$! ! $prec, p_i = 1, w_i = 1$! $r_n \geqq 0, w_i = 1$	! $F, w_i = 1$	
$\sum w_i U_i$	* $r_i \geqq 0, p_i = 1$ * $p_i \leqq p^*$ * $w_i = 1$! ! $prec, p_i = 1, w_i = 1$! $r_n \geqq 0, w_i = 1$	! $F, w_i = 1$	

*: problem in $\mathscr{P}$
?: open problem
!: NP-complete problem
†: NP-completeness proof is given with respect to the id-encoding

(section 4.4.3). NP-completeness for $n|1|prec|\sum c_i$ problems has so far been proved for the unweighted tardiness case under the additional assumption that all p_i are equal to 1 (theorem 4.28). The CLIQUE reduction used to obtain this result does not seem extendable to the $n|1|prec|\sum w_i C_i$ case. Not only do we conjecture NP-completeness of the latter problem, but also of the $n|1|prec, p_i = 1|\sum w_i C_i$ and the $n|1|prec|\sum C_i$ problem, both of which are reducible to $n|1|prec|\sum w_i C_i$. NP-completeness for these two special cases would be in a sense the strongest possible result: the intersection

Table 7.2. References to polynomial-bounded algorithms.

Problem	Reference	Order
$n\|1\|r_i \geqq 0, prec\|C_{\max}$	Section 4.2.1.	$O(n^2)$
$n\|1\|tree\|\Sigma w_i C_i$	Section 4.4.3.	$O(n \log n)$
$n\|1\|prec\|L_{\max}$	Section 4.2.1.	$O(n^2)$
$n\|1\|r_i \geqq 0, p_i = 1, prec\|L_{\max}$	Section 4.2.1.	$O(n^2)$
$n\|1\|p_{i1} \leqq p^*, w_i = 1\|\Sigma w_i T_i$	Section 4.3.2.	$O(n^4 \sum_{i=1}^{n} p_i)$
$n\|1\|r_i \geqq 0, p_i = 1\|\Sigma w_i T_i$	Section 4.4.1.	$O(n^3)$
$n\|1\|r_i \geqq 0, p_i = 1\|\Sigma w_i U_i$	Section 4.4.1.	$O(n^2)$
$n\|1\|w_i = 1\|\Sigma w_i U_i$	Section 4.3.2.	$O(n \log n)$
$n\|1\|p_i \leqq p^*\|\Sigma w_i U_i$	Section 4.3.2.	$O(n \sum_{i=1}^{n} p_i)$
$n\|2\|F\|C_{\max}$	Section 5.1.	$O(n \log n)$
$n\|2\|F, no\ wait\|C_{\max}$	Section 6.4.	$O(n^2)$
$n\|2\|G, n_i \leqq 2\|C_{\max}$	Section 5.1.	$O(n \log n)$
$2\|m\|G\|C_{\max}$	Section 2.4.	$O(m^2)$

Table 7.3. Reductions to NP-complete machine scheduling problems.

Reduction	Reference
KNAPSACK $\propto n\|1\|r_n \geqq 0\|\Sigma C_i$ †	Theorem 4.25.
KNAPSACK $\propto n\|1\|r_n \geqq 0\|\Sigma w_i C_i$	Theorem 4.26.
KNAPSACK $\propto n\|1\|r_n \geqq 0\|\Sigma T_i$	Theorem 4.26.
KNAPSACK $\propto n\|1\|r_n \geqq 0\|L_{\max}$	Theorem 4.8.
KNAPSACK $\propto n\|1\|\|\Sigma w_i T_i$	Theorem 4.14.
KNAPSACK $\propto n\|1\|\|\Sigma w_i U_i$	Section 4.3.2.
KNAPSACK $\propto n\|1\|r_n \geqq 0\|\Sigma U_i$	Section 4.4.1.
KNAPSACK $\propto n\|2\|F, r_n \geqq 0\|C_{\max}$	Theorem 5.12.
KNAPSACK $\propto n\|2\|F, tree\|C_{\max}$	Theorem 5.12.
KNAPSACK $\propto n\|2\|G, n_i \leqq 3\|C_{\max}$	Theorem 5.7.
KNAPSACK $\propto n\|3\|G, n_i \leqq 2\|C_{\max}$	Theorem 5.8.
DIRECTED HAMILTONIAN PATH $\propto n\|m\|F, no\ wait\|C_{\max}$	Theorem 6.8.
DIRECTED HAMILTONIAN PATH $\propto n\|m\|F, no\ wait\|\Sigma C_i$	Section 6.4.
CLIQUE $\propto n\|1\|p_i = 1, prec\|\Sigma T_i$	Theorem 4.28.
CLIQUE $\propto n\|1\|p_i = 1, prec\|\Sigma U_i$	Section 4.3.3.
$n\|1\|r_n \geqq 0\|\Sigma C_i$ † $\propto n\|2\|F\|\Sigma C_i$ †	Section 5.2.
$n\|1\|r_n \geqq 0\|\Sigma w_i C_i \propto n\|2\|F\|\Sigma w_i C_i$	Theorem 5.13.
$n\|1\|r_n \geqq 0\|L_{\max} \propto n\|2\|F\|L_{\max}$	Theorem 5.12.
$n\|1\|r_n \geqq 0\|\Sigma T_i \propto n\|2\|F\|\Sigma T_i$	Theorem 5.13.
$n\|1\|r_n \geqq 0\|\Sigma U_i \propto n\|2\|F\|\Sigma U_i$	Section 5.2.
$n\|2\|F, r_n \geqq 0\|C_{\max} \propto n\|3\|F\|C_{\max}$	Theorem 5.12.

of the two problems, *i.e.* the $n|1|prec, p_i = 1|\sum C_i$ problem, is trivially in $\mathscr{P}$, since every active schedule is optimal.

(ii) $n|1||\sum T_i$

The $n|1||\sum T_i$ problem has been discussed extensively in section 4.3.2. Numerous strong elimination criteria have been developed for this problem. The existence of an $O(n^4 \sum p_i)$ algorithm [Lawler 1975a] proves the problem to be efficiently solvable with respect to a unary encoding of $O(\sum p_i)$ length. It is none the less perfectly possible that the problem is NP-complete with respect to a binary encoding.

Again the KNAPSACK reduction that was used in theorem 4.14 to prove NP-completeness for the $n|1||\sum w_i T_i$ problem could not be extended.

We conjecture, however, that the $n|1||\sum T_i$ problem is binary NP-complete and that an implicit enumeration approach such as the one described in section 4.3.3.2 is essentially unavoidable for this problem.

(iii) $n|2|F, no\ wait|\sum C_i, n|3|F, no\ wait|C_{max}$

With respect to the two open *no wait* problems, we recall that the general $n|m|F, no\ wait|\delta$ problem has been proved to be NP-complete for $\delta = C_{max}$ and $\delta = \sum C_i$ in section 6.4. The special case that $m = 2$ and $\delta = C_{max}$ turned out to be efficiently solvable; it corresponds to a TRAVELLING SALESMAN problem of special structure for which an $O(n^2)$ algorithm is available. No other results for fixed values of m are known. A conjecture with respect to the complexity status of the $n|2|F, no\ wait|\sum C_i$ and $n|3|F, no\ wait|C_{max}$ problem is not obvious. Stimulating prizes await the successful researcher in this area [Lenstra *et al.* 1975].

Let us stress finally that NP-completeness versus membership of $\mathscr{P}$ only yields a very coarse measure of problem complexity. On one hand, it may be questioned if polynomial-boundedness really characterizes 'good' algorithms [Anthonisse and Van Emde Boas 1974]; on the other hand, the practicality of the NP-completeness concept also has not been completely established. For instance, the complexity status of the general linear programming problem is as yet unknown, and NP-completeness of this problem, however unlikely, would seriously devaluate the concept.

In addition, there appear to exist significant differences in complexity within the class of NP-complete problems itself. E.g., in section 6.3 we reported on the successful inclusion of an $n|1|r_i \geqq 0, prec|L'_{max}$ lower bound in a general $n|m|G|C_{max}$ algorithm, although these problems are both NP-complete and thus formally equivalent up to a polynomial-bounded reduction. One possible way to formalize this intuitive difference has been briefly discussed in section 4.3.2, where we looked into the consequences of allowing a unary encoding of problem data. If we allow differentiation between results with respect to unary and binary encoding, the complexity measure varies between binary membership of $\mathscr{P}$ and unary NP-completeness whereas the two other categories may be overlapping (see section 4.3.2). We have concentrated on binary NP-completeness results; however, a further investigation of the complexity consequences of the $p_{ik} \leqq p^*$ assumption seems a useful research topic.

A second way to characterize the complexity of scheduling problems may be through a worst-case analysis of 'simple' heuristics (*e.g.*, priority rules). Previous results in this area indicate that for difficult problems such worst-case results depend on the size of the problem, whereas for simpler problems often a constant upper bound on worst-case behaviour can be obtained (see [Garey and Graham 1975; Graham 1969]). Worst-case analyses of non-trivial heuristics are still lacking for many cases. This aspect again seems worthy of further investigation.

7.2. PRACTICAL SCHEDULING PROBLEMS

Our discussion of the restrictive assumptions implicitly present in the scheduling model (section 2.2) may give the impression that this model corresponds to a somewhat oversimplified picture of reality. The aim of this section is to show that such a simplification does not imply that the theory and algorithms developed in previous chapters are worthless in a practical situation. On the contrary, theoretical results may inspire heuristic solution methods that are more subtle than the very general approaches suggested in section 3.7.

The general heuristic approach that we shall consider here initially involves the determination of the *critical machines* in a problem, i.e. the machines of which the processing order has a crucial influence on the quality of the schedule as a whole. The problem is then decomposed into problems involving one or more of those critical machines; these subproblems are solved by means of methods inspired by the scheduling theory of the preceding chapters. The resulting critical machine schedules are linked by choosing appropriate processing orders on the remaining machines, leading to an overall schedule of reasonable quality.

Rather than discussing this general approach in more detail, we propose to illustrate its use by a small example. Experience obtained with this approach has been very limited and we would only conclude from its performance that it merits further experimentation in varying scheduling situations.

The scheduling problem that we shall describe arises in the context of the production of aluminium airplane parts. The factory in question has been divided into independent production 'streets'. In one of those streets, the most importance machine is a *rubberpress*. Before the metal parts can be pressed into their proper shape, they have to be processed either by a *cutting* or by a high speed *milling* machine, they have to pass through *fitting shops* and they have to spend a full working day of eight hours in an *annealing furnace*. The mild structure caused by this heat treatment can be preserved in a deep freezer during at most 14 days. After the rubberpress the metal parts have to pass through the fitting shops for a second time before being completely finished. The processing time of each operation is known in advance.

Altogether nine operators are available: one of them is required to handle the milling or cutting machine, two are required on the rubberpress and the remaining six are employed in the fitting shops. The annealing furnace requires no attention of personnel; it can be assumed to have an infinite capacity.

We can model this production process as a job-shop involving four machines M_1, M_2, M_3 and M_4 with varying capacities. M_1 represents the cutting/milling machine; its capacity γ_1 is one. M_2 represents the fitting shops; its capacity γ_2 is 6 or, equivalently, we may assume 6 identical machines of this type to be available. M_3 represents the annealing bath which is a non-bottleneck machine of infinite capacity. M_4 represents the rubberpress, again of capacity $\gamma_4 = 1$. After M_4 all jobs return to M_2 for a final operation. If we denote the five operations of J_i by O_{ik} ($k = 1, ..., 5$) with processing times p_{ik} ($k = 1, ..., 5$), typical data for a week's production look like those presented in table 7.4. Some jobs are left over from last week and have completed some of their initial operations.

The prime objective in this scheduling situation is to have the rubberpress occupied as permanently as possible, since idle time on this machine is relatively costly. Hence, M_4 is clearly a critical machine.

If we add the processing times, we find that $\sum_{i=1}^{35} p_{i1} = 56$, $\sum_{i=1}^{35} p_{i2} = 70$, $\sum_{i=1}^{35} p_{i4} = 48.5$, $\sum_{i=1}^{35} p_{i5} = 202$. Clearly, all jobs cannot be processed on M_1 and M_4 within one week of 40 hours and some overflow will result. It seems quite possible to schedule O_{i2} and O_{i3} directly after the completion of O_{i1}, but some waiting time of the jobs before the processing of O_{i4} and O_{i5} seems unavoidable. Furthermore, it is expedient to schedule the O_{i1} in such a way that many jobs are quickly available for further processing, by taking p_{i4} and p_{i5} explicitly into account. Thus, M_1 also becomes a critical machine.

These intuitive considerations lead to the following heuristic algorithm, in which S_{ik} and C_{ik} stand for starting times and completion times of O_{ik} respectively.

Step 1: Schedule jobs on M_1 according to non-decreasing $p_{i1}/(p_{i4} + p_{i5})$ ratio, settling ties by non-increasing $q_{i1} = \sum_{k=2}^{5} p_{ik}$ (cf. theorem 4.11).

Step 2: Schedule jobs on M_2 as early as possible according to non-decreasing C_{i1}.

Step 3: $S_{i3} := 8 \times \lceil C_{i2}/8 \rceil$; $C_{i3} := S_{i3} + 8$.*

Step 4: $r_{i4} := C_{i3}$; $q_{i4} := p_{i5}$. Solve the $n|1|r_i \geq 0|L'_{max}$ problem on M_4, defined by (r_{i4}, p_{i4}, q_{i4}) (cf. section 4.2.1).

Step 5: Schedule jobs on M_2 as early as possible according to non-decreasing C_{i4}.

The resulting schedule for the problem is given in table 7.4 and the corresponding Gantt-chart is drawn in figure 7.1. This schedule compares favorably to several schedules obtained by methods of trial-and-error and rules of thumb. We note, for instance, that the maximum number of time-units that any job has to be postponed because of the capacity constraint on M_2 is 4. In this particular case, the first initial schedule on M_4 found by the procedure 'n1ri0lmaxinit' in step 4 was optimal. Altogether, 11 hours of idle time occur on M_4 before time 48; after that time, new jobs arriving at time 40 will be available to fill the remaining gaps on the rubberpress.

We stress again that this simple example is not meant to validate completely the heuristic approach described in this section. In this particular situation the approach worked rather well, and we think this does indicate the applicability of ideas from scheduling theory even in situations that do not fit the standard model. Especially in view of the frequent complaint about the lack of applicability of scheduling theory the results mentioned above seem to justify further experimentation.

---

* $\lceil x \rceil$ is the minimal integer $\geq x$.

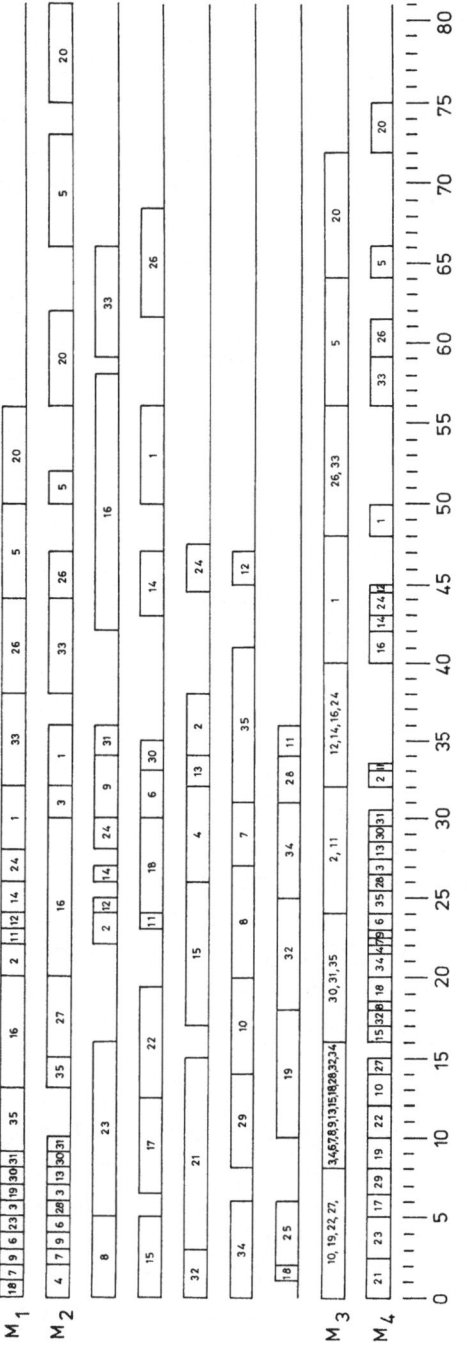

Figure 7.1. A practical scheduling problem: Gantt-chart.

Table 7.4. A practical scheduling problem: data and results.

i	p_{i1}	p_{i2}	p_{i3}	p_{i4}	p_{i5}	$\dfrac{p_{i1}}{p_{i4}+p_{i5}}$	C_{i1}	C_{i2}	C_{i3}	C_{i4}	C_{i5}
1	4	4	8	2	6	.50	32	36	48	50	56
2	2	2	8	1	4	.40	22	24	32	33	38
3	1	1	8	1	2	.33	6	7	16	27.5	32
4	–	2	8	.5	6	–	0	2	16	22	32
5	6	2	8	2	7	.67	50	52	64	66	73
6	1	1	8	1	3	.25	4	5	16	24	33
7	1	1	8	.5	4	.22	2	3	16	22.5	31
8	–	5	8	.5	7	–	0	5	16	18.5	27
9	1	1	8	.5	4	.22	3	4	16	23	34
10	–	–	8	2	6	–	–	0	8	14	20
11	1	1	8	.5	2	.40	23	24	32	33.5	36
12	1	1	8	.5	2	.40	24	25	40	45	47
13	1	1	8	1	2	.33	7	8	16	28.5	34
14	2	1	8	1	4	.40	26	27	40	43	47
15	–	5	8	1	9	–	0	5	16	17	26
16	7	10	8	2	16	.39	20	30	40	42	58
17	–	–	–	1.5	6	–	–	–	0	6.5	12.5
18	1	1	8	1.5	6	.13	1	2	16	20	30
19	–	–	8	2	8	–	–	0	8	10	18
20	6	6	8	3	6	.67	56	62	72	75	81
21	–	–	–	2.5	12	–	–	–	0	2.5	15
22	–	–	8	2	7	–	–	0	8	12	19.5
23	–	–	–	2.5	11	–	–	–	0	5	16
24	2	2	8	1.5	3	.44	28	30	40	44.5	47.5
25	–	–	–	–	4	–	–	–	–	0	6
26	6	3	8	2.5	7	.63	44	47	56	61.5	68.5
27	–	–	8	1	5	–	–	0	8	15	20
28	1	1	8	1	3	.25	5	6	16	26.5	34
29	–	–	–	1.5	6	–	–	–	0	8	14
30	1	1	8	1	2	.33	8	9	24	29.5	35
31	1	1	8	1	2	.33	9	10	24	30.5	36
32	–	3	8	1	7	–	0	3	16	18	25
33	6	6	8	3	7	.60	38	44	56	59	66
34	–	6	8	1.5	6	–	0	6	16	21.5	31
35	4	2	8	1.5	10	.35	13	15	24	25.5	41

7.3. CONCLUSIONS

In this final section we propose to review four inviting directions for future scheduling research. Each of these research areas corresponds to one of the steps typically taken in analyzing a scheduling problem. First, we usually examine the *complexity* of the problem. Based on the outcome of that examination, we then try to develop *optimizing algorithms* for the problem that may be either polynomial-bounded or of the implicit enumeration type. For some problems, complexity results and computational experiments will indicate that the use of *heuristics* is unavoidable. Finally, possible *applications* of the scheduling problem may be considered.

With respect to each of these four aspects we shall now indicate some general research possibilities, inspired by the results obtained in this study.

(i) *Complexity*

The problem classification developed in chapter 2 has turned out to be very useful in characterizing problem complexity. Our complexity results have been summarized earlier in this chapter; some intriguing open problems have been indicated. More urgently, the complexity measure provided by the NP-completeness concept is itself in need of further refinement. As suggested before, such refinements might be obtained by considering the effect of allowing a unary encoding of problem data or by examining the worst-case performance of simple heuristics (see (iii) below). Dependency of worst-case behaviour on the size of the problem would underline the relative complexity of a problem; occasionally, it is even possible to prove that the problem of obtaining a feasible solution within any given percentage of the optimum is NP-complete [Sahni and Gonzalez 1974]. It would be interesting to find out for which scheduling problems the latter strong property holds as well. These and similar refinements point to an important area for future research.

(ii) *Optimizing algorithms*

Complexity results and algorithmic properties are strongly related to each other, as demonstrated by the presentation of chapters 4, 5 and 6. Membership of $\mathscr{P}$ is by definition implied by the existence of a polynomial-bounded algorithm; attempts to find such an algorithm for problems whose complexity status is unknown are of obvious importance. Moreover, even when a problem is known to be in $\mathscr{P}$, it may be possible to improve on the number of steps required for its solution. Research in the latter direction often involves the use of sophisticated data handling techniques, indicating the growing overlap of operations research and computer science with respect to this type of research.

On the other hand, NP-completeness proofs have been used to justify the implicit enumeration approaches presented in this study. Computational experience with several of these algorithms indicates that there is still need for considerable improvement. Inspection of the $n|1|r_i \geq 0|L_{max}$ algorithm of section 4.2.1.2 suggests that its exceptional success may be partly due to the use of a branching rule that exploits the characteristic features of the specific problem under consideration. Construction of such a rule has been attempted without much success for the general job-shop problem in section 6.3.2.2; continuing efforts in this direction, possibly based on alternative problem representations, are required.

Evidently, the disappointing performance of some branch-and-bound algorithms should also be partly ascribed to unsufficiently strong lower bounds. Possible applications of Lagrangian multipliers to lower bound calculations should be investigated more extensively. In the area of general job-shop and flow-shop scheduling, a natural relaxation of the capacity constraints on all but two machines points to a number of NP-complete two-machine problems that are also worthy of further exploration. There is room here for clever branch-and-bound algorithms similar to the $n|1|r_i \geq 0|L_{max}$ approach recalled above, that exploit the properties of the efficient $n|2|F|C_{max}$ algorithm (theorem 5.3).

Generally, branch-and-bound algorithms seem to have reached the stage where most of the immediate ideas have been tried and real ingenuity is required for further improvement.

(iii) *Heuristics*

Given the complexity results and the inevitable limitations of implicit enumeration methods, heuristic methods appear to be unavoidable for many problems. In this study a critical attitude has been adopted towards obvious general heuristics such as the priority rules discussed in section 3.7.1. In our opinion successful solution of practical problems requires a specific and more sophisticated approach; the extensive experiments testing priority rules seem to be neither of mathematical interest nor of much practical value. It would be of interest, though, to prove or disprove these prejudices by a non-heuristic analysis of these heuristics, *i.e.* by examining their worst-case behaviour or by subjecting them to a probabilistic analysis. Both these approaches lead to challenging mathematical problems. Worst-case analyses of heuristics have already been obtained for various combinatorial optimization problems [Graham 1969; Johnson 1973; Rosenkrantz *et al.* 1974; Garey and Graham 1975]; as mentioned previously, the outcome of such analyses further characterizes the complexity of a problem. Probabilistic analysis requires the specification of some probability distribution over the set of problem instances; in spite of this difficulty some impressive results have been obtained in this area [Karp 1975]. It seems safe to predict important advances in this rapidly developing field in the near future.

(iv) *Applications*

The discussion of critical assumptions and restrictions inherent to scheduling models and of the economic significance of optimality criteria (chapter 2) should facilitate the recognition of those actual scheduling problems for which scheduling theory might be a useful solution tool. Moreover, a heuristic approach as sketched in section 7.2 provides a natural way to interpret and apply the results of this study in practical scheduling situations. Thus, awareness of existing theory may yield more practical advantages than seems to be currently thought. The design of general strategies for the application of theoretical results to practical situations should be the major objective of practice oriented scheduling research.

In summary, an abundance of work remains to be done in each of the four above areas. We conclude that healthy interaction between theory and practice should continue to make scheduling problems a challenging research area in the field of operations research.

List of notations*

$\mathcal{O}$	set of operations	2.1.
J_i	job i	2.1.
M_k	machine k	2.1.
$\iota(O_r)$	job-index of O_r	2.1.
$\mu(O_r)$	machine-index of O_r	2.1.
n_i	number of operations of J_i	2.1.
N_i	$\sum_{j=1}^{i} n_j$	2.1.
$O_r \prec O_{r+1}$	O_r directly precedes O_{r+1}	2.1.
$O_r \lll O_s$	O_r precedes O_s	2.1.
p_r	processing time of O_r	2.1
O_{ik}	operation of J_i on M_k, or the k-th operation of J_i	2.1.
p_{ik}	processing time of O_{ik}	2.1.
v_i	permutation of $\{1, \ldots, m\}$ indicating the machine order of J_i	2.1.
$\mathcal{G}$	disjunctive graph	2.1.
$\mathcal{V}$	vertices of $\mathcal{G}$	2.1.
$\mathcal{C}$	conjunctive arcs of $\mathcal{G}$	2.1.
$\mathcal{D}$	disjunctive arcs of $\mathcal{G}$	2.1.
A_0	first operations	2.1.
B_*	last operations	2.1.
$\mathcal{G}^\dagger$	inverse disjunctive graph	2.1.
$\mathcal{G}(D)$	directed graph with vertex set $\mathcal{V}$ and arc set $\mathcal{C} \cup D$	2.1.
F	flow-shop	2.1.
P	flow-shop with same processing order on each machine	2.1.
G	general job-shop	2.1.
G, P	general job-shop with same processing order of jobs on each machine	2.1.

* See also table 2.2.

r_i	release date of J_i	2.2.
$J_i \prec J_j$	precedence constraint between J_i and J_j	2.2.
d_i	due date for J_i	2.2.
v_k	weight for M_k	2.2.
w_i	weight for J_i	2.2.
γ_k	capacity of M_k	2.2.
S_r	starting time for O_r	2.3.1.
C_i	completion time of J_i	2.3.1.
$\mathscr{F}$	set of semi-active schedules	2.3.1.
$c_i(t)$	cost function for J_i	2.3.1.
$c_{\max}$	$\max_i \{c_i(C_i)\}$	2.3.1.
$\sum c_i$	$\sum_{i=1}^{n} c_i(C_i)$	2.3.1.
F_i	flow time $C_i - r_i$ of J_i	2.3.1.1.
W_i	waiting time $C_i - (r_i + \sum_{O_r \in J_i} p_r)$ of J	2.3.1.1.
L_i	lateness $C_i - d_i$ of J_i	2.3.1.2.
T_i	tardiness $\max(0, C_i - d_i)$ of J_i	2.3.1.2.
$\bar{N}_p$	average number of jobs in process	2.3.1.3.
$\bar{N}_w$	average number of waiting jobs	2.3.1.3.
$\bar{N}_f$	average number of finished jobs	2.3.1.3.
$\bar{A}_p$	average amount of work in progress	2.3.1.3.
I_k	idle time $C_{\max} - \sum_{O_r \in M_k} p_r$ on M_k	2.3.1.3.
$\bar{U}$	mean utilization	2.3.1.3.
f_i	value of raw materials for J_i	2.3.3.
g_{ik}	increase in the value of J_i after the k-th operation	2.3.3.
ρ	net return on investment per time unit	2.3.3.
e_i	inventory costs per time unit	2.3.3.
a_i	costs per time unit of late delivery	2.3.3.
b_i	income per time unit of early delivery	2.3.3.
$s :\in S$	s becomes an arbitrary element of S	3.1.
$\mathscr{F}_0$	set of active schedules	3.1.
$\mathscr{X}$	family of subsets Y of feasible solutions arising during branch-and-bound procedure	3.4.
$b(Y)$	subsets created by branching on Y	3.4.
$\mathscr{P}$	class of problems for which a polynomial-bounded algorithm exists	3.6.
$\mathscr{NP}$	class of problems solvable by backtrack search of polynomial-bounded depth	3.6.

$P_1 \propto P_2$	problem P_1 is reducible to problem P_2	3.6.
q_i	tail $c - d_i$ of J_i	4.2.1.
s_i	job dependent set-up time for J_i	4.2.2.
A_i	jobs J_j preceding J_i $(J_j \prec J_i)$	4.2.3.
B_i	jobs J_j following J_i $(J_i \prec J_j)$	4.2.3.
U_i	**if** $C_i \leqq d_i$ **then** 0 **else** 1	4.3.2.
$P(Q)$	$\sum_{i \in Q} p_i$	4.3.3.1.
$C(\sigma, k)$	completion time of the last job of a partial schedule σ on M_k	6.1.1.
$M_{(g,h)}$	non-bottleneck machine corresponding to a sequence $M_g, \ldots, M_h$ of non-bottleneck machines	6.1.2.
$p_{i(g,h)}$	processing time of J_i on $M_{(g,h)}$	6.1.2.
$l_{(g,h)}$	$\min_{i \in S} \{ p_{i(g,h)} \}$	6.1.2.
$\square$	bottleneck machine	6.1.2.
$\triangle$	non-bottleneck machine	6.1.2.
$*$	non-bottleneck machine to be eliminated from the problem	6.1.2.
q_{iu}	$p_{i(u+1,m)}$	6.1.2.
$C_{max}(D_0)$	weight of critical path in $\mathscr{G}(D_0)$	6.3.1.
t_r	earliest possible starting time of O_r in $\mathscr{G}(D)$	6.3.1.
q_r	tail of O_r in $\mathscr{G}(D)$	6.3.1.
T_r	latest possible starting time of O_r in $\mathscr{G}(D)$	6.3.1.
D_{rs}	$D \cup \{(r, s)\}$	6.3.2.2.
$E(D)$	conflicts in $\mathscr{G}(D)$	6.3.2.2.
P_{rs}	$t_r + p_r - T_s$	6.3.2.2.
P_{rs}^*	$\min(P_{rs}, P_{sr})$	6.3.2.2.
$Q_i(k_1, k_2)$	$\sum_{k=k_1}^{k_2} p_{ik}$	6.4.

Appendix 1

The $n|1|r_i \geqq 0$, prec$|L_{\max}$ problem

The two main approaches to the $n|1|r_i \geqq 0$, prec$|L_{\max}$ problem described in sections 4.2.1.1 and 4.2.1.2 and extended in section 4.2.1.3 have been extensively tested and compared.

1.1. IMPLEMENTATION

Implementation of the algorithm described in section 4.2.1.1 is fairly straightforward. Experiments with a jumptrack search strategy revealed a 50–60% increase in solution times as compared to a newest active node strategy, in which jobs were chosen for the $(s + 1)$-st position in the order in which they appeared in the lower bound calculation.

With respect to the implementation of the algorithm described in section 4.2.1.2, the main problem that arises concerns a suitable realization of the precedence constraints $J_h \prec J_j$ ($h \in P_i - \{j\}$). As indicated in section 4.2.1.2, best results from a computational point of view were obtained by allowing non-disjoint subsets $Y' \in b(Y)$, and setting r_j equal to some lower bound on $C_{ji} - p_j$ not less than r_i. This effectuates the single precedence constraint $J_i \prec J_j$, at least for the next node. After some experimentation, it was found that taking $r_j := \max(r_i + p_i, C_i - p_j)$ produced slightly better results than simply putting $r_j := r_i$, as in [McMahon and Florian 1975]. We again used a newest active node search strategy, choosing jobs J_j in the reverse of the order in which they appear in the initial solution.

Precedence constraints were represented by means of the transitive closure of a random graph on $\{1, \ldots, n\}$ (see 1.2 below); implementation of the few changes needed to incorporate precedence constraints in the two algorithms presented no particular problems.

1.2. TEST DATA

For each test problem with n jobs, $3n$ integer values (r_i, p_i, q_i) were generated from uniform distributions between 1 and r_{max}, p_{max} and q_{max} respectively, with $r_{max} = R \cdot p_{max}$, $q_{max} = Q \cdot p_{max}$. These jobs were randomly numbered, and in the precedence graph each arc (i, j) with $i < j$ was included with probability P. Table A.1.1 shows the values of (n, p_{max}, R, Q, P) during our experiments; the values used in previous tests of the algorithms are also given.

Table A.1.1. Values of parameters of test problems.

Parameter	[Baker and Su 1974]	[McMahon and Florian 1975]	h.l.
n	10, 20, 30	20, 50	20, 40, 80
p_{max}	$2000/n$	25	50
R	$.5n$	$.5n, 2n$	$.5, 2, .5n, 2n$
Q	$.75n, .875n, n*$	$.4, 1, 3$	$.5, 2, .5n, 2n$
P	0	0	0, .05, .15, .45

* In this case, the q_i are not distributed uniformly.

For each combination of values (R, Q) with $R \leq Q$ five problems were generated; inversion provided problems with $R \geq Q$. Significant and systematic differences between the solution times of a problem and its inverse would indicate advantages to be gained from problem inversion.

1.3. COMPUTATIONAL RESULTS

The algorithms were coded in ALGOL 60 and run on the Control Data Cyber 73-28 of the SARA Computing Centre in Amsterdam.

Tables A.1.2 and A.1.3 show the computational results in CPU seconds for problems without precedence constraints, *i.e.*, with $P = 0$. Algorithm (4.2.1.1) solves 294 out of 300 problems with up to 80 jobs within the time limit of ten seconds. The limit is never exceeded for problems of the type on which the method has been tested previously. Inspection of the results revealed no obvious rule according to which problem inversion might take place and this additional feature was therefore not incorporated.

Table A.1.2. Computational results for $P = 0$: a survey.

n	P	median solution time			maximum solution time		
		(4.2.1.1)	(4.2.1.2)	(4.2.1.2)′	(4.2.1.1)	(4.2.1.2)	(4.2.1.2)′
20	0	.05	.02	.03	>10:2	.99	.11
40	0	.09	.06	.06	1.09	>10:1	.17
80	0	.23	.16	.15	>10:4	>10:3	.57

Table A.1.3. Computational results for $P = 0$: the influence of R and Q.

n = 80, P = 0, maximum solution time

R↓ Q→	algorithm (4.2.1.1)				algorithm (4.2.1.2)				algorithm (4.2.1.2)′			
	.5	2	.5n	2n	.5	2	.5n	2n	.5	2	.5n	2n
.5	.26	.25	5.54	5.75	.19	.21	1.64	>10:1	.19	.25	.15	.14
	.25				.19				.25			
2		.25	>10:1	4.84		.18	>10:1	>10:1		.22	.19	.16
	.24	.27			.19	.17			.20	.25		
.5n			3.43	3.67			.33	.47			.57	.17
	>10:1	>10:2	3.60		.10	.12	.52		.08	.11	.49	
2n				2.54				.11				.17
	.10	.11	2.51	2.55	.09	.07	.13	.13	.09	.08	.12	.19

Table A.1.4. Computational results: the influence of P.

n	P	median solution time		maximum solution time	
		(4.2.1.2)	(4.2.1.2)′	(4.2.1.2)	(4.2.1.2)′
20	0	.02	.03	.99	.11
	.05	.06	.05	.41	.43
	.15	.07	.07	.14	.15
	.45	.07	.08	.12	.11
80	0	.16	.15	>10:3	.57
	.05	.36	.33	>10:6	>10:4
	.15	.47	.42	.85	.57
	.45	.73	.75	.81	.80

Legend for tables A.1.2, A.1.3 and A.1.4
Solution times in CPU seconds;
$>l:k$: the time limit l is exceeded k times.

Even better results were obtained with algorithm (4.2.1.2), that was previously tested only on the very easiest type of problem. The method performs especially well on problems with $R > Q$. Accordingly, we also tested algorithm (4.2.1.2)' which inverts a problem if

$$\max_i \{r_i\} - \min_i \{r_i\} < \max_i \{q_i\} - \min_i \{q_i\}$$

before applying algorithm (4.2.1.2). This revised algorithm is of remarkable quality, as indicated by tables A.1.2 and A.1.3.

Table A.1.4 shows the effect of precedence constraints, investigated only with respect to algorithms (4.2.1.2) and (4.2.1.2)'. For problems with $P \geq 0.15$, most of the solution time is spent on adjusting the r_i and q_i in accordance with the precedence constraints; this takes 0.06 seconds for $n = 20$, $P = 0.15$ and 0.70 seconds for $n = 80$, $P = 0.45$. Branching occurred very rarely for larger values of P. Inversion leads to some improvement, although not so spectacular as in tables A.1.2 and A.1.3.

We conclude that algorithms (4.2.1.1), (4.2.1.2) and especially (4.2.1.2)' are able to solve $n|1|r_i \geq 0, prec|L'_{\max}$ problems of reasonable size fairly quickly.

Appendix 2

The $n|1||\Sigma c_i$ problem

The $n|1||\Sigma c_i$ algorithm described in sections 4.3.3.1 and 4.3.3.2 has been extensively tested and compared with Shwimer's algorithm and a simple form of lexicographic enumeration.

2.1. IMPLEMENTATION

The $n|1||\Sigma c_i$ algorithm incorporates the *elimination criteria* presented in section 4.3.3.1. It was mentioned in section 4.3.3.1 that precedence cycles can be avoided by continuous updating of A_i and B_i and by restriction to pairs (i, j) with $i \notin B_j \cup A_j$. In principle, all the elimination criteria can be applied in every node: $\bar{S}$ decreases and A_i and B_i increase as we progress through the search tree. This leads, however, to complicated and time-consuming bookkeeping. Therefore, only corollary 4.23 was applied in every node, whereas corollaries 4.16, 4.19, 4.17 and 4.21 are only used in the root node where $S = \emptyset$. They are implemented by running through them in the above order until no further improvement is possible. If after this process $P(B_i) + p_i > d_i$ for some i, we can put $d_i := P(B_i) + p_i$, thereby incurring costs $w_i(P(B_i) + p_i - d_i)$ and increasing the chances on application of corollary 4.23.

The latter corollary is checked in every node. It is also the only elimination criterion incorporated in the lexicographic enumeration algorithm. Shwimer's algorithm employs corollaries 4.16 and 4.23.

Implementation of the *lower bound* has been partly described in section 4.3.3.2. In every node, we have available a feasible dual solution and a partial primal solution. If we want to calculate $LB^*(\bar{S})$, the linear assignment algorithm used for this purpose should preferably make use of these initial solutions and should also yield a sequence of non-decreasing dual solutions, each of which may lead to early elimination of the node. After comparing a number of available algorithms with respect to these desiderata, Dorhout's algorithm [Dorhout 1975] was found to be most suitable. This algorithm can be considered as a synthesis of ideas proposed in [Tabourier 1972] and [Tomizawa 1971]. Essentially, the algorithm works on a complete bipartite graph $G = (\bar{S}, M, E)$ where $\bar{S}$ and M correspond to unscheduled jobs and unfilled positions respectively; edge $e_{ij} \in E$ has weight $w_{ij} = c_{ij} - u_i - v_j$. The algorithm starts with a feasible dual solution (u_i, v_j) and a partial primal solution (x_{ij}), orthogonal to the dual one; (x_{ij}) defines a *matching* on G. The algorithm constructs the shortest path from any *exposed* vertex $i \in \bar{S}$ (*i.e.*, $x_{ij} = 0$ for all j) to the nearest exposed vertex in M, using Dijkstra's shortest path algorithm. The matching is then augmented and the dual solution is changed in such a way that feasibility is maintained and orthogonality is restored.

2.2. TEST DATA

We now describe the way in which we generated random data on which to test these three methods. The reasons for this detailed approach will become apparent as we proceed.

Given the number of jobs n, each problem is completely specified by $3n$ values (p_i, d_i, w_i) $(i = 1, \ldots, n)$. These values correspond to processing times, due dates and weights respectively. We regard the n triples as a three-dimensional sample from a joint distribution with density function $f(x, y, z)$.

In all our tests, the third random variable $\underline{w}$ is independent of p and $\underline{d}$. We have

$$f(x, y, z) = f_{pd}(x, y) f_w(z)$$

where $\underline{w}$ is uniformly distributed over the interval (4.5, 15.5).

In what follows, we shall introduce four parameters that determine $f_{pd}(x, y)$ and that we believed *a priori* to be of possible influence on any algorithm's performance. In fact, three of them are already mentioned as such in [Srinivasan 1971] and [Baker and Martin 1974]. These articles indicate that the choice of a particular function may have a strong influence on the performance of any tardiness algorithm in a way that may be characteristic for the algorithm in question.

The first parameter measures the *correlation between p and $\underline{d}$*, $\rho(\underline{p}, \underline{d})$. It is intuitively plausible that there may be a significant difference between problems where longer jobs also tend to have later due dates, and problems where there is no correlation whatsoever. If $w_i = 1/n$ for all i, then a problem with perfect correlation can be trivially solved by ordering the jobs according to non-decreasing d_i [Emmons 1969]. To investigate the influence of correlation we use two different sorts of functions $f_{pd}(x, y)$. Either

$$f_{pd}(x, y) = f_p(x)f_d(y),$$

in which case p and $\underline{d}$ are independent random variables and $\rho(\underline{p}, \underline{d}) = 0$, or

$$f_{pd}(x, y) = f_p(x)f_{d|p}(y|x),$$

in which case the due date generated depends explicitly on the processing time and $\rho(\underline{p}, \underline{d})$ depends on the particular form of the density functions involved.

In both cases, $\underline{p}$ is normally distributed with expectation μ_p and variance σ_p^2. We arbitrarily fix $\mu_p = 100$. With regards to σ_p^2 however, we have to introduce as the second possibly significant parameter the *relative variation of processing times* $s = \sigma_p/\mu_p$. We introduce s because lower bound $LB^*(\bar{S})$ will presumably be sharper when processing times differ relatively little, as will be obvious from section 4.3.3.2. Hence, we may expect problems with small s to be relatively easy for our algorithm.

In the case of non-correlated $\underline{p}$ and $\underline{d}$, $\underline{d}$ is uniformly distributed with expectation μ_d and variance $\sigma_d^2 = \lambda_d^2/12$, where λ_d denotes the length of the interval on which $f_d(y) > 0$.

We fix μ_d by introducing as a third parameter the *average tardiness factor* $t = 1 - \mu_d/(n\mu_p)$. The value of t roughly indicates the average fraction of jobs that will be late. Problems with $t = 1$ or $t = 0$ tend to be easy; if all jobs are late, then ordering the jobs according to non-decreasing p_i/w_i produces an optimal schedule, and if we find by ordering the jobs according to non-decreasing d_i that no job is late, then clearly this schedule is optimal. In [Srinivasan 1971], problems where t is near 0.65 were found to be most difficult.

Finally, λ_d is fixed by the fourth parameter, the *relative range of due dates* $r = \lambda_d/(n\mu_p)$. Intuitively, a larger r increases the number of times that corollaries 4.19 and 4.21 can be applied, thereby speeding up computations.

In the case of correlated $\underline{p}$ and $\underline{d}$, $\underline{d}/\underline{p} = p$ is again uniformly distributed, with $\mu_{d|p}$ and $\lambda_{d|p}$ specified analogously by $t = 1 - \mu_{d|p}/(np)$ and $r = \lambda_{d|p}/(np)$. Specific values of s, t and r determine the value of $\rho(\underline{p}, \underline{d})$. We have

$$\rho(\underline{p}, \underline{d}) = \frac{1 - t}{\sqrt{(1 + 1/s^2)r^2/12 + (1 - t)^2}},$$

as can be established by straightforward calculations.

Choosing for non-correlated or correlated $\underline{p}$ and $\underline{d}$, and fixing s, t and r, we can generate n triples (p_i, d_i, w_i) and test the three algorithms on the problem so generated. Each generated value is rounded off to the nearest integer, and if a negative d_i is generated, we reset $d_i = 0$, which implies adding a constant to $c_i(t)$ and therefore does not influence the final schedule.

2.3. COMPUTATIONAL RESULTS

We generated a set of 48 problems for $n = 10$ and for $n = 15$ and 24 problems for $n = 20$. The four parameters, defined in 2.2, were set at various values in order to detect their influence on the three algorithms. These algorithms were coded in ALGOL 60 and run on the Control Data Cyber 73-28 computer of the SARA Computing Centre in Amsterdam.

The computational results can be found in tables A.2.1 and A.2.2. As to the measures of performance, we remark that the *solution time* in table A.2.1 is measured in CPU-seconds, the *number of nodes* in table A.2.2 includes eliminated potential descendant nodes, a *median* was calculated only if more than half of the problems finished in time, and a *maximum* only if all problems finished in time.

The results are classified according to the value of the *average tardiness factor t*, this factor having the major influence on the performance of the algorithms. There is a significant difference between 'easy' problems with $t = 0.2$ or $t = 0.4$ and 'difficult' problems with $t = 0.6$ or $t = 0.8$.

On the easy problems, lexicographic enumeration is rather successful and runs quickly through large numbers of nodes. Also Shwimer's algorithm

Table A.2.1. Solution times.

n	t	number of problems	MEDIAN			MAXIMUM		
			Gen. Alg.	Shwimer	Lex. Enum.	Gen. Alg.	Shwimer	Lex. Enum.
10	0.2	24	0.08	0.02	0.02	0.26	0.11	0.04
	0.6	24	0.57	0.77	1.35	3.32	42.41	47.92
15	0.2	12	0.02	0.04	0.02	0.55	0.31	0.28
	0.4	12	0.77	0.57	0.17	8.16	3.86	14.75
	0.6	12	6.29	76.68	>60	121.82	$>300(\,3\times)$	$>60(10\times)$
	0.8	12	45.61	>300	>60	85.56	$>300(12\times)$	$>60(12\times)$
20	0.2	6	0.78	0.17	0.09	1.19	0.32	0.24
	0.4	6	1.10	2.23	1.74	20.31	10.19	21.64
	0.6	6	180.75	>300	>60	$>300(2\times)$	$>300(6\times)$	$>60(6\times)$
	0.8	6	>300	>300	>60	$>300(3\times)$	$>300(6\times)$	$>60(6\times)$

Table A.2.2. Number of nodes.

n	t	number of problems	MEDIAN			MAXIMUM		
			Gen. Alg.	Shwimer	Lex. Enum.	Gen. Alg.	Shwimer	Lex. Enum.
10	0.2	24	1	2	6	8	14	64
	0.6	24	56	132	3239	456	12284	96328
15	0.2	12	1	1	1	28	69	572
	0.4	12	44	86	305	541	586	36231
	0.6	12	647	13066	–	9564	–	–
	0.8	12	4532	–	–	9952	–	–
20	0.2	6	9	12	105	29	29	580
	0.4	6	25	281	3564	1206	1130	57671
	0.6	6	11105	–	–	–	–	–
	0.8	6	–	–	–	–	–	–

performs well, notably for $n = 15$ and $t = 0.4$. In fact, Shwimer tested his method only on problems where $t = (n - 1)/2n$, *i.e.* $t = 0.47$ for $n = 15$. The general $n|1||\sum c_i$ algorithm exhibits a satisfactory and steady behaviour. Both the median and maximum numbers of nodes examined by this method are significantly smaller than the numbers for the other two methods, so the lower bound $LB^*(\bar{S})$ is indeed more effective in pruning the search tree. For these problems, however, it seems hardly worthwhile to spend much time on the computation of sophisticated lower bounds.

Turning to the difficult problems, we see that the general algorithm is by far superior to the other algorithms. This is most clearly shown by the results for the problems with 15 or 20 jobs. Of the latter set of twelve problems, lexicographic enumeration and Shwimer's method do not finish any problem at all; the other algorithm succeeds in finishing seven of them. The measures of performance become completely worthless in this situation. It is of interest to note, however, that the best solutions to unfinished problems, found by the general algorithm, are better than Shwimer's. Our results seem to contradict Srinivasan's remark that problems with $t = 0.65$ are the most difficult ones; problems with $t = 0.8$ are clearly the most difficult here.

We will now discuss the influence of the remaining three parameters ρ, s and t on the performance of the algorithms.

As to the *correlation ρ*, no influence at all could be demonstrated.

The *relative variation of processing times s* has a significant influence for problems with 15 or 20 jobs, as demonstrated by the sign test ($\alpha < 0.02$).

For $n = 20$, eleven out of twelve problems with $s = 0.05$ were finished with a median solution time of 8 seconds, while only eight out of twelve problems with $s = 0.25$ were finished with a median of 150 seconds. On the average, 70 percent of the nodes were eliminated by the underestimate LB' or by Elmaghraby's lemma when $s = 0.05$, and only 40 percent when $s = 0.25$. Furthermore, the first complete schedule, corresponding to the assignment in the root node, was at worst 1 percent from the optimum when $s = 0.05$ and at worst 20 percent when $s = 0.25$. As expected $LB^*(\bar{S})$ depends heavily on s.

Finally, the *relative range of due dates r* has a considerable influence. Problems with $r = 0.95$ are significantly easier than problems with $r = 0.20$.

Appendix 3

The $n|m|P|C_{\max}$ problem

The computational performance of the elimination criteria and lower bounds presented in sections 6.1.1 and 6.1.2 has been extensively investigated.

3.1. IMPLEMENTATION

In this section we shall discuss in detail the implementation of each lower bound that was tested. For all lower bounds except $LB(Z, (\triangle\square\triangle))$ we replaced r_{iu} by $C(\sigma, u)$; since each of these bounds only involves $\min_{i \in S} \{r_{iu}\}$ very little is gained and, in fact, solution times are increased by using r_{iu} instead of $C(\sigma, u)$.

In each case we applied a recursive search strategy of the restricted flooding type where descendant nodes are chosen in order of nondecreasing lower bounds. Hence, we can distinguish two types of calculations:
- calculations performed once in the root node of the search tree;
- calculations performed in the node corresponding to σ in order to obtain lower bounds $LB(W, \Omega)$ for all σi $(i \in \bar{S})$.

(i) $LB(Z, (*\square*))$
- In the root node q_{iu} is calculated for all (i, u) in $O(mn)$ steps.
- For each M_u, $\sum_{i \in S} p_{iu}$ is calculated and indices i'_u and i''_u with

$$q_{i_u', u} = \min_{i \in S} \{q_{iu}\},$$

$$q_{i_u'', u} = \min_{i \in S - \{i_u'\}} \{q_{iu}\}$$

are found in $O(\bar{s})$ steps. For each choice $i \in \bar{S}$, $LB(u, u, (*\square*))$ is then calculated in $O(1)$ steps as

$$\max(C(\sigma, u), C(\sigma i, u - 1)) + \sum_{i \in S} p_{iu} + \begin{cases} q_{i_{u'}, u} & \text{if } i \neq i_u', \\ q_{i_{u''}, u} & \text{if } i = i_u'. \end{cases}$$

Altogether, calculation of $LB(Z, (*\square*))$ for all σi $(i \in \bar{S})$ requires $O(m\bar{s})$ steps.

(ii) $LB(Z, (*\square\triangle))$

We do not consider $LB(Z, (\triangle\square*))$; this bound performed very poorly in some initial testing.

- In the root node the q_{iu} are calculated and, for all u, ordered into a non-decreasing sequence in $O(mn \log n)$ steps.
- For each choice $i \in \bar{S}$, $LB(u, u, (*\square\triangle))$ is calculated in $O(\bar{s})$ steps by processing $\{J_j | j \in \bar{S} - \{i\}\}$ according to the ordering found in the root node. Calculation of $LB(Z, (*\square\triangle))$ for all σi $(i \in \bar{S})$ requires $O(m\bar{s}^2)$ steps.

(iii) $LB(Z, (\triangle\square\triangle))$

- In the root node the q_{iu} are calculated and ordered in $O(mn \log n)$ steps.
- Calculation of $LB(Z, (\triangle\square\triangle))$ for all σi $(i \in \bar{S})$ requires the solution of $O(m\bar{s})$ $n|1|r_i \geq 0|L'_{\max}$ problems.

(iv) *Job-based bound*

- In the root node $p_{i(u,m)}$ and $\min(p_{iu}, p_{im})$ are calculated for all (i, u) in $O(mn)$ steps.
- The job-based bound for σi on M_u can be rewritten as follows:

$$C(\sigma i, u) + \max_{j \in S - \{i\}} \{p_{j(u,m)} + \sum_{h \in S - \{i, j\}} \min(p_{hu}, p_{hm})\}$$

$$= C(\sigma i, u) + \tau_u - \min(p_{iu}, p_{im}) + \max_{j \in S - \{i\}} \{v_{ju}\}$$

where

$$\tau_u = \sum_{h \in S} \min(p_{hu}, p_{hm}),$$

$$v_{ju} = p_{j(u,m)} - \min(p_{ju}, p_{jm}).$$

Accordingly, for each M_u, τ_u and v_{ju} $(j \in \bar{S})$ and indices i_u' and i_u'' with

$$v_{i_{u'}, u} = \max_{j \in S} \{v_{ju}\},$$

$$v_{i_{u''}, u} = \max_{j \in S - \{i_{u'}\}} \{v_{ju}\}$$

are found in $O(\bar{s})$ steps. For each choice $i \in \bar{S}$, the bound on M_u is then calculated in $O(1)$ steps as

$$C(\sigma i, u) + \tau_u - \min(p_{iu}, p_{im}) + \begin{cases} v_{i_u', u} & \text{if } i \neq i_u', \\ v_{i_u'', u} & \text{if } i = i_u'. \end{cases}$$

Altogether, calculation of the job-based bound for all σi ($i \in \bar{S}$) requires $O(m\bar{s})$ steps.

(v) $LB(W, (*\square \triangle \square*))$
(v-i) $W^* = \{(u, m) | u = 1, \ldots, m - 1\}$.
(v-ii) W^{**} consists of m pairs of critical machines for which $\sum p_{iu}$, $\sum p_{iv}$ and $\sum (p_{iu} + p_{iv})$ are relatively high; these pairs are determined in $O(mn)$ steps.

- In the root node the $p_{iu} + p_{i(u+1, v-1)}$ and $p_{i(u+1, v-1)} + p_{iv}$ are calculated and an optimal order of the jobs with respect to $LB^*(u, v, (*\square \triangle \square*))$ is found for all $(u, v) \in W$ in $O(mn \log n)$ steps.
- Note that for any subset of unscheduled jobs an optimal order with respect to $LB^*(u, v, (*\square \triangle \square*))$ has been determined in the root node. Calculation of $LB(W, (*\square \triangle \square*))$ for all σi ($i \in \bar{S}$) can now easily be seen to require $O(m\bar{s}^2)$ steps.

The value of the best solution found during the tree search provides an upper bound on the value of the optimal solution. In the root node a heuristic method is used to obtain an initial upper bound. Two well-known methods are available for this purpose.

(a) [Palmer 1965]
Calculate *slope indices*

$$\zeta_i \triangleq \sum_{k=1}^{m} \left(k - \frac{m+1}{2} \right) p_{ik} \qquad\qquad (i = 1, \ldots, n),$$

order the jobs according to nondecreasing ζ_i and evaluate the resulting $n|m|P|C_{\max}$ schedule. This procedure requires $O(\max(mn, n \log n))$ steps.

(b) [Campbell *et al.* 1970]
For $l = 1, \ldots, m - 1$, apply the $n|2|P|C_{\max}$ algorithm using processing times $\sum_{k=1}^{l} p_{ik}$ and $\sum_{k=m+1-l}^{m} p_{ik}$ ($i = 1, \ldots, n$) and evaluate the resulting processing order as an $n|m|P|C_{\max}$ schedule. Choose the best solution value as initial upper bound. This procedure requires $O(mn \log n)$ steps.

The second method turned out to produce superior results. In the case of $LB(W, (*\Box\triangle\Box*))$ it also outperformed evaluation of the optimal $LB^*(u, v, (*\Box\triangle\Box*))$ schedule for all $(u, v) \in W$. Accordingly, in each implementation heuristic (b) was chosen to provide an initial upper bound.

The elimination criteria were combined with some of the more successful lower bounds.

In order to find out if σi is dominated by σji, it is sufficient to check condition (v) of section 6.1.1. It follows easily that in that case

$$(A.3\text{-}1) \quad p_{j1} \leqq p_{jk} \qquad\qquad (k = 2, \ldots, m).$$

The dominance relation is transitive; however, the stronger condition (v) need not be transitive and we have to check (v) for each pair (i, j) such that (A.3-1) holds for j. Dominance cycles can occur and have to be avoided. Altogether, application of elimination criterion (v) for all $i, j \in \bar{S}$ requires $O(m\bar{s}^2)$ calculations.

3.2. TEST DATA

For each test problem with n jobs and m machines, mn integer data p_{ik} were generated from uniform distributions between α_{ik} and β_{ik}. The parameters α_{ik} and β_{ik} are determined by the following two aspects, thought to be of possible influence on an algorithm's performance:
- *correlation* between the processing times of a job, in the sense that the p_{ik} ($k = 1, \ldots, m$) are consistently relatively large or relatively small; for problems with correlation, n additional integers ε_i were randomly drawn from $\{1, 2, 3, 4, 5\}$;
- a *trend* within the processing times p_{ik} as k increases.

For each chosen combination of n and m, four groups of three problems each were generated according to Table A.3.1. A second set of twelve problems was obtained by inversion, *i.e.*, by renumbering M_k as M_{m+1-k} for $k = 1, \ldots, m$; thus, problems with a positive trend are transformed into problems with a negative trend.

Table A.3.1. Test data.

$\alpha_{ik}: \beta_{ik}$	no trend		positive trend	
no correlation	1	: 100	$12\frac{1}{2}(k-1)+1$	$: 12\frac{1}{2}(k-1)+100$
correlation	$20\varepsilon_i+1:$	$20\varepsilon_i+20$	$2\frac{1}{2}(k-1)+20\varepsilon_i+1:$	$2\frac{1}{2}(k-1)+20\varepsilon_i+20$

3.3. COMPUTATIONAL RESULTS

The algorithms were coded in ALGOL 60 and run on the Control Data Cyber 73-28 of the SARA Computing Centre in Amsterdam. Tables A.3.2, 3, 4, 5 show the computational results.

First, all lower bounds were tested on three sets of problems with $n|m$ equal to $6|3$, $6|5$ and $6|8$ respectively. These experiments indicate that the 'one-machine bounds' $LB(Z, (*\square*))$, $LB(Z, (*\square\triangle))$ and $LB(Z, (\triangle\square\triangle))$ produce inferior results. Furthermore, the job-based bound can be combined quite successfully with $LB(Z, (*\square*))$ or $LB(Z, (*\square\triangle))$; the latter combination dominates the former one but leads to increased solution times.

Consequently, only the bound $LB(McM) \triangleq \max(LB(Z, (*\square*))$, job-based bound) from [McMahon 1971] and both 'two-machine-bounds' $LB(W^*, (*\square\triangle\square*))$ and $LB(W^{**}, (*\square\triangle\square*))$ were compared on larger problems with $n|m$ equal to $10|3$, $10|5$, $15|3$, $20|3$, $20|5$ and $50|3$. Since $LB(W^*, (*\square\triangle\square*))$ dominates $LB(McM)$, the search tree created by the former bound is in most cases smaller than the tree created by the latter bound. However, $LB(W^*, (*\square\triangle\square*))$ is computationally more expensive. The behaviour of $LB(W^{**}, (*\square\triangle\square*))$ is rather erratic. Note that quite often these two-machine bounds achieve the minimum number of nodes, which is equal to $n + 1$ in the case that the initial upper bound is optimal and $\frac{1}{2}n(n + 1)$ otherwise.

An increase in the number of machines drastically increases the solution times. Less than half of the $20|5$ problems could be solved within one minute.

The same three bounds were combined with the elimination criteria. Previous research [McMahon 1971] indicates that these criteria have a positive influence on solution times only for small problems. In our experiments this was confirmed only with respect to $LB(McM)$. An explanation of this phenomenon might be that the computational requirements of the elimination criteria are of a larger order of magnitude than the requirements of this lower bound. In combination with $LB(W, (*\square\triangle*))$, however, use of elimination criteria leads to significant decreases in solution times and numbers of unsolved problems. Apparently, the elimination criteria eliminate nodes that would be eliminated by lower bounds in any case, but do so with less computational effort.

Altogether, the best results were obtained with algorithms incorporating the elimination criteria and $LB(W, (*\square\triangle*))$. Table A.3.4 indicates that if one minute running time is available to solve a particular problem, it should be allocated to such an algorithm.

Table A.3.2. Median solution times.

EC LB	− (i)	− (ii)	− (iii)	− (iv)	− (ii, iv)	− (i, iv)	− (v-i)	− (v-ii)	+ (i, iv)	+ (v-i)	+ (v-ii)
6|3	.17	.26	.38	.08	.13	.07	.05	.06	.07	.05	.06
6|5	.63	1.18	2.57	.18	.26	.15	.16	.39	.14	.13	.32
6|8	1.03	1.39	3.17	.18	.28	.19	.22	1.06	.18	.25	.86
10|3						.20	.25	.34	.21	.18	.25
10|5						.91	.40	6.22	1.09	.42	3.62
15|3						.34	.57	.89	.48	.41	.49
20|3						.55	.62	.81	2.99	.36	.54
20|5						−	−	−	−	−	−
50|3						3.73	31.60	28.98	−	13.94	27.29

Table A.3.3. Median number of nodes.

EC LB	− (i)	− (ii)	− (iii)	− (iv)	− (ii, iv)	− (i, iv)	− (v-i)	− (v-ii)	+ (i, iv)	+ (v-i)	+ (v-ii)
6|3	69	64	60	46	19	23	7	7	16	7	7
6|5	208	203	179	47	33	35	30	54	29	22	36
6|8	260	212	167	26	23	23	16	136	23	19	97
10|3						55	55	55	55	55	55
10|5						290	55	971	220	55	599
15|3						129	120	120	120	120	120
20|3						219	116	116	978	116	116
20|5						−	−	−	−	−	−
50|3						1681	2356	1275	−	1275	1275

Table A.3.4. Numbers of unsolved problems.

EC LB	− (i, iv)	− (v-i)	− (v-ii)	+ (i, iv)	+ (v-i)	+ (v-ii)
6|3	0	0	0	0	0	0
6|5	0	0	0	0	0	0
6|8	0	0	0	0	0	0
10|3	1	1	1	1	1	1
10|5	3	0	8	2	0	7
15|3	7	2	1	5	2	1
20|3	10	6	5	10	2	2
20|5	15	14	19	13	13	18
50|3	11	10	9	12	8	10

Table A.3.5. Numbers of unsolved problems for all $n|m$.

EL LB	(i, iv)		(v-i)		(v-ii)	
correlation → trend ↓	no	yes	no	yes	no	yes
no	1	9	1	6	1	8
no	4	8	3	5	5	8
positive	0	9	0	7	0	8
negative	7	9	4	7	5	8

Legend

Each entry in Tables A.3.2, 3, 4 (Table A.3.5) represents 24 (27) test problems.

Solution times: CPU seconds on a Control Data Cyber 73-28.

Numbers of nodes: including eliminated nodes.

Numbers of unsolved problems: with a time limit of 60 seconds.

EC: elimination criteria; see section 6.1.1. A '+' indicates that criterion (v) was incorporated.

LB: lower bound; see section 6.1.2. If more than one bound is indicated, the maximum of the two lower bound values has been used.

   (i)   : $LB(Z, (* \square *))$;

   (ii)   : $LB(Z, (* \square \triangle))$;

   (iii) : $LB(Z, (\triangle \square \triangle))$;

   (iv)   : *Job-based bound*;

   (v-i) : $LB(W*, (* \square \triangle \square *))$;

   (v-ii) : $LB(W**, (* \square \triangle \square *))$.

$n|m$: number of jobs | number of machines.

Finally, table A.3.5 indicates that both correlation and trends influence the computational performance. Problems with correlation are definitely more difficult. Also, problems with a negative trend are more difficult than problems with a positive trend, confirming earlier impressions [McMahon 1971] that it is helpful to invert a problem if that leads to 'fuller' machines M_k for $k > \frac{1}{2}m$.

Appendix 4

The $n|m|G|C_{\max}$ problem

The two approaches to the general job-shop problem sketched in sections 6.3.1 and 6.3.2 have been the subject of some limited computational experiments.

4.1. IMPLEMENTATION

Algorithm (6.3.2.1), obtained by combining $LB_k^*(D)$ with the procedure 'actsched', has been implemented with a restricted flooding search strategy. For all test problems $|J_i \cap M_k| \leq 1$, so that $LB_k'''(D)$ and $LB_k^*(D)$ provide equally strong lower bounds. From previous computational experiments, it appears useful to find a feasible schedule heuristically in some or all nodes of the search tree in order to adjust the upper bound. Evaluation of the optimal one-machine schedules found during the calculation of $LB_k'''(D)$ turned out to produce bad results. Accordingly, a priority rule was used, whereby highest priority was granted to the scheduleable operation

$$O_r \in Q = \{O_s | t_s < t_{r_0} + p_{r_0} = \min\{t_q + p_q | O_q \in S\}, \mu(O_s) = \mu(O_{r_0})\}$$

minimizing $\max(H_r, H_r')$, where

$$H_r \overset{\triangle}{=} t_r + \sum_{\substack{\mu(O_s)=\mu(O_r) \\ O_s \in T}} p_s$$

$$H_r' \overset{\triangle}{=} \max_{O_s \in Q - \{O_r\}} \{t_r + p_r + \sum_{\substack{\iota(O_q)=\iota(O_s) \\ O_q \in T}} p_q\}.$$

Algorithm (6.3.2.2), obtained by combining $LB_k^*(D)$ with the branching rule described in section 6.3.2.2, was implemented with a newest active node search strategy; in the upper levels of the search tree lower bounds $LB(D_{rs})$ and $LB(D_{sr})$ are mostly equal in any case. In this particular implementation, machines on which a conflict exists were explicitly identified during the

Table A.4.1. Test problems.

problem	130404			130504			360606		
n	4			5			6		
m	4			4			6		
optimum	35			13			55		
source				[Nemeti 1964]			[Muth and Thompson 1963 p. 236]		

r	$\iota(O_r)$	$\mu(O_r)$	p_r	$\iota(O_r)$	$\mu(O_r)$	p_r	$\iota(O_r)$	$\mu(O_r)$	p_r
1	1	1	6	1	1	2	1	3	1
2	1	3	9	1	2	3	1	1	3
3	1	4	5	2	1	3	1	2	6
4	2	2	7	2	3	3	1	4	7
5	2	3	6	2	2	2	1	6	3
6	2	4	7	3	1	1	1	5	6
7	3	2	3	3	2	3	2	2	8
8	3	1	7	3	4	2	2	3	5
9	3	4	6	4	1	4	2	5	10
10	3	3	4	4	4	1	2	6	10
11	4	2	9	4	3	3	2	1	10
12	4	1	6	5	4	4	2	4	4
13	4	4	5	5	3	4	3	3	5
14							3	4	4
15							3	6	8
16							3	1	9
17							3	2	1
18							3	5	7
19							4	2	5
20							4	1	5
21							4	3	5
22							4	4	3
23							4	5	8
24							4	6	9
25							5	3	9
26							5	2	3
27							5	5	5
28							5	6	4
29							5	1	3
30							5	4	1
31							6	2	3
32							6	4	3
33							6	6	9
34							6	1	10
35							6	5	4
36							6	3	1

calculation of $LB_k^*(D)$; among these the machine M_k maximizing $LB_k^*(D)$ was chosen for the branching operation. A branching pair $\{r_0, s_0\}$ was chosen either by maximizing $\min(t_r + p_r - t_s, t_s + p_s - t_r)$ (strategy B1) or by maximizing P_{rs}^* over all conflicts (strategy B2).

For each of these two possibilities, the choice between D_{rs} or D_{sr} for further exploration was made by minimizing either $t_r + p_r - t_s$ (strategy S1) or $P_{rs} = t_r + p_r - T_s$ (strategy S2). Hence, four variations on this approach were tested altogether. We note that the use of additional conditions embodied in theorem 6.7 mainly resulted in further increases in running time.

4.2. TEST DATA

The algorithms were tested on three problems, two of which appear in the literature. The data for these problems are presented in table A.4.1.

4.3. COMPUTATIONAL RESULTS

The algorithms were coded in ALGOL 60 and run on the Control Data Cyber 73-28 of the SARA Computing Centre in Amsterdam.

Table A.4.2 shows the results obtained with algorithm (6.3.2.1) on the three test problems. In strategy E1 no attempts were made to find good feasible schedules in order to adjust the upper bound. In strategy E2, the one-machine schedules obtained during the calculation of $LB_k'''(D)$ were used for this purpose; evaluating them as an overall schedule produced rather bad results. Use of the priority rule introduced in section 4.2 in every node (E3) produced slightly better results. Strategy E4 involves the use of this heuristic on four levels of the search tree; this produced still better results, as will be clear from table A.4.2.

Table A.4.2. Results for algorithm (6.3.2.1).

problem	solution time				number of nodes			
	E1	E2	E3	E4	E1	E2	E3	E4
130404	.21	.27	.45	.35	19	8	8	8
130504	.30	.28	.28	.21	22	11	5	5
360606	5.39	9.15	6.87	2.83	279	279	62	62

Table A.4.3. Results for algorithm (6.3.2.2).

	problem	solution time		number of nodes	
		S1	S2	S1	S2
B1	130404	.92	.93	23	23
	130504	.40	.32	13	11
	360606	29.88	15.91	347	175
B2	130404	.59	.58	15	15
	130504	.51	.28	17	11
	360606	36.39	15.24	411	181

Results obtained with algorithm (6.3.2.2) are collected in table A.4.3. The choice of B1 or B2 only has a minor influence on the algorithm's performance. On the other hand, strategy S2 based on the penalties P_{rs} is clearly superior to strategy S1 based on $t_r + p_r - t_s$. Altogether, algorithm (6.3.2.2) is clearly worse than algorithm (6.3.2.1). On somewhat larger problems (*e.g.*, the $10|10|G|C_{max}$ problem and the $20|5|G|C_{max}$ problem given in [Muth and Thompson 1963]) both algorithms failed conspicuously to produce an optimal schedule within 5 minutes running time. In view of the fact that previous experiments [McMahon and Florian 1975] confirm that algorithm (6.3.2.1) is the currently best $n|m|G|C_{max}$ algorithm, this clearly indicates that in spite of some progress a large amount of work in this area remains to be done.

References

AGARWAL, A. K. (1975), 'Multiple reversal procedure in an implicit enumeration algorithm for machine sequencing via disjunctive graphs', unpublished manuscript.

AGIN, N. (1966), 'Optimum seeking with branch and bound', *Management Science*, vol. 13, pp. B-176-185.

ANTHONISSE, J. M. and VAN EMDE BOAS, P. (1974), 'Are polynomial algorithms really good?', Report BW 40, Mathematisch Centrum, Amsterdam.

ARTHANARI, T. S. and MUKHOPADHYAY, A. C. (1971), 'A note on a paper by W. Szwarc', *Naval Research Logistics Quarterly*, vol. 18, pp. 135-138.

ASHOUR, S. (1970), 'A branch-and-bound algorithm for flow-shop scheduling problems', *AIIE Transactions*, vol. 2, pp. 172-176.

ASHOUR, S. (1972), *Sequencing Theory*, Berlin, Springer-Verlag.

ASHOUR, S. and HIREMATH, S. R. (1973), 'A branch-and-bound approach to the job-shop scheduling problem', *International Journal of Production Research*, vol. 11, pp. 47-58.

ASHOUR, S. and PARKER, R. G. (1971), 'A precedence graph algorithm for the shop scheduling problem', *Operational Research Quarterly*, vol. 22, pp. 165-175.

ASHOUR, S., CHIN, K. Y. and MOORE, T. E. (1973), 'An optimal schedule time of a job shop-like disjunctive graph', *Networks*, vol. 3, pp. 333-349.

ASHOUR, S., MOORE, T. E. and CHIN, K. Y. (1974), 'An implicit enumeration algorithm for the nonpreemptive shop scheduling problem', *AIIE Transactions*, vol. 6, pp. 62-72.

BAGGA, P. C. and CHAKRAVARTI, N. K. (1968), 'Optimal m-stage production schedules', *Journal of the Canadian Operations Research Society*, vol. 6, pp. 71-78.

BAKER, K. R. (1973), 'Procedures for sequencing tasks with one resource type', *International Journal of Production Research*, vol. 11, pp. 125-138.

BAKER, K. R. (1974), *Introduction to Sequencing and Scheduling*, New York, Wiley.

BAKER, K. R. and MARTIN, J. B. (1974), 'An experimental comparison of solution algorithms for the single-machine tardiness problem', *Naval Research Logistics Quarterly*, vol. 21, pp. 187-199.

BAKER, K. R. and MERTEN, A. G. (1973), 'Scheduling with parallel processors and linear delay costs', *Naval Research Logistics Quarterly*, vol. 20, pp. 793-804.

BAKER, K. R. and SU, Z. S. (1974), 'Sequencing with due-dates and early start times to minimize maximum tardiness', *Naval Research Logistics Quarterly*, vol. 21, pp. 171-176.

BALAS, E. (1967), 'Discrete programming by the filter method', *Operations Research*, vol. 15, pp. 915-957.

BALAS, E. (1968), 'A note on the branch-and-bound principle', *Operations Research*, vol. 16, pp. 442-445.

BALAS, E. (1969), 'Machine sequencing via disjunctive graphs: an implicit enumeration algorithm', *Operations Research*, vol. 17, pp. 941-957.

BALAS, E. (1970), 'Machine sequencing: disjunctive graphs and degree-constrained subgraphs', *Naval Research Logistics Quarterly*, vol. 17, pp. 1-10.

BALAS, E. (1970a), 'Project scheduling with resource constraints', in: Beale, E. M. L. (ed.), *Applications of Mathematical Programming Techniques*, The English Universities Press.

BELLMORE, M. and NEMHAUSER, G. L. (1968), 'The traveling salesman problem: a survey', *Operations Research*, vol. 16, pp. 538–559.

BENNINGTON, G. E. and MCGINNIS, L. F. (1973), 'A critique of project planning with constrained resources', in: Elmaghraby, S. E. (ed.), *Symposium on the Theory of Scheduling and Its Applications*, Berlin, Springer-Verlag.

BORNSTEIN, C. M. (1973), private communication.

BOWMAN, E. H. (1959), 'The schedule-sequencing problem', *Operations Research*, vol. 7, pp. 621–624.

BRATLEY, P., FLORIAN, M. and ROBILLARD, P. (1971), 'Scheduling with earliest start and due-date constraints', *Naval Research Logistics Quarterly*, vol. 18, pp. 511–519.

BRATLEY, P., FLORIAN, M. and ROBILLARD, P. (1973), 'On sequencing with earliest starts and due dates with application to computing bounds for the $(n|m|G|F_{max})$ problem', *Naval Research Logistics Quarterly*, vol. 20, pp. 57–67.

BROOKS, G. H. and WHITE, C. R. (1965), 'An algorithm for finding optimal or near optimal solutions to the production scheduling problem', *Journal of Industrial Engineering*, vol. 16, pp. 34–40.

BROWN, A. P. G. and LOMNICKI, Z. A. (1966), 'Some applications of the "branch-and-bound" algorithm to the machine scheduling problem', *Operational Research Quarterly*, vol. 17, pp. 173–186.

BRUNO, J., COFFMAN, E. G. and SETHI, R. (1974), 'Scheduling independent tasks to reduce mean finishing time', *Communications of the ACM*, vol. 17, pp. 382–387.

CAMPBELL, H. G., DUDEK, R. A. and SMITH, M. L. (1970), 'A heuristic algorithm for the *n* job, *m* machine sequencing problem', *Management Science*, vol. 16, pp. B-630–637.

CHARLTON, J. M. and DEATH, C. C. (1970), 'A generalized machine-scheduling algorithm', *Operational Research Quarterly*, vol. 21, pp. 127–134.

CHARLTON, J. M. and DEATH, C. C. (1970a), 'A method of solution for general machine-scheduling problems', *Operations Research*, vol. 18, pp. 689–707.

COFFMAN, E. G. (ed.) (1975), *Computer and Job-Shop Scheduling Theory*, New York, Wiley.

COFFMAN, E. G. and DENNING, P. S. (1972), *Operating Systems Theory*, Englewood Cliffs, New Jersey, Prentice-Hall.

COFFMAN, E. G. and GRAHAM, R. L. (1972), 'Optimal scheduling for two-processor systems', *Acta Information*, vol. 1, pp. 200–213.

CONWAY, R. W., MAXWELL, W. L. and MILLER, L. W. (1967), *Theory of Scheduling*, Reading, Massachusetts, Addison-Wesley.

COOK, S. A. (1971), 'The complexity of theorem-proving procedures', in: *Proceedings of the 3rd Annual ACM Symposium on the Theory of Computing*.

CUNNINGHAM, A. A. and TURNER, I. B. (1973), 'Decision analysis for job shop scheduling', *Omega*, vol. 1, pp. 733–746.

DANNENBRING, D. G. (1974), 'An evaluation of flow shop sequencing heuristics', Research report, University of North Carolina.

DAVIS, E. W. (1966), 'Resource allocation in project network models – a survey', *Journal of Industrial Engineering*, vol. 17, pp. 177–188.

DAVIS, E. W. (1973), 'Project scheduling under resource constraints – historical review and categorization of procedures', *AIIE Transactions*, vol. 5, pp. 297–313.

DAVIS, E. W. and HEIDORN, G. E. (1971), 'An algorithm for optimal project scheduling under multiple resource constraints', *Management Science*, vol. 17, pp. B-803–816.

DAY, J. and HOTTENSTEIN, M. P. (1970), 'Review of sequencing research', *Naval Research Logistics Quarterly*, vol. 17, pp. 11–39.

DESSOUKY, M. I. and MARGENTHALER, C. R. (1972), 'The one-machine sequencing problem with early starts and due dates', *AIIE Transactions*, vol. 4, pp. 214–222.

DORHOUT, B. (1975), 'Experiments with some algorithms for the linear assignment problem', Report BW 39, Mathematisch Centrum, Amsterdam.

DUTTA, S. K. and CUNNINGHAM, A. A. (1975), 'Sequencing two-machine flow-shops with finite intermediate storage', *Management Science*, vol. 21, pp. 989–996.

DUTTON, J. M. (1964), 'Production-scheduling – a behavioural model', *International Journal of Production Research*, vol. 3.

EASTMAN, W. L. (1959), 'A solution to the traveling salesman problem', *Econometrica*, vol. 27, p. 282.

EASTMAN, W. L., EVEN, S. and ISAACS, I. M. (1964), 'Bounds for the optimal scheduling of n jobs on m processors', *Management Science*, vol. 11, pp. 268–279.

EDMONDS, J. (1965), 'Paths, trees and flowers', *Canadian Journal of Mathematics*, vol. 17, pp. 449–467.

EDMONDS, J. (1965a), 'The chinese postman's problem', *Operations Research*, vol. 13, suppl. 1, p. B-73.

ELMAGHRABY, S. E. (1968), 'The machine scheduling problem - review and extensions', *Naval Research Logistics Quarterly*, vol. 15, pp. 205–232.

ELMAGHRABY, S. E. (1968a), 'The one-machine sequencing problem with delay costs', *Journal of Industrial Engineering*, vol. 19, pp. 105–108.

ELMAGHRABY, S. E. and PARK, S. H. (1974), 'Scheduling jobs on a number of identical machines', *AIIE Transactions*, vol. 6, pp. 1–12.

EMMONS, H. (1969), 'One-machine sequencing to minimize certain functions of job tardiness', *Operations Research*, vol. 17, pp. 701–715.

EMMONS, H. (1973), 'One machine sequencing to minimize mean flow time with minimum number tardy', Technical Memorandum no. 295, Case Western Reserve University.

EMMONS, H. (1974), 'A note on a scheduling problem with dual criteria', unpublished manuscript.

FISHER, M. L. (1973), 'Optimal solution of scheduling problems using Lagrange multipliers, part I', *Operations Research*, vol. 21, pp. 1114–1127.

FISHER, M. L. (1973a), 'Optimal solution of scheduling problems using Lagrange multipliers, part II', in: Elmaghraby, S. E. (ed.), *Symposium on the Theory of Scheduling and Its Applications*, Berlin, Springer-Verlag.

FISHER, M. L. (1974), 'A dual algorithm for the one-machine scheduling problem', to appear in *Mathematical Programming*.

FLORIAN, M., TRÉPANT, P. and MCMAHON, G. B. (1971), 'An implicit enumeration algorithm for the machine scheduling problem', *Management Science*, vol. 17, pp. B-782–792.

FUJII, M., KASAMI, T. and NINOMIYA, K. (1969), 'Optimal sequencing of two equivalent processors', *SIAM Journal on Applied Mathematics*, vol. 17, pp. 784–789.

GAPP, W., MANKEKAR, P. S. and MITTEN, L. G. (1965), 'Sequencing operations to minimize in-process inventory costs', *Management Science*, vol. 11, pp. 476–484.

GAREY, M. R. and GRAHAM, R. L. (1975), 'Bounds for multiprocessor scheduling with resource constraints', *SIAM Journal on Computing*, vol. 4, pp. 187–200.

GAREY, M. R. and JOHNSON, D. S. (1975), 'Scheduling tasks with non-uniform deadlines on two processors', Bell Laboratories, New Jersey.

GAREY, M. R., JOHNSON, D. S. and SETHI, R. (1975), 'The complexity of flowshop and jobshop scheduling', Technical Report 168, The Pennsylvania State University.

GELDERS, L. and KLEINDORFER, P. R. (1974), 'Coordinating aggregate and detailed scheduling decisions in the one-machine job shop: part I. Theory', *Operations Research*, vol. 22, pp. 46–60.

GELDERS, L. and KLEINDORFER, P. R. (1975), 'Coordinating aggregate and detailed scheduling decisions in the one-machine job shop: II-computation and structure', *Operations Research*, vol. 23, pp. 312–324.

GERE, W. S. (1966), 'Heuristics in job shop scheduling', *Management Science*, vol. 13, pp. 167–190.

GIFFLER, B. and THOMPSON, G. L. (1960), 'Algorithms for solving production scheduling problems', *Operations Research*, vol. 8, pp. 487–503.

GILMORE, P. C. and GOMORY, R. E. (1964), 'Sequencing a one state-variable machine: a solvable case of the traveling salesman problem', *Operations Research*, vol. 12, pp. 655–679.

GLOVER, F. (1967), 'Maximum matching in a convex bipartite graph', *Naval Research Logistics Quarterly*, vol. 14, pp. 313–317.

GONZALES, T. and SAHNI, S. (1975), 'Flow-shop and job-shop schedules', Technical Report, University of Minnesota.

GORENSTEIN, S. (1972), 'An algorithm for project (job) sequencing with resource constraints', *Operations Research*, vol. 20, pp. 835–850.

GOYAL, S. K. (1973), 'A note on the paper: On the flow-shop sequencing problem with no wait in process', *Operational Research Quarterly*, vol. 2, pp. 130–133.

GOYAL, S. K. (1975), 'Job-shop sequencing problems with no wait in process', *International Journal of Production Research*, vol. 13, pp. 197–206.

GRABOWSKI, J. and SYSLO, M. M. (1973), 'On some machine sequencing problems (I)', *Zastosowania Matematyki*, vol. 13, pp. 340–345.

GRAHAM, R. L. (1969), 'Bounds on multiprocessing timing anomalies', *SIAM Journal on Applied Mathematics*, vol. 17, pp. 416–429.

GRAHAM, R. L. (1972), 'Bounds on multiprocessing anomalies and related packing anomalies', in: *Proceedings of the 40th AFIPS Conference*.

GREENBERG, H. H. (1968), 'A branch-bound solution to the general scheduling problem', *Operations Research*, vol. 8, pp. 352–361.

GUPTA, J. N. D. (1971), 'Economic aspects of production scheduling systems', *Journal of the Operations Research Society of Japan*, vol. 13, pp. 169–193.

GUPTA, J. N. D. (1971a), 'The generalized n job, m machine scheduling problem', *Opsearch*, vol. 8, pp. 173–185.

HAEHLING VON LANZENAUER, C. and HIMES, R. C. (1970), 'A linear programming solution to the general sequencing problem', *Journal of the Canadian Operations Research Society*, vol. 18, pp. 129–134.

HARDGRAVE, W. W. and NEMHAUSER, G. L. (1963), 'A geometric method and a graphical algorithm for a sequencing problem', *Operations Research*, vol. 12, pp. 655–679.

HECK, H. and ROBERTS, S. (1972), 'A note on the extension of a result on scheduling with secondary criteria', *Naval Research Logistics Quarterly*, vol. 18, pp. 403–405.

HELD, M. and KARP, R. M. (1962), 'A dynamic programming approach to sequencing problems', *Journal of SIAM*, vol. 10, pp. 196–210.

HELLER, J. (1959), 'Combinatorial, probabilistic and statistical aspects of an $M \times J$ scheduling problem', AEC Research and Development Report, New York.

HELLER, J. (1966), 'Some numerical experiments for an $M \times J$ flow-shop and its decision theoretical aspects', *Operations Research*, vol. 8, pp. 178–184.

HORN, W. A. (1972), 'Single-machine job sequencing with treelike precedence ordering and linear delay penalties', *SIAM Journal on Applied Mathematics*, vol. 23, pp. 189–202.

HORN, W. A. (1974), 'Some simple scheduling algorithms', *Naval Research Logistics Quarterly*, vol. 21, pp. 177–185.

HSU, N. C. (1966), 'Elementary proof of Hu's theorem on isotone mappings', *Proceedings of the American Mathematical Society*, vol. 17, pp. 111–114.

HU, T. C. (1961), 'Parallel sequencing and assembly line problems', *Operations Research*, vol. 9, pp. 841–848.

IGNALL, E. and SCHRAGE, L. (1965), 'Application of the branch-and-bound technique to some flow-shop scheduling problems', *Operations Research*, vol. 13, pp. 400–412.

ISAAC, A. M. and TURBAN, E. (1968), 'Some comments on the traveling salesman problem', *Operations Research*, vol. 17, pp. 543–546.

JACKSON, J. R. (1955), 'Scheduling a production line to minimize maximum tardiness', Research Report, University of California at Los Angeles.

JACKSON, J. R. (1956), 'An extension of Johnson's results on job lot scheduling', *Naval Research Logistics Quarterly*, vol. 3, pp. 201–203.

JOHNSON, D. S. (1973), 'Approximation algorithms for combinatorial problems', in: *Proceedings of the 5th Annual ACM Symposium on the Theory of Computing*.

JOHNSON, S. M. (1954), 'Optimal two- and three-stage production schedules with set-up times included', *Naval Research Logistics Quarterly*, vol. 1, pp. 61–68.

JOHNSON, S. M. (1958), 'Discussion: sequencing n jobs on two machines with arbitrary time lags', *Management Science*, vol. 5, pp. 299–303.

KARP, R. M. (1972), 'Reducibility among combinatorial problems', in: Miller, R. E. and Thatcher, J. W. (eds.), *Complexity of Computer Computations*, New York, Plenum Press.

KARP, R. M. (1975), unpublished manuscript.

KNUTH, D. E. (1973), *The Art of Computer Programming*, Vol. III, Reading, Massachusetts, Addison-Wesley.

KNUTH, D. E. (1974), 'A terminological proposal', *SIGACT News*, vol. 6, pp. 12–18.

KOHLER, W. H. and STEIGLITZ, K. (1975), 'Exact, approximate and guaranteed accuracy algorithms for the flow-shop problem $n|2|F|\bar{F}$', *Journal of the ACM*, vol. 22, pp. 106–114.

KRONE, M. J. and STEIGLITZ, K. (1974), 'Heuristic programming solution of a flow-shop scheduling problem', *Operations Research*, vol. 22, pp. 629–638.

LAGEWEG, B. J. (1975), private communication.

LAGEWEG, B. J., LENSTRA, J. K. and RINNOOY KAN, A. H. G. (1975), 'The job-shop scheduling problem', unpublished manuscript.

LAND, A. H. and DOIG, A. G. (1960), 'An automatic method for solving discrete programming problems', *Econometrica*, vol. 28, pp. 497–520.

LAWLER, E. L. (1963), 'The quadratic assignment problem', *Management Science*, vol. 9, pp. 586–599.

LAWLER, E. L. (1964), 'On scheduling problems with deferral costs', *Management Science*, vol. 11, pp. 280–288.

LAWLER, E. L. (1973), 'Optimal sequencing of a single machine subject to precedence constraints', *Management Science*, vol. 19, pp. 544–546.

LAWLER, E. L. (1975), 'Sequencing to minimize the weighted number of tardy jobs', to appear in: *Revue Française d'Automatique, Informatique et Recherche Operationelle*.

LAWLER, E. L. (1975a), 'A "quasi-polynomial" algorithm for sequencing jobs to minimize total tardiness', unpublished manuscript.

LAWLER, E. L. (1975b), 'Optimal sequencing of jobs subject to series parallel precedence constraints', Report BW 54, Mathematisch Centrum, Amsterdam.

LAWLER, E. L. (1976), *Combinatorial Optimization: Networks and Matroids*, New York, Holt, Rinehart and Winston.

LAWLER, E. L. and MOORE, J. M. (1969), 'A functional equation and its application to resource allocation and sequencing problems', *Management Science*, vol. 16, pp. 77–84.

DE LEEDE, E. and RINNOOY KAN, A. H. G. (1975), unpublished manuscript.

LENSTRA, J. K. (1976), *Sequencing by Enumerative Methods*, Mathematisch Centrum, Amsterdam.

LENSTRA, J. K. and RINNOOY KAN, A. H. G. (1973), 'Towards a better algorithm for the jobshop scheduling problem I', Report BN 22, Mathematisch Centrum, Amsterdam.

LENSTRA, J. K. and RINNOOY KAN, A. H. G. (1975), 'A recursive approach to the generation of combinatorial configurations', Working Paper WP/75/25, Graduate School of Management, Delft.

LENSTRA, J. K., RINNOOY KAN, A. H. G. and BRUCKER, P. (1975), 'Complexity of machine scheduling problems', to appear in *Annals of Discrete Mathematics*.

LIU, C. L. (1971), 'A combinatorial study of some scheduling algorithms', Department of Computer Science, University of Illinois.

LIU, C. L. (1972), 'Optimal scheduling on multiprocessor computing systems', in: *Proceedings of the 13th Annual Symposium on Switching and Automata Theory*.

LOFTS, N. R. (1974), 'Multiple allocation of resources in a network – an optimal scheduling algorithm', *Informatica*, vol. 12, pp. 25–38.

LOMNICKI, Z. A. (1965), 'A branch-and-bound algorithm for the exact solution of the three-machine scheduling problem', *Operational Research Quarterly*, vol. 16, pp. 89–100.

MANNE, A. S. (1960), 'On the job shop scheduling problem', *Operations Research*, vol. 8, pp. 219–223.

MASON, A. T. and MOODIE, C. L. (1971), 'A branch and bound algorithm for minimizing cost in project scheduling', *Management Science*, vol. 18, pp. B-158–173.

MCMAHON, G. B. (1969), 'Optimal production schedules for flow shops', *Journal of the Canadian Operations Research Society*, vol. 7, pp. 141–151.

MCMAHON, G. B. (1971), *A Study of Algorithms for Industrial Scheduling Problems*, Ph.D. Thesis, University of New South Wales.

MCMAHON, G. B. and BURTON, P. G. (1967), 'Flow-shop scheduling with the branch-and-bound method', *Operations Research*, vol. 15, pp. 473–481.

MCMAHON, G. B. and FLORIAN, M. (1975), 'On scheduling with ready times and due dates to minimize maximum lateness', *Operations Research*, vol. 23, pp. 475–482.

MCNAUGHTON, R. (1959), 'Sequencing with deadlines and loss functions', *Management Science*, vol. 6, pp. 1–12.

MELLOR, P. (1966), 'A review of job shop scheduling', *Operational Research Quarterly*, vol. 17, pp. 161–171.

MITTEN, L. G. (1958), 'Sequencing *n* jobs on two machines with arbitrary time lags', *Management Science*, vol. 5, pp. 293–298.

MITTEN, L. G. (1970), 'Branch-and-bound methods: general formulation and properties', *Operations Research*, vol. 18, pp. 24–34.

MOODIE, C. L. and MANDEVILLE, D. E. (1965), 'Project resource balancing by assembly line balancing techniques', *Journal of Industrial Engineering*, vol. 17, pp. 377–383.

MOORE, J. M. (1968), 'An *n* job, one machine sequencing algorithm for minimizing the number of late jobs', *Management Science*, vol. 14, pp. 102–109.

MÜLLER-MERBACH, H. (1970), *Optimale Reihenfolgen*, Berlin, Springer-Verlag.

MUTH, J. F. and THOMPSON, G. L. (1963), *Industrial Scheduling*, Englewood Cliffs, New Jersey, Prentice-Hall.

NABESHIMA, I. (1963), 'Sequencing on two machines with start lag and stop lag', *Journal of the Operations Research Society of Japan*, vol. 5, pp. 97–101.

NABESHIMA, I. (1971), 'General scheduling algorithms with applications to parallel scheduling and multiprogramming scheduling', *Journal of the Operations Research Society of Japan*, vol. 14, pp. 72–99.

NEMETI, L. (1964), 'Das Reihenfolgeproblem in der Fertigungsprogrammierung und Linearplanung mit logischen Bedingungen', *Mathematica*, vol. 6, pp. 87–99.

NEPOMIASTCHY, P. (1973), 'Application of the penalty technique to solve a scheduling problem and comparison with combinatorial methods', Rapport de Recherche no. 7, Institut de Recherche d'Informatique et d'Automatique.

NICHOLSON, T. A. J. (1971), 'A method for optimizing permutation problems and its industrial applications', in: Welsh, D. J. A. (ed.), *Combinatorial Mathematics and Its Applications*, Academic Press.

PALMER, D. S. (1965), 'Sequencing jobs through a multi-stage process in the minimum total time – a quick method of obtaining a near optimum', *Operational Research Quarterly*, vol. 16, pp. 101–106.

PIEHLER, J. (1960), 'Ein Beitrag zum Reihenfolgeproblem', *Unternehmensforschung*, vol. 4, pp. 138–142.

PORTER, D. B. (1968), 'The Gantt chart as applied to production scheduling and control', *Naval Research Logistics Quarterly*, vol. 15, pp. 311–317.

PRITSKER, A. A. B., WATTERS, L. J. and WOLFE, P. M. (1969), 'Multiproject scheduling with limited resources: a zero-one programming approach', *Management Science*, vol. 16, pp. 93–108.

RAIFFA, H. and SCHLAIFER, R. (1961), *Applied Statistical Decision Theory*, Boston, Graduate School of Business Administration, Harvard University.

RAIMOND, J. F. (1969), 'Minimaximal paths in disjunctive graphs by direct search', *I.B.M. Journal of Research and Development*, vol. 13, pp. 391–399.

RANDOLPH, P. H., SWINSON, G. and ELLMEYSEN, C. (1973), 'Stopping rules for sequencing problems', *Operations Research*, vol. 21, pp. 1309–1315.

RAU, J. G. (1970), 'Minimizing a function of permutations of n integers', *Operations Research*, vol. 18, pp. 237–240.

REDDI, S. S. and RAMAMOORTHY, C. V. (1972), 'On the flow shop sequencing problem with no wait in process', *Operational Research Quarterly*, vol. 23, pp. 323–331.

REDDI, S. S. and RAMAMOORTHY, C. V. (1973), 'A scheduling problem', *Operational Research Quarterly*, vol. 24, pp. 441–446.

REDDI, S. S. and RAMAMOORTHY, C. V. (1973a), 'Reply to Dr. Goyal's comments', *Operational Research Quarterly*, vol. 24, pp. 133–134.

REDWINE, C. N. and WISMER, D. A. (1974), 'A mixed integer programming model for scheduling orders in a steel mill', *Journal of Optimization Theory and Applications*, vol. 14, pp. 305–318.

REITER, S. and SHERMAN, G. (1965), 'Discrete optimizing', *Journal of SIAM*, vol. 13, pp. 864–889.

RINNOOY KAN, A. H. G. (1974), 'On Mitten's axioms for branch-and-bound', Working paper, Graduate School of Management, Delft.

RINNOOY KAN, A. H. G., LAGEWEG, B. J. and LENSTRA, J. K. (1975), 'Minimizing total costs in one-machine scheduling', *Operations Research*, vol. 23, pp. 908–927.

ROOT, J. G. (1965), 'Scheduling with deadlines and loss functions on k parallel machines', *Management Science*, vol. 11, pp. 460–475.

ROSENKRANTZ, D. J., STEARNS, R. E. and LEWIS, P. M. (1974), 'Approximate algorithms for the traveling salesperson problem', in: *Proceedings of the 15th Annual Symposium on Switching and Automata Theory*.

ROTHKOPF, M. H. (1966), 'Scheduling independent tasks on parallel processors', *Management Science*, vol. 12, pp. 437–447.

ROY, B. (1971), 'Problems and methods with multiple objective functions', *Mathematical Programming*, vol. 1, pp. 239–267.

ROY, B. and SUSSMANN, B. G. (1964), 'Les problèmes d'ordonnancement avec contraintes disjonctives', note D.S. no. 9 bis, SEMA, Montrouge.

SAHNEY, V. K. (1972), 'Single-server, two machine sequencing with switching time', *Operations Research*, vol. 20, pp. 24–36.

SAHNI, S. K. and GONZALEZ, T. (1974), 'P-complete problems and approximate solutions', in: *Proceedings of the 15th Annual Symposium on Switching and Automata Theory*.

SANG, N. and FLORIAN, M. (1970), 'A note on lower bounds for the machine scheduling problem', publication # 49, Departement d'Informatique, Université de Montréal.

SCHILD, A. and FREDMAN, I. J. (1962), 'Scheduling tasks with deadlines and non-linear loss functions', *Management Science*, vol. 9, pp. 73–81.

SCHRAGE, L. (1970), 'Solving resource-constrained network problems by implicit enumeration – non-preemptive case', *Operations Research*, vol. 18, pp. 263–278.

SCHRAGE, L. (1970a), 'A bound based on the equivalence of min-max-completion time and min-max-lateness scheduling objectives', Report 7042, Center for Mathematical Studies in Business and Economics, Department of Economics and Graduate School of Business, University of Chicago.

SCHRAGE, L. (1971), 'Obtaining optimal solutions to resource constrained network scheduling problems', unpublished manuscript.

SHWIMER, J. (1972), 'On the *n*-job, one-machine, sequence-independent scheduling problem with tardiness penalties: a branch-bound solution', *Management Science*, vol. 18, pp. B-301–313.

SIDNEY, J. B. (1975), 'Decomposition algorithms for single-machine sequencing with precedence relations and deferral costs', *Operations Research*, vol. 23, pp. 283–298.

SMITH, W. E. (1956), 'Various optimizers for single-stage production', *Naval Research Logistics Quarterly*, vol. 3, pp. 59–66.

SMITH, R. D. and DUDEK, R. A. (1967), 'A general algorithm for solution of the *n*-job, *M*-machine sequencing problem of the flow shop', *Operations Research*, vol. 15, pp. 71–82.

SMITH, R. D. and DUDEK, R. A. (1969), 'Erratum', *Operations Research*, vol. 17, p. 756.

SRINIVASAN, V. (1971), 'A hybrid algorithm for the one machine sequencing problem to minimize total tardiness', *Naval Research Logistics Quarterly*, vol. 18, pp. 317–327.

STURM, L. B. J. M. (1970), 'A simple optimality proof of Moore's sequencing algorithm', *Management Science*, vol. 17, pp. B-116–118.

SUSSMAN, B. G. (1972), 'Scheduling problems with interval disjunctions', *Zeitschrift für Operations Research*, vol. 16, pp. 165–178.

SYSLO, M. M. (1974), 'On some machine sequencing problems (II)', *Zastosowania Matematyki*, vol. 14, pp. 93–97.

SZWARC, W. (1968), 'On some sequencing problems', *Naval Research Logistics Quarterly*, vol. 15, pp. 127–155.

SZWARC, W. (1971), 'Elimination methods in the $m \times n$ sequencing problem', *Naval Research Logistics Quarterly*, vol. 18, pp. 295–305.

SZWARC, W. (1973), 'Optimal elimination methods in the $m \times n$ flow-shop scheduling problem', *Operations Research*, vol. 21, pp. 1250–1259.

TABOURIER, Y. (1972), 'Un algorithme pour le problème d'affectation', *Revue Française d'Automatique, Informatique et Recherche Operationelle*, vol. 6, pp. 3–15.

TOMIZAWA, N. (1971), 'On some techniques useful for solution of transportation network problems', *Networks*, vol. 1, pp. 173–194.

TREMOLIÈRES, R. (1973), 'Scheduling in continuous time and with tardiness costs', Working Paper 73-23, European Institute for Advanced Studies in Management.

ULLMAN, J. D. (1972), 'Polynomial complete scheduling problems', in: *Proceedings of the 4th Symposium on Operating System Principles*.

VAN DEMAN, J. M. and BAKER, K. R. (1974), 'Minimizing mean flowtime in the flow shop with no intermediate queues', *AIIE Transactions*, vol. 6, pp. 28–34.

WAGNER, H. M. (1959), 'An integer programming model for machine scheduling', *Naval Research Logistics Quarterly*, vol. 6, pp. 131–140.

WIEST, J. D. (1967), 'A heuristic model for scheduling large projects with limited resources', *Management Science*, vol. 13, pp. B-359–377.

WISMER, D. A. (1972), 'Solution to the flow shop scheduling problem with no intermediate queues', *Operations Research*, vol. 20, pp. 689–697.

Author index

Agarwal, A. K., 120
Agin, N., 40
Anthonisse, J. M., 134
Arthanari, T. S., 97
Ashour, S., 16, 52, 112, 117

Bagga, P. C., 108
Baker, K. R., 15, 62, 71, 87, 130, 147, 151
Balas, E., 14, 39, 40, 120
Bellmore, M., 66
Bennington, G. E., 14
Bornstein, C. M., 24
Bowman, E. H., 36
Bratley, P., 16, 62, 118
Brooks, G. H., 117
Brown, A. P. G., 112
Brucker, P., 14, 15, 16, 83, 100, 134
Bruno, J., 14, 15
Burton, P. G., 112, 113

Campbell, H. G., 158
Chakravarti, N. K., 108
Charlton, J. M., 117, 120
Chin, K. Y., 117
Coffman, E. G., 14, 15
Conway, R. W., 11, 23, 28, 34, 51, 58, 68, 89, 100
Cook, S. A., 46
Cunningham, A. A., 125

Davis, E. W., 14
Day, J., 51
Death, C. C., 117, 120
Denning, P. S., 15
Dessouky, M. I., 62
Doig, A. G., 40
Dorhout, B., 78, 102, 150, 151
Dudek, R. A., 107, 108, 158
Dutta, S. K., 125

Dutton, J. M., 52
Dijkstra, E. W., 151

Eastman, W. L., 15, 40
Edmonds, J., 31, 46, 48
Elmaghraby, S. E., 14, 36, 75
van Emde Boas, P., 134
Emmons, H., 16, 68, 70, 71, 75
Even, S., 15

Fisher, M. L., 14, 71, 79
Florian, M., 16, 62, 117, 118, 120, 146, 147, 166
Fujii, M., 14

Garey, M. R., 15, 52, 87, 100, 141
Gelders, L., 76, 78
Gere, W. S., 51
Giffler, B., 32
Gilmore, P. C., 128
Glover, F., 66
Gomory, R. E., 128
Gonzalez, T., 52, 140
Gorenstein, S., 14
Goyal, S. K., 125, 128
Grabowski, J., 125
Graham, R. L., 14, 15, 52, 141
Greenberg, H. H., 117
Gupta, J. N. D., 24, 39

Haehling von Lanzenauer, C., 37
Hardgrave, W. W., 29
Heck, H., 16
Heidorn, G. E., 14
Held, M., 44
Heller, J., 52, 55
Himes, R. C., 37
Hiremath, S. R., 117
Horn, W. A., 14, 60, 87

Hottenstein, M. P., 51
Hsu, N. C., 14
Hu, T. C., 14

Ignall, E., 102, 107, 112
Isaac, A. M., 66
Isaacs, I. M., 15

Jackson, J. R., 57, 58, 59, 93
Johnson, D. S., 87, 100, 141
Johnson, S. M., 89, 90, 95, 105

Karp, R. M., 44, 46, 47, 48, 70, 142
Kasami, T., 14
Kleindorfer, P. R., 76, 78
Knuth, D. E., 46, 58
Kohler, W. H., 102
Kroese, H. E. S., iii
Krone, M. J., 52

Lageweg, B. J., 75, 77, 78, 83, 123
Land, A. H., 40
Lawler, E. L., 26, 44, 58, 66, 70, 83, 85, 87, 134
de Leede, E., 55
Lenstra, J. K., 14, 15, 16, 40, 66, 75, 77, 78, 79, 83, 100, 119, 123, 134
Lewis, P. M., 141
Liu, C. L., 15
Lofts, N. R., 14
Lomnicki, Z. A., 112

Mandeville, D. E., 14
Manne, A. S., 38
Margenthaler, C. R., 62
Martin, J. B., 71, 151
Mason, A. T., 14
Maxwell, W. L., 11, 23, 28, 34, 51, 58, 68, 89, 100
McGinnis, L. F., 14
McMahon, G. B., 14, 62, 107, 108, 109, 112, 113, 117, 118, 120, 146, 147, 160, 162, 166
Merten, A. G., 15
Miller, L. W., 11, 23, 28, 34, 51, 58, 68, 89, 100
Mitten, L. G., 40, 105
Moodie, C. L., 14
Moore, J. M., 26, 44, 70
Moore, T. E., 117
Mukhopadhyay, A. C., 97
Muth, J. F., 38, 164, 166

Nabeshima, I., 105, 117
Neméti, L., 117, 164
Nemhauser, G. L., 29, 66
Nepomiastchy, P., 39
Nicholson, T. A. J., 35
Ninomiya, K., 14

Palmer, D. S., 158
Park, S. H., 14
Parker, R. G., 117
Piehler, J., 125, 127
Porter, D. B., 32
Pritsker, A. A. B., 37

Raiffa, H., 50, 53
Raimond, J. F., 39
Ramamoorthy, C. V., 125, 127, 128
Rau, J. G., 35, 36
Reddi, S. S., 125, 127, 128
Redwine, C. N., 37
Reiter, S., 35
Rinnooy Kan, A. H. G., 14, 15, 16, 40, 55, 75, 77, 78, 79, 83, 100, 119, 123, 134
Roberts, S., 16
Robillard, P., 16, 62, 118
Root, J. G., 14
Rosenkrantz, D. J., 141
Rothkopf, M. H., 14
Roy, B., 6, 16

Sahney, V. K., 13
Sahni, S., 52, 140
Sang, N., 117
Schlaifer, R., 50, 53
Schrage, L., 102, 107, 112, 117
Sethi, R., 14, 15, 100
Sherman, G., 35
Shwimer, J., 75, 78, 79, 150, 153, 154
Sidney, J. B., 87
Smith, M. L., 158
Smith, R. D., 107, 108
Smith, W. E., 16, 30, 35, 67
Srinivasan, V., 71, 151, 154
Stearns, R. E., 141
Steiglitz, K., 52, 102
Sturm, L. B. J. M., 70
Su, Z. S., 62, 147
Sussmann, B. G., 6, 117
Syslo, M. M., 125
Szwarc, W., 105, 108, 109

Tabourier, Y., 151
Thompson, G. L., 32, 38, 164, 166

Tomizawa, N., 151
Tremolières, R., 80
Trépant, P., 117, 120
Turban, E., 66

Ullman, J. D., 15

Van Deman, J. M., 87, 130

Wagner, H. M., 37
Watters, L. J., 37
White, C. R., 117
Wiest, J. D., 14
Wismer, D. A., 37, 125
Wolfe, P. M., 37

Subject index

Active schedule, 32
Assembly type production, 13
Average tardiness factor, 152, 153

Backtracking, 39
Bayesian analysis, 31, 50, 52
– approach, 55
Binary encoding, 45, 70, 134
Block, 63
Bottleneck assignment problem, 66
– transportation problem, 65
Bounding rule, 40
Branch-and-bound, 31, 39, 66, 71, 76, 85, 95, 99, 100, 106, 115, 141
Branch-and-exclude, 39
Branching, 12, 87
– pair, 121
– rule, 40, 119

Capacity, 14, 136
Capital costs, 24
Classification, 28
Clique problem, 47, 87, 132, 133
Commodity, 5
Completion, 106
– time, 16, 18
Complexity, 3, 16, 29, 31, 45, 131, 139, 140
Computational results, 147, 153, 160, 165
Conflict, 121, 122
Conjunctive arcs, 6
Cost function, 17
Critical job, 64
– machine, 50, 135, 136
– path, 21, 126

Depth-first search, 41
Descendant, 40
Directed hamiltonian circuit problem, 47, 48

– hamiltonian path problem, 47, 85, 129, 133
Disjunctive arcs, 7, 120
– constraint, 39
– graph, 6
Dispatching procedure, 52, 81
Due date, 13, 18
Dynamic programming, 31, 43, 44, 45, 71

Earliness, 26
EDD rule, 51, 57, 68
Efficient algorithm, 31
Elimination criteria, 42, 70, 71, 100, 107, 108, 150, 159, 160, 162
Euclidean, 127

Facility, 5
FCFS rule, 51
Feasible sequence, 8
FIFO rule, 51
Flow-shop, 2, 8, 106, 127, 141
Flow time, 18
Frontier search, 41

Gantt-chart, 7, 32, 137, 138
Good algorithm, 31, 46

Heuristic method, 31, 50, 62, 140

Id-encoding, 81, 83, 100
Identical machines, 14
Idle time, 20, 25, 56
Implementation, 146, 150, 156, 163
Implicit enumeration, 40
Intermediate storage, 13, 125
Inventory costs, 19, 24, 25
Inverse disjunctive graph, 7, 21
– problem, 8, 59, 64, 99
Inversion, 147
Iterative heuristic, 52

Job, 1, 5, 29
Job-based bound, 113, 157
Job dependent set-up time, 15, 66, 84
– lot, 5
Job-shop, 2, 10, 106, 136, 141
Job splitting, 15, 56, 62

Knapsack problem, 47, 61, 69, 81, 84, 93,
    94, 98, 99, 133, 134

Lagrangian multipliers, 71, 141
Lateness, 18, 19, 22
Likelihood, 53
Linear assignment problem, 76, 78, 80, 86,
    101
– transportation problem, 76, 79
Lower bound, 40, 43, 62, 63, 76, 77, 86, 95,
    101, 109, 112, 116, 150, 156, 162

Machine, 1, 5, 29
Make-span, 18
Matching, 151
Mathematical programming models, 36

Neighbourhood structure, 35
Newest active node search, 41, 62, 78, 146
Non-bottleneck machine, 15, 59, 110, 111,
    114
Non-delay schedule, 34
NP-complete, 46, 47, 49, 61, 65, 69, 71, 81,
    84, 85, 87, 93, 94, 97, 100, 128, 130, 133,
    141

Operations, 1, 5
Optimality criterion, 16, 29

Parallel machines, 14
Partition problem, 47
Penalty, 122
Permutation schedule, 10
Polynomial-bounded algorithm, 46, 133,
    134
Posterior distribution, 53, 54
Precedence constraints, 12, 64, 66, 71, 87,
    117, 118, 120, 121, 131, 146, 149
– cycle, 75, 150
– graph, 12, 87, 147
Preemption, 15
Prior distribution, 52, 54
Priority rule, 31, 50, 51, 135, 163, 165
Processing order, 6
– times, 6
Process stage, 5

Production center, 5
– lot, 5

Quadratic assignment problem, 85

Random rule, 51, 52
Ready time, 11
Reducible, 46
Regular measures, 16, 23, 24, 27, 119
Release date, 11
Resource constrained project scheduling,14
Restricted flooding, 41, 156, 163
Restrictive assumptions, 10, 11

Satisfiability problem, 46
Schedule, 2
Scheduleable operations, 51, 120, 163
Schedule time, 18
Search strategy, 40, 64
– tree, 43, 121, 156, 163
Semi-active schedule, 17
Sequence, 2
Sequence dependent change-over times, 15,
    66, 84, 119
Settled pair, 8
Single pass procedure, 52, 81
Slacktime, 51, 58
SOT rule, 51
SPT rule, 51, 68
Starting times, 16
Switching argument, 35

Tail, 59, 116
Tardiness, 19, 22
Tasks, 5
Test data, 147, 151, 159, 165
Time lag, 105
Total production time, 18
Transitive closure, 121
– kernel, 12
Travelling salesman problem, 47, 48, 66,
    127, 128, 134

Unary encoding, 45, 70, 134
Upper bound, 40, 64, 77, 158, 165
Utilization, 19, 20

Waiting time, 18
Weight, 13
Workload, 51
Work station, 5
Worst case analysis, 15, 52, 135